Creative Therapy

for Children with Autism, ADD, and Asperger's

Janet Tubbs

SQUAREONE
PUBLISHERS

The information and advice in this book are based on the training, personal experiences, and research of the author. Its contents are current and accurate; however, the information presented is not intended to substitute for professional advice. Should you have any questions regarding the appropriateness of the material contained in this book, the author and the publisher suggest you consult with a qualified professional prior to using any methodologies presented within.

Throughout the book, case studies and personal accounts of children whom the author has worked with are included. Clients' names have been changed to protect their privacy.

Cover Designer: Jeannie Tudor
Editor: Elaine Weiser
In-House Editor: Eric Motylinski
Typesetter: Gary Rosenberg

Square One Publishers
115 Herricks Road
Garden City Park, NY 11040
(516) 535–2010 • (877) 900–BOOK
www.squareonepublishers.com

Library of Congress Cataloging-in-Publication Data
Tubbs, Janet.
   Creative therapy for children with autism, ADD, and Asperger's : using
artistic creativity to reach, teach, and touch our children / Janet Tubbs.
       p. ; cm.
   Includes bibiographical references and index.
   ISBN 978-0-7570-0300-4 (quality pbk.)
1. Autism—Treatment. 2. Attention-deficit hyperactivity disorder—Treatment.
3. Asperger's syndrome—Treatment. 4. Creation (Literary, artistic,
etc.)—Therapeutic use. 5. Art therapy. 6. Music therapy. I. Title.
   [DNLM: 1. Autistic Disorder—therapy. 2. Asperger Syndrome—therapy. 3.
Attention Deficit Disorder with Hyperactivity—therapy. 4. Child. 5.
Psychotherapy—methods. 6. Sensory Art Therapies—methods. WM 203.5 T885c 2007]
RC553.A88T83 2008
618.92'858906—dc22   2007015463

Printed in the United States of America

10   9   8   7   6   5   4   3   2   1

Contents

PART TWO

Activities to Enrich Body, Mind, and Spirit

This book is dedicated
to Donald W. Gill,
whose wisdom, humor, and compassion
are a constant inspiration.

Acknowledgments

To Kathy Koewler, who has been with me from the beginning of this writing adventure. Her proofing and support were greatly appreciated.

To my dear friend Geri Johnson, for her Internet sleuthing that tracked down obscure pieces of information.

To Elaine Weiser, my editor, who has held my hand through the monumental process of assembling and editing this book. Somehow she knew my thoughts as I struggled to express them in print and made suggestions that perfectly echoed my sentiments.

Above all, I am deeply indebted to Rudolf Steiner who, as a visionary, has given us a legacy of his deeply spiritual nature and compassion for children, disabilities, and the creative arts. He left over 6,000 books and lectures on dozens of topics when he died in 1925, and his work is as valid today as it was 100 years ago.

One further note:
To avoid long and awkward phrasing within sentences, the use of male and female pronouns when referring to a child will alternate. Odd-numbered chapters in Part One will use male pronouns; even-numbered chapters in Part One will use female pronouns. Part Two will use male pronouns, and the Introduction and the Conclusion will use female pronouns.

*I*ntroduction

Do you sometimes have the feeling that your child is different from her siblings or other children her age? She may have odd mannerisms, like spinning a spoon on the floor for hours or having a tantrum if you decide to take a different route to the store. She might insist on having her crayons lined up in a row and won't look you in the eye. In fact, she may have stopped talking and not want you to hug her anymore. If you can relate to any of these unusual behaviors, you are not alone.

We all want our children to be "perfect," but sometimes they aren't. It is second nature for friends to compare their children, hoping theirs is taller or smarter than the rest of the toddlers in child care or nursery school. When they aren't, we are told that they will catch up and that some babies are slower than others. You cling to that, all the while knowing that something isn't quite right with your child. You don't want to believe that there could be anything wrong. Even when the pediatrician recommends testing, you resist; it might prove that your worst fears are realized.

Your daughter's kindergarten teacher may call for yet another meeting about her annoying behavior. This time you are told that she has to be removed from the school for pinching, biting, kicking, and insolence. When the teacher says your daughter needs help, you are defensive, but after a great deal of thought and consideration, you finally agree that at times she is out of control. Your search begins for something quick and easy that will make her behave more like other girls her age.

Your doctor may recommend testing by a psychologist or a Developmental Pediatrician, and while you are apprehensive, you feel sure whatever it is can be easily fixed with a shot or a pill to make the symptoms disappear. You are still relatively calm about the outcome, but when the specialist tells you that your child has a neurological disorder, probably autism, you are suddenly thrust into a world you didn't know existed. You will likely experience a range of emotions from disbelief to anger to overwhelming despair.

It is important to understand that you are not alone. Help is out there for you and your child, whether in a clinical setting or through support groups. You will find many parents who have been in your situation and who are eager to help you through this difficult time. Once you get past that initial shock, it is natural to want to learn everything about this disorder so you can help your child.

You will find that there are millions of boys and girls with autism and soon recognize the symptoms in your child and other children. You will also discover that, in addition to autism, there are other, related neurological disorders, known as Autism Spectrum Disorders, which are increasingly common and easily recognized, and which share some of the characteristics of autism but are clearly distinct classifications. These include Asperger's Syndrome as well as Attention Deficit Disorder (ADD) and Attention Deficit Hyperactivity Disorder (ADHD). Throughout this book, the closely related conditions of ADD and ADHD are frequently lumped together as "ADD" to avoid long and awkward phrasing of sentences. References to ADD are not meant to exclude ADHD unless specifically noted.

APPROACHING THE PROBLEM

The purpose of this book is to show you how to help your child reach her fullest potential through mutual respect, verbal and non-verbal communication, and an understanding of the power of the creative arts. The first step is to believe that there's a purpose to her life with autism, just as there's a purpose to all life. When we believe that, accepting the diagnosis is less difficult. The second step is to realize that since your child is non-traditional (compared to whatever the norm is), traditional therapies aren't as effective as they could be. She needs something that will speak to her spiritual nature.

The third step is knowledge of the three-fold nature of a human being: body, mind, and spirit. There are many books about working with our body, with our mind, or with our spirit, but finding one that speaks to all three of these elements as a cohesive whole is difficult. And trying to find this information for a child with autism, Asperger's, ADD, or ADHD can be even more daunting. This book stresses the spiritual nature of a child for one reason: Without it the child can never be complete. It is the sensitive, feeling, spiritual nature that propels the other two elements of body and mind to function to the best of their ability.

If one of those three aspects is missing, we're unbalanced and out of alignment. Think of such imbalance in your family as having a car with a wobbly left wheel. It works and gets you where you're going if you stay under 40 mph, but all of the passengers are jostled and shaken if you want to speed up a little. You finally accept that you need professional help and so you search for a good mechanic who can fix the wheel. This may take time but when you find one you trust, she tells you there's a broken axel that has to be replaced first. This is a setback mentally, emotionally, and financially, because the entire procedure may be expensive. But the end result will be a smooth ride with the kids sleeping peacefully in the back instead of punching and yelling at each other.

Your child's spiritual nature is the "wobbly wheel" that is put back into alignment. Conventional therapies, as we know them, treat only the body or only the mind. Some treat both, but it's rare to find an effective therapy that treats all three: body, mind, and spirit. It's your child's spiritual nature that flashes through in times of joy or interest. It's this aspect that is moved by classical music or beautiful colors and encourages her to paint wonderful pictures. In this book, you will learn to look beyond the obvious, to know that there's a spiritual part of your child that is responding to everything you say, do, and yes—think.

As a child, music, singing, dance, and puppetry fascinated me. In addition to being a hospital administrator, my father was a puppeteer and amateur magician. His "tricks" intrigued me, and at the tender age of nine, I became his assistant. The rabbit my father pulled from the hat during an evening performance was my pet during the day. His sleights of hand and materializations were illusions, and I knew there was something else that the audience wasn't seeing that was actually influencing the outcome of my father's "amazing" tricks. The fact that they were tricks and he was a master illusionist prompted me from that time to look beyond the obvious. We've all heard the sayings, "You can't tell a book from its cover" and "Things aren't always what they seem." These phrases apply to just about everything, but they have great significance when we consider children on the Autism Spectrum because we have a sense that these boys and girls are much more aware than they may seem.

> Parental involvement is paramount to the success of remedial and creative therapies because parents can facilitate changes in their child by using many of the same techniques a therapist does.

Parental involvement is paramount to the success of remedial and creative therapies because parents can facilitate changes in their child by using many of the same techniques a therapist does. As a parent, you've probably seen occasional moments of awareness, understanding, and humor in your child that surprised and delighted you. We have to look beyond the obvious, and in autism, the obvious is the body and mind, with one's spiritual nature being hidden and unobtrusive. When all three are synchronized, we have an integrated human being, which is the goal of each of us. This holistic approach is key to understanding autism, Asperger's, and ADD, since the most common therapies address a child through only the physical or mental states.

As a parent, you can help your child by being actively involved in programs designed by therapists, and, on a daily basis, you can continue the momentum gained in the weekly sessions.

When parents accept responsibility for their child and want to work with her at home, both mothers and fathers have the opportunity to take part in the process. This is especially important for those who may have limited contact with their child due to work demands or other reasons.

Another advantage of working with the child at home is involvement of the extended family of relatives. Most want to help but do not know how, or think that only a therapist can work with a child on the Spectrum. Anyone can do the basic exercises provided in Part Two of this book and utilize techniques of therapists by understanding the reasoning behind using music, art, drawing, massage, speech, music, toning, and sensory integration. Siblings can have a part in their brother's or sister's therapy through play, which helps create a stronger bond between them.

Grandparents often feel "out of the loop" because Autism Spectrum Disorders are relatively new and unfamiliar to them. They have little or no frame of reference and when they see abnormal behavior in their grandchildren, they tend to be puzzled, irritated, and impatient. By being actively involved, they are educating themselves in what may have been perceived as mere lack of discipline or perhaps mental retardation. They begin to enjoy the hands-on participation and feel a sense of accomplishment and empowerment.

When the family all works together in an integrative process that includes teachers, therapists, and medical professionals, the child improves because her three-fold nature of body, mind, and spirit is brought into balance to create a healthy, whole child.

WHAT'S IN THIS BOOK

The non-traditional approach described in this book has been successfully used with my clients for over twenty-five years. In Part One you will learn about the characteristics of children on the Autism Spectrum and the research on and theories and treatments of these neurological disorders.

Chapter 1 will provide you with a better understanding of the three-fold nature of a whole person—body, mind, and spirit.

Possible causes for the prevalence of autism, as well as potential remedies, will be presented in Chapter 2.

Chapters 3, 4, and 5 explain the criteria for diagnoses, and typical characteristics, of children with various Spectrum Disorders.

Chapter 6 will discuss the importance of nutrition for Spectrum kids.

Chapter 7 explores the importance of art in our lives, the innate spirituality of artistic creation, and benefits of Art Therapy.

You'll learn about the four temperaments in Chapter 8. Of particular interest will be how to identify which of the four temperaments is most apparent in your child, and the most effective ways of reaching and teaching each one.

Chapter 9 explores the tremendously positive impact of fairy tales on young minds.

The spiritual connection with music cannot be ignored. Chapter 10 explains the benefits of Music Therapy, and how rhythm is everywhere.

Color is something that is largely taken for granted. However, as Chapter 11 will explain, it has a hidden impact on our lives, and color can be used therapeutically to help children in a variety of ways.

Children on the Spectrum often have trouble with speech and hearing. Chapter 12 shows how children with such impairments can be helped, and the need to choose our words carefully.

The magic of puppetry is explored in Chapter 13. You'll learn how to create your own puppets, and how the most basic of puppets can help even a non-verbal child communicate and express her feelings.

Chapter 14 introduces you to additional therapies that are also fun and effective, but used only occasionally, as compared to the methods explored in previous chapters, which can and should be used extensively.

Part Two contains a variety of specific exercises that implement the ideas of the creative therapies you'll read about in Part One. These are activities that you, the parent, can easily do at home with your child. If you're a teacher or therapist, you may want to use them in your classroom or sessions. These are fun exercises that will appeal to a child's body, mind, and spiritual nature.

Each may be considered "just" a game, yet there is a method and an objective for each activity. Kids will know only that they're having fun. Your child will enjoy these activities and attain specific goals, some of which will include learning to express and communicate feelings and emotions in various creative ways and improving fine and gross motor skills, observation skills, memory, and attention span.

These activities are perfect for all of your children because siblings are affected more than we know by an autistic brother or sister. They often resent the attention that parents give to a child with special needs, and these feelings of anger are usually suppressed. The same therapeutic methods and activities described in this book for children on the Autism Spectrum are appropriate for their brothers and sisters, since they offer a multitude of ways to express feelings in a non-judgmental way.

In chapters to follow, you will read about methods and reasoning that may be unfamiliar to you. They are different from traditional therapies because they are designed for your non-traditional child. They are given to you as keys that will unlock your child's hidden potential.

By the time you are finished reading this book, you will have an opportunity to discover your child's untapped abilities. By applying the suggested methods, you will have the power to create real magic, not

By the time you are finished reading this book, you will have an opportunity to discover your child's untapped abilities.

sleight of hand, to take your child far beyond what she already knows. Your child will recognize her progress and have the motivation to take the next step towards the integration of her inner world and the world in which we live.

PART ONE

A Creative Approach to Autism Spectrum Disorders

CHAPTER 1

*U*nlocking Your Child's Hidden World

Autism, a serious neurological disorder, was first identified over fifty years ago. For the first few decades, a relatively small number of physicians knew of it. For too long the clinical treatment of children with neurological disorders was off-limits to parents, who were given scant information about what actually had taken place behind closed doors. It was for the professional to know what was being done for—or to—the child, and parents were patronizingly believed to be unable to comprehend such advanced thinking. This book changes that outmoded practice by providing you, the parent, with tools and techniques necessary to work with your child in your home.

Today we can learn about autism, Attention Deficit Disorder (ADD) and Attention Deficit Hyperactivity Disorder (ADHD), and Asperger's Syndrome (three common disorders on the Autism Spectrum) from Internet message boards, chat rooms, newsletters, support groups, and books. Parents are educating themselves about their child's disorder and therapies that are available to them. However, few know that they can implement most methods in their own home once they learn which are the most effective for their son or daughter and how to use them.

There are methods of reaching children on the Autism Spectrum, and in this chapter, we will explore the three elements that make up your child's world: body, mind, and spirit. If just one of those elements is out of balance with the other two, disorder may prevent the assimilation of the whole child. You will learn how to take a proactive role in your child's improvement by recognizing that you have the right and responsibility to take on a major part of his therapy. For the most effective results, you will want a therapy program designed to combine the creative arts and the healing arts. Creative arts are designated in this book as art, energetic drawing, music, rhythmic massage, sculpture, puppetry, and handwork, e.g. knitting. (Initially, it was believed that music was the only form of effective therapy available.) Healing arts may include physical and psychological testing, nutritional consultation, and medical treatment. These will all be discussed in subsequent chapters.

By using a combination of methods as you work with your child, you will see significant changes including improvement in fine motor, verbal, and social skills. In this chapter you will learn how children with ADD, autism, and Asperger's Syndrome are different from their peers. You will then have another key to their hidden world, which will help you to help them function on all levels: physical, emotional, mental, and spiritual.

Parents who participate in their child's therapy play an enormous part in his growth and development. Everyone who participates in at-home therapy will have a sense of contribution, achievement, and excitement as results are seen. It is a big step for you to assume a large part of your child's treatment, one that may be intimidating at first. You will need strength, time, presence of mind, and courage of heart to accept that responsibility, but the rewards will far outweigh the time and effort you are investing in your child's growth.

As you continue reading and exploring unfamiliar territory, you will become more confident and at peace with yourself and your child. Although improvement may seem glacially slow, it helps to keep in mind that all changes are not immediately visible. Also, your child has set patterns and he may resist change. Children with autism typically like routine. Your child may signal his resistance by crying or ignoring all efforts to communicate. Be patient. As you persist in learning about this disorder, you will realize that your child is one of many who are autistic, a fact that is reassuring to all family members.

Adults often do not like change, either, so adapting to a holistic approach and new ideas about the various arts may be foreign to you and, at first, seem an insurmountable challenge. However, you will soon understand and become more familiar with what will be a new and exciting approach to reaching your child and helping him develop to his fullest potential.

HOW CAN YOU HELP YOUR CHILD?

If you are like most parents, you probably have asked, "Why did this happen to my child?" It is a first response for most people. After the shock of a diagnosis wears off, the next question should be—and remain—"How can I help my child?" It may take a while to find the right combination of psychologist, pediatrician, and/or therapist you feel is absolutely right for your child and his particular disorder. If at any time, for any reason, you feel uncomfortable, you have the right to see someone else. It is your feeling nature, your sensitivity or intuition that is guiding you, so trust it, keep looking, and you will find a perfect match.

You can play a big part in the overall improvement in your child by working with him at home every day. Make it a game instead of a chore. Be a child again and get down to his level, on the floor and on your stomach as you paint or color. Don't tower over him like an ogre, telling him what to do. Instead be with him and have fun. It's much easier for him to look at you when you are at eye level than if you are several feet above him.

Siblings, grandparents, uncles and aunts, and other family members can all participate in a child's improvement by painting, playing memory games, dancing, massaging, and talking with him. The goal is to keep him constantly stimulated mentally, physically, emotionally, and spiritually. A child needs continual activity that alternates between passive and active times. That is, cuddling while reading a story and then coloring, or alternating massage with kicking a ball. It is important to change his perception of the environment by moving from the dining room table to the floor to standing at an easel and then to a small child's table. In each setting his eyes and limbs are using different muscles as he observes his surroundings with a new perspective. When a child is kept involved, he is unable to retreat to his inner world. His time spent in activities begins to increase and he spends less time within and isolated.

It is vital to your child's improvement that you talk all the time with him as you work together. Talk about anything. Be enthusiastic and descriptive about things you have done and places you have been. Engage him and ask questions. He may not answer verbally but you will have triggered an internal response. Don't hesitate to talk to your child if he seems inattentive or uninterested, because he is listening to and hearing everything that is said, which can stimulate a desire to emulate you.

Engage your child in activities that address his mind, his body, and his spirit. This means physical exercise, even if it's moving slightly to music or going for a walk because his muscles need movement. Stimulate him mentally by talking to him and asking questions. Surround him with the spiritual qualities of truth, beauty, and goodness. This is done in many ways by being a role model. Your child will absorb your morals, ethics, and love of the arts without lessons or lectures, and these attributes will become second nature. The importance of various art forms and suggestions for creative exercises will be discussed in detail later in the book. The methods described in this book will help your child to control what is within his power to control and to strengthen his areas of weakness.

Engage your child in activities that address his mind, his body, and his spirit.

Fill your home with color, music, and soft words; all of these are necessary to your child's feeling nature or sensitivity. Combined with necessary physical care and remedial therapies, a home free of arguments and yelling creates the most positive environment for the blossoming young child. By taking an industrious role and working with him as often as possible, each day you will be keeping his three-fold nature active. You will be helping him to grow safely into a healthy life.

Working parents obviously can't spend all day working with their child. The next best thing is to tell caregivers and therapists the procedures you would like to have implemented while in your home. In a clinical setting, therapists may be willing to include some of these methods in their sessions.

You can take an assertive role by eliminating electronic gadgets and toys that do all of your kids' thinking for them. Reduce or eliminate television and encourage your children to rely on their creativity and interaction with siblings and peers for entertainment. As parents, you will have to rely on your own ingenuity and imagination to spur the interest of your child. This can be daunting at first, but you will soon find that you are having fun while helping your child to improve his skills.

The Perils of Our High-Tech Society

We live in an era where our will to achieve and express ourselves is stifled by input from radio, television, movies, video games, and computers, as we absorb other people's thoughts and creations. This passivity deadens our feelings and weakens our will to create. It results in an unbalanced focus of interest and often an observable weakness in a child. Electrical impulses originating from these sources affect the electro-magnetic currents of the brain and generate an erratic rhythm in the neurological development of the young child. It is not unheard of for children to experience seizures after playing video games or watching television for long periods, so obviously something in such electronic devices is responsible for the neurological collapse of these healthy, normal children.

Electronic gadgets and games with rigid directions that leave no room for creativity are slowly taking the imagination of children away from them. When I was a child, entire families gathered around the radio in the early evening to listen to their favorite programs. The wonderful thing about radio was that we automatically used our imagination to picture the characters and the story. Some would picture a girl's hair black, another blonde, and there was no right or wrong. When the soundman made the noise of a horse galloping, we could see that horse galloping. Today, television and movies show us in excruciating detail more than we really want to know and more than children should know. It's rarely necessary to be imaginative in this kind of environment. For this reason, we should give children books that have no words at all, but simply pictures awaiting a plot to unfold around them. A child then makes up his own story every time he opens the book, and each one can be a new adventure.

In a high-tech society such as ours, materialistic impulses are very strong, leading us to lives sadly lacking in artistic expression. When this happens to a society as a whole, immoral and illegal acts become rampant because the spiritual impulse is smothered by desires for the material world. As a result, our will is subjugated and struggles to assert itself by either developing a one-sided approach to life and activities or simply fading into the background and weakening the body and mind.

The Autism Spectrum

ADD/ADHD*	ASPERGER'S	AUTISM	FRAGILE X	RETT	LANDAU-KLEFFNER
Often: allergic to dairy products, unable to focus on tasks, gifted, artistic, and hyperactive.	Often: bursts of temper, poor social skills, obsessions; very artistic, curious, and intelligent.	Often: lack of eye contact; tactilely defensive, non-verbal, observant, and intelligent.	Most common inherited cause of mental impairment. Adverse to sound, socializing, and touch.	Mostly girls. Cessation or regression of development at 6–18 months. Small head; difficulty walking.	Usually diagnosed at age 3–7. Symptoms similar to those of autism; poor language skills.

The Spectrum is a grouping of pervasive developmental disorders that range from very mild (ADD) to Asperger's Syndrome to the more severe autism, all of which are the subject of this book. Beyond autism are three rare disorders with some traits of autism: Fragile X, Rett, and Landau-Kleffner Syndromes.

Between ADD and autism is a large category of undefined disorders that do not meet the criteria of any known disorders on the Spectrum and are designated as Pervasive Development Disorders—Not Otherwise Specified.

PERVASIVE DEVELOPMENT DISORDER—NOT OTHERWISE SPECIFIED (PDD–NOS)

Children with PDD–NOS demonstrate some characteristics of ADD, ADHD, Asperger's, and autism but do not precisely meet the clearly defined criteria for a diagnosis of any of these disorders. They may be tactilely defensive and have allergies, poor social skills, and an inability to focus on tasks. They are therefore categorized as a separate group on the Autism Spectrum and may eventually be diagnosed as having autism.

---

*Some contend that ADD/ADHD should not be on the Autism Spectrum. Children with ADD/ADHD, however, do have some traits in common with autism—for instance, minor behavioral problems and an inability to sustain focus.

WHAT IS THE AUTISM SPECTRUM?

The Autism Spectrum is the term for a range of neurological disorders, classified from mild to severe, from Attention Deficit Disorder (ADD) to Asperger's Syndrome to what is known as "classic autism." Think of the Spectrum as a straight line with a dot at each end and one in the middle. Although along the bar there are other, less common disorders, this book will focus on these three increasingly prevalent ones. The dot at the left end is ADD, the mildest form of neurological disorder in the Spectrum. At the far right is classic autism, the most involved or severe form of these disorders. In the middle of this hypothetical line is a dot for Asperger's Syndrome, which has some characteristics of ADD and some of autism but does fit properly into either category.

Children with ADD are easily distracted and have trouble focusing on tasks unless it's something of great interest. ADD children are often accused of daydreaming and are restless in school because they are bored. They love to explore but sometimes their enthusiasm is distracting to other children. If they are overly active, running around the classroom, constantly at the window to see what's going on outside, or in general disrupting the teacher, they are known as "hyperactive" and labeled as having ADHD or Attention Deficit Hyperactivity Disorder.

Right in the middle of our invisible bar is Asperger's Syndrome, which has become increasingly prevalent as it is being more easily recognized. The immediately noticeable signs of an "Aspie," as kids with Asperger's Syndrome like to call themselves, are obsessions with things like timetables and train and plane schedules, a fiery temper, and poor social skills. Aspies are intriguing, challenging, funny, brilliant, and often moody. They are very creative but usually have a short attention span, like kids with ADD. They start to do something, are attracted to something else, and never finish what they started. On the more serious side, Aspies often threaten to harm themselves or others. Until a decade or so ago, kids with Asperger's Syndrome (most commonly boys) were thought to be unruly trouble makers who simply needed discipline.

At the far right of the bar is classic autism, the most severe condition on the Spectrum. There are different degrees of autism, but the most common form is slightly to the left of the edge of the bar. Children in this range are very intelligent, observant, and sensitive to their surroundings, and are not given enough credit for their intelligence. They hear and understand everything that is taking place around them. Everything registers even though they may give no outward sign of hearing, seeing, or understanding anything. Children with autism may be non-verbal, shun receiving or giving affection, and may not look you in the eye. They may have elective mutism, literally shutting off their hearing because the noise in their environment is unbearably loud and painful.

Current statistics estimate that 1 in every 150 American children is diagnosed with autism. In the United Kingdom, the statistic is 1 in 84. Autism is a life-altering problem that can have a profound impact upon a child's behavior, learning ability, and future—as well as the lives of family members.

While each disorder on the Autism Spectrum shares one or more characteristics of autism, they are each separate and distinct. Despite the severity of symptoms, most children on the Spectrum are intelligent and observant. It may appear otherwise because of an inability to verbalize their thoughts, needs, love, fear, pain, and anger, but at a deep spiritual level, they are very much aware. Perhaps the body or the brain doesn't quite "work," yet the spirit shines through. It may show in their eyes, a slight smile, or their body language when they are engaged in an activity they enjoy or listening intently to someone or something that has attracted their attention.

FINDING THE KEY TO THE AUTISTIC CHILD

A child with autism is an enigma, a puzzle that is waiting to be solved. Although there are many things we don't know about this disorder, we do know that autistics respond to all forms of art, something that can originate only from a sensitive or feeling nature. How can we unlock the puzzle of autism when children live for the most part totally within themselves, isolated from physical, verbal, or visual contact with other people? We begin by being observant because they will show definite, if almost imperceptible, pleasure from painting or listening to music. Your child may be more attentive when you play one piece of music rather than others. He may listen more closely when you describe a trip to a state park where you saw deer and waterfalls. Obviously there is something stirring in children when they are actively or passively involved with the arts. The goal of remedial and creative therapies is to stimulate that inner "something" with purposeful exercises and techniques that embrace the child's three-fold nature of body, mind, and spirit. Without this synergy or harmonious collaboration, it is impossible for anyone to reach his fullest potential.

As you learn to do this, it is important to talk with your child and tell him that you love him. However, it's equally important that you teach by example. For example, don't just say "I love you." Show it in very definite ways. Be gentle and speak softly. Think good thoughts, because "thoughts are things." We all project energy constantly, and if you do one thing but think another, your child will know. If you say, for example, "Let's play your favorite music! Wouldn't that be fun?" but you're thinking, "If I have to listen to that one more time I will scream!" you aren't fooling him. If you tell him you love and respect him but talk disparagingly about him while he is in the next room, you have forgotten his incredibly sensitive hearing. If people did that to us, we would refuse to associate with them—but your child can't do that, so he closes down further and retreats to his own safe, hidden world.

Children need to be included in conversation and never talked about in their presence as if they were incapable of understanding what is being said. Children with this neurological disorder not only understand but feel and sense deeply. We know this from boys and girls who have suddenly begun to speak or communicate through writing. Parents tend to think that what they say to their child doesn't register because he doesn't reply. In reality, he soaks up everything—good and bad—like a sponge. For this reason, your home needs to be a haven, a place of refuge for everyone in the family, but especially for a child with special needs.

As you read this book, you will discover many ways to help your child attain wholeness. You will read how to excite the feeling nature of your child by immersing him in color, classical music, pleasant surroundings, intelligent conversation, good books, humor, and love. Every child will bloom in this environment, and children with autism are no different. They not only like it; they need it because feelings are nourishment to the spirit as food is to the physical body. To nourish the whole child—physically, mentally, emotionally, and spiritually—we must remember that he absorbs everything he sees, hears, touches, tastes, and senses. Children thrive as their feeling nature is energized by the truth, beauty, and goodness in their lives.

Children thrive as their feeling nature is energized by the truth, beauty, and goodness in their lives.

**TRUTH,
BEAUTY, AND
GOODNESS**

The universe is changing; our bodies are changing; our lives, advertising, clothing, cars, businesses, and the environment are all changing and evolving—yet most therapy for children is stuck in the past. This is a disaster for children with disabilities because their three-fold nature is changing, and some of the programs that may have worked for autistics years ago aren't as effective as they could be today. We have learned a lot in the past twenty years about the intelligence of children with autism, Asperger's, and ADD, and by taking into consideration the spiritual nature of children, all conventional therapies could be enhanced.

Even though we have to keep up with changes around us, there are some things that never change. Parents and therapists who work with autistic children and have documented results are communicating with these boys and girls on a very deep level, which is possible only when adults demonstrate three spiritual traits that remain constant. These three spiritual traits are truth, beauty, and goodness.

Truth

Always be honest with children. They will know if you aren't and will completely ignore you. They aren't deaf; they simply want nothing to do with you. Autistic children are exquisitely perceptive because they are able to cancel out the world around them, including the false personalities of people who may be trying to help. They can then zero in on the true qualities of peers, parents, teachers, and therapists.

Beauty

If you don't truly appreciate the beauty of a sunset, a rainbow, a piece of fine art, or the great music of the classics, you won't be able to fully communicate with autistic children on a spiritual level, because they relate to beauty in all of its forms. Art is more than coloring or painting on a piece of paper. It springs from deep within, and the intent is to bring this quality into one's consciousness.

Goodness

Children learn from role models. If parents, caregivers, and therapists don't demonstrate love, compassion, integrity, and respect, children won't either. Goodness is an innate quality that is nourished by one's thoughts and actions.

These three spiritual attributes help establish non-verbal relationships with others, and are especially important when working with autistic children who will understand and absorb them into their sensitive, feeling nature. They are the basics of trust and respect, which are vital to the improvement of children with disorders found on the Spectrum.

Body, mind, and spirit are the three elements of the whole individual. Although we can devote a great deal of time to our body, mind, or spirit, undue emphasis on only one aspect doesn't allow similar growth in the other two elements. In this book, the spiritual nature of a child is stressed for one reason: Without it the child can never be complete. It is the sensitive, feeling, spiritual nature that propels the other two elements of body and mind to function to the best of their ability.

THE THREE ELEMENTS OF A WHOLE CHILD

The components of a whole child are also related to our ability to act, to think, and to feel. We say "I had a thought" or "I had a feeling," with the difference being its origin. Thoughts are mental and can be analyzed intellectually. Feelings, on the other hand, are from one's spiritual nature and can't be analyzed. As soon as we begin to dissect it, a feeling becomes a thought. Let's look at each of these elements of a whole person and see its importance in the life of a child on the Autism Spectrum.

Thoughts are mental and can be analyzed intellectually. Feelings, on the other hand, are from one's spiritual nature and can't be analyzed.

Body—The First Element

The body is the most easily recognized because it is material and visible; yet if it isn't taken care of, it degrades and dies just like every other living thing. We nurture our body with good food, exercise, fresh air, and avoidance of anything that isn't healthy to our system. Any one of these can be taken to the extreme, and the results of excesses are easily seen in the physical form. Obviously, over-eating makes us fat and under-eating makes us thin and ill. Over-exercise can strain or injure various parts of the body and too little weakens our muscles and contributes to obesity. In Chapter 6, you will find information on eating with consciousness and why nutrition is so important to all of us. If we are not well-fed, our thoughts are disconnected, "fuzzy," and sometimes incomprehensible and we may find it difficult to function at all.

Less obvious is the allergic reaction many people have to common foods. Our body reacts to things that affect our good health, and if we ignore it, the result can be a deterioration of the body and constant feelings of discomfort or outright pain. Most kids with ADD or ADHD have allergies—as do kids with autism and Asperger's Syndrome. If not treated in some way, allergies can cause serious health issues. It is in our best interests always to be aware of things in food and the environment that can cause medical problems.

We live in a world that is greatly affected by advertising. We are surrounded by commercials for beautifying the body. Naturally, these commercials are meant to make money for the seller and are not necessarily considerate of the overall health of the consumer. For this reason, we need to educate ourselves about what is available to our children and to us. The products and treatments being advertised for autism are no different. In fact, we need to look at everything with a critical eye so that our bodies respond to only the best foods, therapy, and medications. As a parent, you must take care of your child's body, or the other two elements of mind and spirit will be affected and unable to do their part in building a healthy, whole person.

Mind—The Second Element

The mind is the holder of all of our thoughts, dreams, and memories. Regardless of all the modern technology that can measure the brain and its functions, the reality is that nobody really knows how our mind works. There may be some uniformity in brain size, substance, and development, but your mind is unique to you. Nobody else has your thoughts. For this reason, psychological therapy is generally helpful to most people but unfortunately not to everyone. Similarly, remedial arts show greater benefits to some children than to others. Any individually developed program has to be flexible. It must be designed to find a way to speak to your child's mind in a language that he can understand, because the mind of a child with autism, ADD, or Asperger's Syndrome works very differently from a typical child's. Equally important to reaching your child's mind is finding a way to communicate with and nurture his spirit.

The Global Junk Food Epidemic

The physical body is frequently assaulted by what can be called the junk food epidemic. At one time, the United States was the only country that had a category of "junk food." Today, unfortunately, other countries have imported our favorite dining pastime, and their health is also declining while obesity is increasing. A diet of unhealthy food affects the body, the senses, and the spirit. It is imperative that every child be given food free of pesticides, additives, and artificial color. This is especially true for those on the Spectrum, who usually have a number of allergies.

Poor nutrition weakens the body and mind, and the diet of most children in the majority of homes is lacking in nourishment. We live in a world where we are surrounded by fast food restaurants, in which food is plentiful, tasty, and cheap. This is very appealing to our busy lives, but when it becomes our daily lunch and dinner, we are in danger of being malnourished on all levels. It is the worst possible food for children on the Autism Spectrum because almost all of it has preservatives and other additives, as well as high fat and sodium content and empty calories.

When a therapy program is designed for your child, it may include nutritional guidance from a therapist, physician, or dietician. This will help the entire family understand the value of good food. It takes work and commitment to make dietary changes, but the results will be worth it. It is one of the first steps you can take to help your child. For helpful suggestions on nutrition, see Chapter 6.

Spirit—The Third Element

We feel through our spirit. We may see with our eyes and think with our mind, but we can feel only through the spiritual part of our self. We hear with our ears, and our brain tells us it is music. But only our spirit can feel the pain or experience the joy that the artist is conveying through his work. Music and art are the language of the spirit. It is this element of ourselves that responds to truth, beauty, and goodness, all of which are embedded in remedial artistic therapies. For this reason, knowledge of the hidden, sensitive side of a child is imperative to the development of any therapeutic program designed for a child on the Autism Spectrum.

Each person has an intrinsic quality or disposition that embraces who he is as an individual. It's the part of him that makes him unique. It's what sets him apart from others because of his ability. For example, Mozart was described by his father as "a miracle that God allowed to be born in Salzburg." He composed his first music at the age of four and his first symphony at the age of eight. He was unparalleled in his mastery of the piano, which alone is a feat, but to compose an entire symphony at such a young age was an ability that went far beyond other people's talents. This unique sense is the spiritual nature of a child.

Today we call a person with such unusual and unexplained gifts a "savant." The movie *Rain Man* was one of the first to introduce savants to the general public. Unlike Mozart, the autistic character in the movie, played so accurately by Dustin Hoffman, was a mathematical savant with an attraction to all things with numbers. However, not all autistic children are savants and not all savants are autistic. Fortunately, these children are no longer called "idiot savants," a term coined in 1887 by Dr. J. Langdon Down, who also described Down syndrome. The autistic savants we hear or read about have displayed unexplainable talents. They did not necessarily study music or play an instrument and in many cases were not exposed to music in their homes. How can we explain such amazing talent? The unique ability shown by these individuals can come only from some unseen source such as the spirit.

Our ability to feel—the sensitive part of us—is the spiritual component of our three-fold nature that is galvanized by the beauty of the arts in all of its many forms, from painting and music to sculpture and poetry. By working with the whole child and using specific exercises, the hemispheres of the brain begin to balance by developing a mid-pole, which is lacking in autistic children. This will be discussed in more detail in Chapter 3.

When we see a beautiful sunset we're moved, sometimes to tears. We might say, "It warmed my heart." It isn't our physical body that produces that response, nor is it our brain, which tends to analyze everything. If we

Each person has an intrinsic quality or disposition that embraces who he is as an individual.

examine and dissect the colors of the sky or a rainbow, we lose an unexpected moment of pleasure or joy. But when our deep, sensitive, feeling nature sees a sunset, rainbow, or beautiful painting, we truly experience it as a creation of something that delights us just by being there. Fine music has the same effect and we are transported to deep within, if only for a few brief minutes. That's all it takes to reach and excite the spirit because sound and color are language to a child with autism. When children are continually exposed to truth, beauty, and goodness, such as is found in nature and the arts, they can grow, learn, and evolve, which are goals shared by each of us.

The most effective and compassionate parent, therapist, or teacher must acknowledge that human beings are more than a physical body and a physical brain. We have a spiritual essence that, like our mind, can't be seen or intellectually defined. However, like the mind, it plays an important part in our growth. Our feeling nature strives for perfection, which is its ultimate goal. At the same time, the Law of Polarity demands the opposite: complete indifference to one's spiritual betterment and attachment to the status quo. (For example, this Law identifies the opposites of day and night, sun and moon, good and bad, as well as right and left, up and down, and everything else we can think of that has "two sides.")

"Spiritual" in this context has no religious connotation; rather, it involves the development of spiritual qualities that begin before birth. These qualities combine with the body and mind to form our three-fold nature that is responsible for all areas of development. This differs from what is often viewed as "religious." Religious beliefs are most often associated with the teachings and doctrines of an organized movement. Therefore, one can be spiritual without having a formal religion, just as one can regularly attend a place of worship without being spiritual.

Remedial creative therapies and intelligent dialogue can transform the negative into the positive through enjoyable activities that help balance the hemispheres of the brain.

When the spirit of an individual is an influence in his life, negative qualities of human nature are transformed into positive, caring, beneficial acts of kindness and generosity. Remedial creative therapies and intelligent dialogue can transform the negative into the positive through enjoyable activities that help balance the hemispheres of the brain. As this happens, the three elements of body, mind, and spirit merge into an integrated, whole person. Parents can help their child to achieve that wholeness in the comfort of their home.

As you learn about the three elements of a whole person, you will understand how important it is for your child to be exposed to all things positive. You will further realize that each of the three aspects—body, mind, and spirit—has to be nourished in its own way. Then it will be apparent that the third factor, one's spirit, is usually overlooked in assembling a program to meet the needs of a child with autism. All of these add up to a belief that there must be a meaning to life. If there were no meaning to life, there would be no mention of one's spirit throughout recorded history. We would be nothing more than animals with the ability to talk and reason. It is the spirit that responds to the good, the true, and the beautiful, qualities that are to be found in nature, in the arts, and in many people.

Children in today's chaotic world are different from boys and girls of previous generations. Many are brilliant with an innate desire to explore and learn, and many are on the Autism Spectrum. Because they are different, a new form of therapy has to be explored, one with a holistic purpose that speaks to the child's ability to will, to think, and to feel. The words "to will" aren't commonly used, yet no action is ever taken without first having the intent. The intent is one's will, which is different from a thought. We may think about going for a walk in the park but until it becomes our intention, it's only a thought and our will is not being used. Once we leave the house, go to the park, and begin walking, our will has become our strength. You already know your child has a strong will when you ask him to do something and he refuses. The remedial and creative therapies in this book help to strengthen the three-fold nature of a child so that his willing, thinking, and feeling are all called into action when needed and aren't simply an instinctive reaction.

Children with ADHD and Asperger's often feel that people don't understand them because their supercharged minds work rapidly and in many directions. Their minds are constantly active, always wanting to learn and research. They are insatiably curious, willful, and inventive, eager to move ahead into areas that intrigue them, even though they may not be considered "the norm," especially in school. Teachers don't know how to deal with this new type of child who is always "on." Parents, who come home from work tired, hungry, and out of patience, are annoyed and frustrated by their child who is raring to go. Both teachers and parents often welcome medication for these children because it makes their lives easier by reducing hyperactive and destructive behavior. Unfortunately, it may diminish their curiosity, individuality, and desire to explore as well.

Change Is Inevitable

We have to accept change because it is inevitable. Our world is changing and we are evolving and changing, too. We are more intelligent than previous generations because we have had to adapt to increasing changes in our social, business, and personal lives. We have only to look at how computers have affected our lives. We had to learn how to use them and now they are found in most homes and offices. Our civilization is evolving, as

THE WILL TO CHANGE

When kids feel respected and supported, they want to improve, and their feelings about being different are not as overwhelming.

it always has, and it will continue to evolve until the end of time. Why should children not change along with everyone and everything else?

We can see this change in the influx in the last thirty years of many boys and girls who are brilliant, creative, and articulate alongside others who have the limitations of autism and Asperger's. We can now identify these states of mind as gifted or challenged. To help children achieve their greatest potential, we need to support differences and encourage abilities. Most of all, we need to let all children know we respect and love them. When kids feel respected and supported, they want to improve, and their feelings about being different are not as overwhelming.

The major difference in this new generation is the spiritual nature of these children. We might ask:

- Why have there been so many different kinds of therapies developed in the past ten or twenty years?

- Why is there such an emphasis on music, art, and movement, all of which affect our feelings?

- Why do children respond so well to these therapies?

The answer is, because these children are different. An interesting study by Eric Courchesne, PhD; Ruth Carper, PhD; and Natacha Akshoomoff, PhD was reported in the July 26, 2003 issue of the *Journal of the American Medical Association (JAMA)*. Their research indicated that the heads of many children with autism at birth are smaller than the average newborn's. It went on to say that while there was no difference in length and weight, there was a notable difference in head circumference. However, several months after birth there was a rapid and excessive increase in the size of the head, which might be a marker for autism. This growth slowed during late childhood and by the time an autistic reached adulthood, their heads were comparable to others'.

Why does this happen? We don't know the answer, but we do know that it happens as the brain is being formed, in about the third month of development. The study reported in *JAMA* rules out infections or diseases of the mother, environmental toxins, or any other physical contributory factors that might affect a child in his later years. Nothing else is physically affected in these children but their brain size.

The article made it clear that not all babies with small heads are autistic and not all autistic children have small heads. The research is worthy of attention, though, because this might be an early warning sign of autism. If this is the case, very early intervention is necessary when the brain is still elastic and capable of inputting information that increases brain growth.

Difference Can Be Good

Kids with autism and Asperger's know they're different and tell us they don't like being different from other kids. Once everybody understands that "different" isn't necessarily negative, no one will consider such neurological disorders incurable and debilitating conditions. Parents will also change as they accept that their child may be different from their siblings and perhaps from all other children they know. Difference can be good because it creates a transformation in people, and there is no growth without it. Here is how autism can transform our way of thinking:

- Mothers: Perhaps you were a person who saw a child acting up in a store and said to another shopper, "That child needs discipline." Now that you have an autistic child who throws himself on the floor and screams in the supermarket, you have more compassion for embarrassed mothers who are trying desperately to quiet their children. So, you have changed and grown.

  Or, by improving your child's diet, you may have learned the value of nutrition and changed the way you shop and prepare meals. Consequently, the entire family has benefited.

- Fathers: Most fathers have high hopes for their infant sons and may look forward to the day when they can toss a football or shoot some hoops on the driveway together. When they learn that their young son is autistic or their older boy would rather paint and dance, some fathers may be deeply disappointed or angry. Change may be a little slower in these fathers, but most begin to realize that there are many different kinds of people in this world and not all are interested in sports.

- Siblings: Siblings of children with autism are often protective and may show compassion towards other children—who may have been the object of their ridicule before their brother or sister was diagnosed with a Spectrum Disorder. As peers notice this improved attitude, their outlook changes and they begin to have a better understanding of disabilities. It becomes a process of educating other young people.

- Teachers: Teachers are learning how to identify temperaments that clearly make children different from each other. (See Chapter 8 for more information on temperaments.) As a result, they're changing the way in which children had previously been lumped into one group called "normal."

- Medical Professionals: Autism has spurred medical research that may never have happened. Drug companies have removed preservatives from MMR (mumps/measles/rubella) vaccines that are suspected causes of autism. (As of this writing, thimerosal, the preservative in the MMR vaccine, is still used in some American flu vaccines, though never those for infants.) You will read more about MMR and mercury (possible, though unproven, contributors to autism) in Chapter 2.

SUMMARY

There has been a worldwide increase in autism cases, and many children on the Autism Spectrum are not recognized as possibly being gifted and very intelligent. Although we don't know exactly how or why this increase is happening, we do know that conventional treatment methods are not as effective as they could be. By addressing a child's three-fold nature of body, mind, and spirit, and understanding the need for truth, beauty, and goodness to create mutual respect and trust, we can treat the whole child.

When a treatment program is developed for your child, you are entitled and urged to participate in his therapy by working with him at home. By filling your home with fine music, art, good food, and conversation, you will create an environment that is pleasing to your child's feeling nature, his spirit. Your selection of toys and games is important as well, because anything that gives step-by-step instructions on how to play removes all desire to be inventive and creative.

In the next chapter, we will explore autism more fully and discuss some of the theories and findings relating to its causes and treatments—for example, the importance of nutrition, how the environment may contribute to Spectrum Disorders, and the intriguing subjects of gut issues and stem cells.

CHAPTER 2

*F*inding the Keys to Autism Spectrum Disorders—

Exploring Possible Causes and Treatments

Despite the advances that have been made in diagnosis and treatment over the past twenty years, autism is still a mystery. Because autism and Autism Spectrum Disorders are relatively new conditions, as opposed to polio, for example, there is a great deal of conjecture about the causes of, and the care for children with, such neurological disturbances. We don't know how or why it happens. We do know that Spectrum Disorders are global in nature and no respecter of social strata, nationality, wealth, education, race, or anything else that tends to separate people. Although it can be confusing to the medical profession and parents, at least people are talking and speculating about Spectrum Disorders.

This chapter will explore some of the major culprits believed to be at least partially responsible for autism and other Spectrum Disorders, as well as some methods that have been used to treat these puzzling conditions. It is suggested that an integrative approach of medicine and the creative arts is the most effective means of reaching and teaching children on the Spectrum.

You will learn about precautions parents can take to make their homes safer for the entire family by recognizing chemicals in common household products that may be harmful.

This chapter also discusses two controversial topics of global interest: the use of stem cells for research and treatment, and mercury as a possible cause of autism. Both are impartially presented and provide information for much thought and discussion.

WHAT CAUSES AUTISM?

There are many theories about the cause of autism, including genetics, the environment, vaccines, and viral inflammations such as encephalitis. Although all have some validity, the major trauma is a gap or break—an *infraction*—in part of the brain. This break is responsible for incomplete transmission of thoughts from one section of the brain to another, through what are known as *neuropathways*. Development of these pathways occurs in the first three months in the uterus, when the brain is being wired and may be contaminated by other factors that complicate research and treatment. For example, another theory is that the infraction may be the result of toxins in the mother's body that are transferred to the developing embryo.

Although it is not known exactly what causes this disruption of the neuropathways' development, it is obvious that children on the Spectrum share similar characteristics. For example, they may all show some degree of difficulty focusing on tasks, poor social skills, lack of organizational ability, and/or a tendency to withdraw, with alternating periods of excessive activity. These boys and girls require early remedial work that engages the whole body, energizing the brain to re-establish neuropathways and creating healing from within. Involving children in activities that stimulate organs and the autonomic nervous system generates new brain cells. And, by creating new cells, synapses (or connections) are formed that bridge the gap. This allows information to flow through neuropathways, as it should.

SEARCHING FOR EFFECTIVE THERAPIES

There are many therapies available to parents of children on the Spectrum, the most effective being a combined approach that addresses the whole child. For example, a program designed specifically for each child should include some or all of the following:

- Remedial, artistic therapies (music, painting, sculpture, drawing, and movement)

- Medical treatment, if necessary

- Nutritional evaluation and change of diet

- Rhythmic massage

- Speech therapy

- Sensory integration

- Exercises designed to help balance the hemispheres of the brain and create new neuropathways

By using a comprehensive program that combines traditional and non-traditional methods, you will be reaching and teaching the whole child. This approach works on her three-fold nature to create changes in the body, which seeks to heal itself. Remedial, creative therapies are designed to initiate changes in a child with neurological disorders, since each art form stimulates a different aspect of her three-fold nature of body, mind, and spirit. The innate intelligence of your child's body tries to reach a point of constant normal rhythm instead of simply functioning in an abnormal, out-of-sync, and disorderly manner.

When conventional therapies are combined with the less-known but very effective artistic remedial therapies, we find noticeable improvements in a number of areas. The readily apparent results of this multimodality method are a desire to draw, paint, dance, and work with clay. This is a huge step for tactilely defensive children because their interest shows an inner activity manifesting in an outer expression—the goal of all therapists and parents of autistic children.

You will find more information in upcoming chapters on all of these ways of helping your child. For your child's best interests, be sure traditional therapy will also include the non-traditional methods described in these chapters for a truly holistic program designed specifically for your child.

POTENTIAL CULPRITS AND CURES

Over the years there have been many theories, discoveries, and therapies developed to help Spectrum children overcome their limitations, but so far, no one has been able to say without any doubt that there is one specific cause or one miraculous therapy. There are, however, some helpful treatments as well as common-sense suggestions for creating a safe environment for children with ADD, autism, and Asperger's. With such a complex array of symptoms, it's unlikely that there's only one culprit or cure in the following list of potentials.

Biomedicals/Nutritionals

This category may sound intimidating, but it simply means a combination of biology, medicine, and nutrition. It mainly focuses on how food affects the body and changes that should be made to the diet in addition to medical treatment. Children on the Spectrum are highly sensitive to certain ingredients in common foods. Most offenders are in the foods we eat every day, such as soup and bread.

Aspartame and Monosodium Glutamate (MSG)

Aspartame and MSG are two of the most controversial substances in diets of people today. Neither is necessary for good nutrition and both are suspect in a number of illnesses.

A lot of restaurant food contains additives like aspartame and MSG, both of which can have unpleasant or serious side effects. (You will read more about additives in Chapter 6.) Aspartame, a sweetener and sugar substitute, and MSG, a "flavor enhancer," might be responsible for brain damage. Glutamate and asparatate are amino acids (found in MSG and aspartame) that are naturally produced by the body, but when too much

The New Kids on the Block

Many children born since the last quarter of the twentieth century are uncommonly intelligent and alert. They must be given every opportunity to grow creatively through the arts and to pursue their interests so they can tap into their optimum potential.

A large number of this new generation of children can be generally divided into four groups.

The Gifted

The first group, the gifted, learn quickly and remember what they have read, heard, seen, felt, or experienced, but are unorganized and scattered in many areas. Most are gifted, articulate, and self-assured, even arrogant. They are impatient with routine and structure, yet they need both to function in the world as we know it. They are excitable because new people, new books, and new ideas are waiting to be explored. To them, focusing on one subject that isn't riveting is a waste of time when they could be thinking about three or four other things at once.

The children in this group are born artists with a great imagination and love of music and art. Because of their exuberance and sensitive body that is often ravaged by unrecognized allergies, and because teachers and parents don't know how to relate to this new "species," they are labeled "abnormal." If they are overly active, they are prescribed Ritalin or other psychotropic drugs. They are children with a label of ADD or ADHD, and their uniqueness is slowly and systematically being destroyed by people who want no deviation from the norm of mediocrity.

The Intelligent Who Lack Verbal Skills

There is a second group of children, most of whom are very intelligent but lacking in verbal skills or ability. They, too, respond to art, music, and movement. Many parents say that their children began life as happy, healthy babies and toddlers, and then suddenly, between eighteen months and two-and-a-half years, a dramatic change occurred. Terrified parents saw their toddlers regress into infancy. Speech, language, and eye contact were gone. Socialization and recognition of parents were non-existent and the urge to explore was lost. These children are labeled "autistic" and their involvements range from relatively mild to severe. Nevertheless, they show signs of awareness at times by a sideways look, a slight smile, a beautiful painting, or a great interest in someone or something.

The Creative Who Lack Social Skills

The third group shares some characteristics of ADD and autism. The easily recognized signposts of poor social skills, fiery temper, and obsessive behavior identify children with Asperger's Syndrome. They are very intelligent, artistic, articulate, and aware that they are "different" from their peers. Because of this, once a therapist is accepted and trusted, improvement is rapid and noticeable to their parents, teachers, and physicians. Asperger's Syndrome is usually not recognized until around the age of six, when a child enters school and her behavior is clearly inappropriate.

It is sad but true that Asperger's Syndrome is still unknown to many people, including those in the medical profession. It has been overlooked for so long because of the "boys will be boys" attitude that dismisses an actual neurological disorder as simply childish masculine behavior. However, when a child starts school and is with a group of other children of the same age, it becomes obvious to teachers that explosive outbursts of temper, failure to associate with peers, and threats of bodily harm are not normal and need professional attention.

These three groups share a common bond of intelligence and love of the arts. They are different from other children and perhaps from their siblings. They all march to a different drummer and can be difficult to communicate with. And they are all on the Autism Spectrum.

Children with ADD are usually very articulate while those with autism are more withdrawn, yet both groups respond to love, compassion, respect, and the creative arts. These polar opposites meet in the middle of the bar—Asperger's. These three groups of children are "a different breed," and timeworn therapies must change to meet that difference. We need to bring back not only the arts of the great civilizations, but also the deep reverence that inspired them. Today, we are starting once again to swing rapidly towards knowledge of truth, beauty, and goodness. To help our children grow safely into a healthy life, we have to accept this wisdom, bring it into our culture, and give it to the people who desperately need it.

The Average Child

The fourth and largest group is of children with no debilitating disorder. They are "average" or "typical" and basically need no special care other than the love, nurturing, and respect of their parents. Many children in this fourth group are brilliant and receptive to their inspirational thoughts that emanate from the feeling aspect of their three-fold nature. They are assertive and firm in their opinions. They want to know why they have to do certain things, like obey rules. When they ask questions, they want answers.

Many are incredibly gifted in music and art. They play instruments, sing, and speak in a style far beyond their years. They are self-assured, have a good sense of humor, and appear destined to be leaders in whatever field they choose.

Each of these four groups is "different" and together they are changing the world by forcing us to change our outmoded way of stereotyping young boys and girls. They bring new awareness to the medical profession, which is constantly searching for answers to these natural variations in children.

is present in the brain, they can cause nerve cells to overexcite and destroy themselves.

Although there is no definite connection between aspartame and autism, there is enough proof that this substance causes distress, from nausea to mimicking the symptoms of multiple sclerosis and lupus. Also known as NutraSweet, aspartame is responsible for over ninety documented ailments resulting from its use. This is discussed more fully in Chapter 6. Many believe that the use of aspartame during pregnancy has an effect on the developing child. More than one expert on the subject states that there is absolutely no reason for its use, including Lewis Mehl-Madrona, MD, PhD, of the University of Saskatchewan College of Medicine.

Monosodium glutamate (MSG) is virtually unknown in cultures that use spices in their cooking, and there is no logical reason to add it to food. This additive is known to cause a variety of problems, including diarrhea, bloating, nausea, depression, hyperactivity, migraines, and breathing problems—to name just a few.

According to the Association for Freedom of Choice and Correct Information, John Erb, the author of *The Slow Poisoning of America*, discovered there are many disturbing repercussions from consuming MSG. Mr. Erb met with Dr. Thomas Ward, Nova Scotia's Deputy Minister of Health, a pediatrician who specialized in Neonatology. After Erb detailed the dangers of MSG, Dr. Ward responded, "I know how awful the stuff is. I would never touch it." Naturally, Erb stressed the necessity of removing MSG from all food; however, Dr. Ward said that the federal government would have to be in charge of such a task.

The only way to protect yourself and your children from additives is to read the labels of boxes, bags, and cans to be sure the product doesn't contain aspartame or MSG. Like aspartame, there appears to be no direct connection between MSG and autism. However, there is no point in eating or drinking substances that are known to cause numerous physical problems.

The FDA outlawed the use of aspartame in 1984, but then approved it sixteen years later—and it is still in use today, even though the hazards of this substance are well known.

Gluten

While aspartame is an additive to foods, gluten is a natural substance found in the countless food products containing wheat. Gluten is the elastic protein substance in wheat that gives it body and is found in many foods, such as bread and other baked goods. Gluten intolerance is not unusual, especially among children on the Spectrum who may have violent reactions, such as irrational behavior, to gluten.

In an article in the *Journal of Neurology, Neurosurgery, and Psychiatry*, "Gluten Sensitivity as a Neurological Illness," by M. Hadjivassiliou, R.A. Grünewald, and G.A.B. Davies-Jones of the Department of Neurology, The Royal Hallamshire Hospital, the authors stated, "Our original study concluded that gluten sensitivity played an important part in neurological illness." They further stated that some researchers think that gluten may trigger other autoimmune disease.

Ataxia is the loss of muscle coordination, a condition that is not uncommon in autism. Gluten ataxia is the neurological condition that results from sensitivity to gluten. Not all children who are sensitive to gluten have ataxia; however, weakening or loss of fine and gross motor skills is common in children on the Spectrum. Some have a puzzling rash that is relieved when wheat is removed from their diet, while others have reduced behavioral problems such as hyperactivity. In the publication of the American Academy of Neurology, Dr. Hadjivassiliou wrote: "Gluten ataxia is a common neurological manifestation of gluten sensitivity."

Although there is no direct link to Spectrum Disorders, there is evidence that removal of gluten from a child's diet correlates with rapid improvement in physical symptoms such as ataxia, inability to focus on tasks, headaches, stomach distress, and problematic behavior. Physicians usually recommend a slow removal of wheat from the diet, since there may be withdrawal.

It is important for you or your physician to confer with an allergist to determine what foods should be eliminated from your child's diet.

According to the American Academy of Neurology, the cerebellum, which is the part of the brain responsible for coordination, is most affected by gluten ataxia.

It is important for you or your physician to confer with an allergist to determine what foods should be eliminated from your child's diet. Many children on the Autism Spectrum have allergies, and dietary changes should be made. This is one of the first steps you can personally take towards developing the wholeness of your child. It may not be the easiest, however, because children on the Spectrum often have their favorite foods and will eat nothing else. In Chapter 6, the chapter on nutrition, you will find some good ideas about substituting healthy foods for your child's unhealthy favorites.

Heavy Metals and Chelation

The symptoms of mercury poisoning are similar to those of autism, as stated in the Direct Laboratory Services, Inc. Newsletter of February 27, 2004. Most children on the Spectrum test positively for mercury in their system. Many also have lead, aluminum, and arsenic in their bodies, but in much smaller amounts than mercury. The source of mercury is often believed to be the preservative formerly used in infant vaccines or possibly fish the mother ate while pregnant. Another theory is that mercury from the mother's dental fillings "leaked" from her teeth to the developing child. As with the disorder of autism, causes and theories are often speculative and always controversial.

In addition to having heavy metals in their systems, children on the Spectrum usually have digestive problems and bowel problems. The metals have to be removed because they negatively affect the brain and the body. A large number of professionals state that a link exists between heavy metals and Spectrum disorders. The symptoms of heavy metal poisoning are the same symptoms noted in children on the Spectrum. They include inability to focus, digestive upsets, allergies, headaches, and fatigue.

Nicola McFadzean, ND, states that mineral deficiencies are seen to play a significant role in ADHD behaviors.

In her article, "Heavy Metal Toxicity and Autism," Meredith Lazaroff, PhD, Neuroscientist, Developmental Disabilities Resource Center, writes, "Mercury poisoning and autism spectrum disorders share similar traits including loss of speech or failure to develop speech, poor concentration, language comprehension difficulties, sensory disturbances, and sleep difficulties." Since most complaints are relieved or eliminated when metals are removed, it is logical to assume there is a direct connection.

A common way of removing the presence of metals from the body is to use chelation, or a chelator. This word comes from *chele*, a Greek word meaning "claw." It paints a vivid picture of this substance reaching out and grabbing lead or mercury from the system and eliminating it through the urine.

In an article dated August 29, 2005, and updated March 2006, the Autism Research Institute states, "Chelation is not used to treat autism, but rather to treat heavy metal overload (lead, mercury, cadmium, etc), which is a major cause of autism and retardation."

All metals but mercury remain in the blood and can be detected by blood tests for quite some time. Although mercury seems to disappear from the body, a small amount remains hidden in brain tissue. Mercury has a shorter stay of a few weeks or months, at which time it migrates to the organs and brain. A biopsy of the organs will tell for certain if there's mercury in them, but this is a rather drastic step when the physician can tell by symptoms how toxic the child is. (See page 40 for more information on mercury.)

Before treatment can be started, hair and urine samples are sent to a laboratory for analysis, since they are reflective of the blood. If the results show high levels of metals, such as arsenic, aluminum, lead, cadmium, and mercury, chelation seems to help get rid of them. In this process, an agent, such as DMSA, is introduced orally or transdermally (by gel through the skin) that binds the metals to it, and they are then passed out of the body in the urine.

DMSA was approved by the FDA and is used by a number of doctors. However, other physicians object to the use of this drug and cite cases of seizures and nervous system dysfunction due to the redistribution of mercury in vital organs, including the brain. Chelation is a controversial procedure that should be done under a doctor's supervision. Many parents whose children have gone through the process are very enthusiastic about the improvements they've noticed after chelation.

Chemical Culprits in Our Environment

There is no escaping our environment, which is filled with toxins that we eat, drink, and breathe. Chemicals are widespread in our immediate home, school, and work environments. Chemicals saturate our surroundings, and this has created a new classification of allergies called Multiple Chemical Sensitivity (MCS). People with MCS are highly sensitive to dozens of things, and an increasing number of people are continuously ill just trying to survive in their homes. Adults and non-autistic children may articulate how they feel or move someplace else, but autistic kids can't do those things. They are affected, too, but nobody knows why they cry or vomit, or are hyperactive or lethargic.

Phthalates (pronounced without the "ph") are dangerous chemicals that are more common than we think. They are found in everyday products such as cosmetics, shower curtains, wallpaper, raincoats, detergents, hair spray, and nail polish. Animal studies have shown that phthalates have caused abnormalities in the male reproductive system. The FDA has called for a review of this softening chemical.

Too few doctors recognize the effects of environmental poisoning and may dismiss repeated complaints as either psychosomatic or lack of response to traditional treatment. Fortunately for all of us, the number of researchers studying Multiple Chemical Sensitivity is increasing as more cases come to their attention. This is especially important for children on the Spectrum, who have very sensitive constitutions.

Bernard Weiss (Department of Environmental Medicine, University of Rochester School of Medicine and Dentistry) and Philip J. Landrigan (Department of Community and Preventive Medicine, Mount Sinai School of Medicine), in a joint paper in *Environmental Health Perspectives*, state, "We know the causes of fewer than 25% of neurodevelopmental disabilities." However, they continue, "We have come to understand that chemicals in the environment can cause a wide range of developmental disabilities in children."

Many cases of fatigue, muscle ache, allergies, muddled thinking, hyperactivity, and miscellaneous complaints can be directly traced to our surroundings. With ever-present chemicals in our house, where we work or go to school, and in the things we eat, drink, breathe, or are exposed to, it's no wonder many people feel under par much of the time.

Our homes, schools and offices are often the source of Multiple Chemical Sensitivity in children on the Spectrum. When we consider a school, for example, we have to take into account the paint and cleaning solutions used to maintain the building. Furniture and carpeting are sources of fumes from the manufacture of these products. In the past two decades,

Too few doctors recognize the effects of environmental poisoning and may dismiss repeated complaints as either psychosomatic or lack of response to traditional treatment.

Don't Use Bug Sprays!

Pesticide poisoning is a major cause of toxicity in children, and sprays are commonly used in homes, parks, schools, businesses, and food. Insect sprays are the easiest toxins to eliminate from your home environment. Just don't use them. They carry fumes throughout the house, and when used in the kitchen, contaminate food and utensils. Children are more at risk because their small bodies absorb just as much as that of an adult, but the toxins get more concentrated. Their fingers are frequently in their mouths, and absorption of poison is probable. Symptoms of pesticide poisoning are often mistaken for the flu and later may show as neurological impairment. Such neurological impairment may manifest as Spectrum Disorders.

To reduce your exposure to pesticides, you can take several precautions. First of all, don't walk barefoot on lawns that have been sprayed. Whenever possible, buy organic produce. It is more expensive, but much safer to consume than non-organic. Peel non-organic fruits and vegetables, and always wash all produce prior to using. Try washing fruits and vegetables with Fit, a natural product that is said to remove more chemicals and wax than water alone. Instead of using pesticide sprays, use the old-fashioned household methods of black pepper to get rid of ants and boric acid powder for roaches.

Some heavily roach-infested cities in the Southwest United States spray sewers with a boric acid solution. This powder is available in drugstores and can be sprinkled in cabinets, but for hard-to-reach places, here's a "recipe" that will stop roaches in their tracks using common kitchen ingredients. Strange as it sounds, this is the best bug killer to use around the house.

Sauté some onion and mix with enough peanut butter to make a cookie consistency. Add a generous amount of boric acid powder to the mixture and roll into balls. Freeze and then roll the balls under the refrigerator or stove, and in the backs of cabinets. Roaches are attracted to the food and are killed by the boric acid. This is an easy, safe, and effective alternative to dangerous roach sprays.

more and more people are prey to the "sick building syndrome" that causes illness from mild to severe.

Speaking to the Multiple Chemical Sensitivity Symposium held in May 2001, Nicholas A. Ashford, PhD, JD, stated, "Increasingly, evidence links chemicals and autoimmune diseases (including lupus, scleroderma, and rheumatoid arthritis), attention deficit hyperactivity disorder (ADHD), autism (one out of six children in the U.S. has autism, aggression, or ADHD), depression, asthma (which has doubled in incidence in the last 10 years)."

Essential Fatty Acids (EFAs)

Most children on the Spectrum are deficient in essential fatty acids (EFAs), which are vitally important to keeping the body in balance. Essential fatty acids are necessary for good health in everyone, but especially for children on the Autism Spectrum. EFAs are good fats, which we need to nourish brain tissue and neurons. They also help to strengthen weakened gut tissue. We can't create these fats within our bodies as we can with many other substances, so we have to get them from food or supplements.

One well-known example of an essential fatty acid is omega-3. Good sources of EFAs are flaxseed oil, fish oil, evening primrose oil, canola oil, soybean oil, and nuts, especially walnuts. (However, doctors today caution against using too much fish oil because of the high amount of mercury being found in fish.) Symptoms of an EFA deficiency include dry skin, dry scalp, dry hair, excessive thirst, Attention Deficit Hyperactivity Disorder, and dyslexia.

Parents have found that when their Spectrum children take EFAs every day they sleep better, have fewer behavioral problems, and sometimes show improved speech.

A study at Oxford University of forty-one children between ages eight and twelve who had dyslexia and ADHD was launched to test the effects of key fatty acid nutrients. Some children received a placebo of a garlic oil capsule; others received highly unsaturated fatty acids (HUFAs). At the end of twelve weeks, the children who had been given the placebo showed no improvements, while the children who had taken the HUFAs showed improvement in attention and cognitive skills.

Parents have found that when their Spectrum children take EFAs every day they sleep better, have fewer behavioral problems, and sometimes show improved speech.

You should check with your physician about vitamins, supplements, EFAs, probiotics, digestive enzymes, calcium/magnesium, and immune support products. Many children on the Spectrum are given one or more of these aids, which are found in health food stores.

Gastrointestinal Impairment

Gastrointestinal problems are common in children with autism. These are often referred to, within the autism community, as "gut" issues, or "leaky gut." We're just beginning to learn from how the Chinese have been approaching the treatment of autism for many years: by focusing on the child's gastrointestinal (GI) and immune systems. No prescription drugs are used in their treatment, which is based on the belief that autistic children have an impaired digestive system that prevents the body from absorbing nutrients needed for brain development. Physicians around the world are in agreement that children with autism have gut problems.

Autistic children have abnormal gastrointestinal systems, perhaps stemming from improper pancreatic function or viral infections. As a result, proteins aren't completely broken down, leaving a residue of undigested amino acids called peptides, which are similar to opiates, the use of which can cause some of the familiar symptoms of autism. The biggest offenders that produce peptides are milk, oats, barley, wheat, and rye, which are usually removed from the diet of children on the Spectrum. Ordinarily, peptides would be eliminated through the stool, but in this case, they're absorbed by a weakened gut lining before proceeding into the bloodstream and eventually the brain, perhaps through a weakened blood-brain barrier. This membrane keeps toxins and metals from entering the brain, but mercury can pass through the blood-brain barrier of children. (It is for this reason that chelation may be recommended. See page 31 for information on chelation.)

Research supports this connection between autism and gastrointestinal problems. English gastroenterologist Dr. Andrew Wakefield (with colleagues), in a colonoscopy study reported in the *American Journal of Gastroenterology* of sixty children with developmental disorders, including fifty

---

Methyl-B12: An Encouraging Vitamin Therapy

Dr. James Neubrander, at the Autism One conference on May 29, 2005, presented a promising vitamin therapy treatment for autism and other neurodevelopmental disorders. He discovered that methyl-B12 has a profound effect on autism and related conditions.

B12 (cobalamin) is described as a vitamin "family" with five specific members, each having different functions. Methylcobalamin, or methyl-B12, is the only member able to activate the methionine/homocysteine biochemical pathway directly. This pathway is responsible for the body's entire sulfur-based detoxification system, and for the formation of S-adenosylmethionine (SAMe), the universal methyl donor.

Neubrander stated that many children using methyl-B12, in combination with other biomedical and non-biomedical therapies, lost their diagnosis of having neurodevelopmental impairment.

Dr. Neubrander's presentation indicated that 94 percent of children had been found to respond to methyl-B12 therapy. Awareness, cognition, appropriateness, eye contact, and other characteristics present in neurotypical children were improved in about 90 percent of children. Various speech and language skills were developed in 80 percent of children; these skills included the presence of spontaneous language, more complex sentences, and increased vocabulary. Approximately 70 percent of the children showed improvements in socialization and emotion. These children initiated and engaged in interactive play. Emotions were felt and understood, apparently for the first time or at a greater neuro-typical level.

He went on to say that it is important for parents and clinicians to understand that the maximum results from methyl-B12 therapy occur over years of use. Initial results may be apparent within the first five weeks; however, methyl-B12's power is derived from its long-term use.

Increased activity levels, sleep disturbances, and increased mouthing of objects were the most common side effects of methyl-B12 therapy.

Dr. Neubrander's discovery is highly encouraging; however, methyl-B12 is a treatment, not a cure.

with autism, concluded: "A new variant of inflammatory bowel disease is present in this group of children with developmental disorders." Harvard researchers studied 500 gastrointestinal biopsies and discovered that more than half of autistic children had gut disorders. Gut disorders can include diarrhea, constipation, gas, and foul stools.

We know the average child is given a variety of drugs and antibiotics in her short life. Children with autism have large amounts of yeast in their intestines, most likely from the use of a broad-spectrum antibiotic given routinely for earaches. This medication removes both the bad and good bacteria in the gut, which then have to be replaced with probiotics to restore the natural flora.

Suggestions for helping gut disturbances may include lactobacillus, yogurt, and/or a gluten-free/casein-free (GFCF) diet. (See page 30 for more about gluten.) Be sure your child drinks plenty of water, because she has to keep hydrated. Distilled water contains nothing but pure water, causing some to object that beneficial minerals are removed in the distillation process, along with the chlorine, pesticides, and heavy metals found in some drinking water. Other supplements can always be added to the child's diet. Discuss these options with a trusted professional, such as a medical practitioner or a nutritionist.

Genetics

Dr. Leo Kanner, who first identified autism as Associate Professor of Psychiatry at Johns Hopkins Medical Center in 1943, noted that in most cases the child's behavior was abnormal from early infancy, and he suggested the presence of an inborn, presumably genetic, defect. A genetic link may be overlooked in families because many people are unfamiliar with the signs of autism. Some parents don't want to believe their child's disorder can be genetic and feel that admitting autism "runs in the family" is something to be ashamed of. They look to other causes, like the environment or vaccines.

Because some characteristics of autism often appear in several members of the same family, there appears to be a genetic link that shows itself in different ways. It's not uncommon for an autistic child to have, for example, an eccentric uncle who has a large train collection, or an aunt who collects pieces of string. Some relatives may show musical genius; others may be unable to hold a conversation.

Siblings may or may not be affected. Twins are often autistic, but sometimes one has the disorder and the other doesn't. That would seem to indicate that it is not environmental, but it could also mean that one twin has a stronger immune system. In some families there are two sets of

Some parents don't want to believe their child's disorder can be genetic and feel that admitting autism "runs in the family" is something to be ashamed of. They look to other causes, like the environment or vaccines.

There is a strong tendency for autism to cluster in families, although children with this disorder tend more often to be the first and only child.

twins, each of whom has autism. Because there is no proof one way or the other, we need to explore all possibilities and proceed with a program that treats the whole child.

Visible clues relating a child to a relative who has "quirks" characteristic of that same disorder are more common with Asperger's than with autism. Children with autism do not have overtly autistic parents. That is, mother or father may have some autistic tendencies such as an intense sensitivity to noise. They may dislike being touched and think that hugging is distasteful. They may feel a need to separate food on their plate, leaving a space between each vegetable. These are often considered mere idiosyncrasies, but at some point in their research for information about autism, parents usually begin to see a vague similarity to their child's more pronounced behavior. (The characteristics of autism are described in detail in Chapter 3.)

There is a strong tendency for autism to cluster in families, although children with this disorder tend more often to be the first and only child. A study by S. Folstein and M. Rutter, obtained from the database Online Mendelian Inheritance in Man (OMIM) at Johns Hopkins University, stated that if there are other children, only about 2 percent of siblings are affected, most commonly with speech delays. The researchers went on to say that there were no recorded cases in which "an autistic child had an overtly autistic parent." However, they noted that people with autism rarely marry and rarely give birth.

Because Asperger's Syndrome and ADD/ADHD are less severe than autism, the genetic factor is usually overlooked until similarities are brought to parents' attention. The characteristics of brief attention span, inability to focus on tasks, mood swings, tantrums, or feelings of inadequacy are often considered a normal part of childhood. And they are to a certain extent. It is the degree of anger or the time spent staring into space that are clues that such behavior is not developmentally appropriate. It is not unusual to find several children in the same family demonstrating a variety of characteristics that are symptomatic of Spectrum Disorders other than autism.

Vaccine Dangers

Vaccinations can have a positive effect on the health of the public and have saved many lives over the years. However, in the past there were some potential dangers in some infant vaccines, based upon the presence of *thimerosal* (also known as *thiomersal* or *thimerosol*).

In the past, the most compelling evidence regarding the relationship of vaccinations and developmental disorders was the coincidental time line. Many parents stated that their child had been developing normally until being vaccinated, at which time she began regressing. Because this was so often the case, it was difficult to declare that anything other than the vaccine (such as the MMR vaccine) was the culprit. However, since autism is a global event, and people in other parts of the world do not receive as many shots, there must have been something more than vaccinations involved. This was such a relatively new phenomenon, it is impossible to say with certainty that mercury in the vaccine had been the sole cause. It has been, however, a primary cause of concern in the autism community. The chapter on autism, Chapter 3, has more details about this.

Years ago a child didn't get her first shot until two months of age. Now, within days of birth, infants are vaccinated. According to an article by Donald G. McNeil, Jr. published November 30, 2002 in the New York *Times*, children often receive up to twenty vaccines in the first two years of life. Whether infants can handle so many vaccines at once is subject to debate; many feel that these shots should be given at intervals rather than together. In any case, one of these vaccines, routinely given at a very young age, is for MMR (the childhood illnesses of measles, mumps, and rubella). Until recently, this triple shot contained thimerosal, a preservative that is a suspected cause of autism.

Childhood Illnesses Before Vaccinations

At one time doctors and the general public believed that childhood illnesses were called that for a reason—that they are meant to occur in childhood (when symptoms typically will be milder) because they inoculate people against more serious illnesses as they get older. Until the ascendancy of the drug industry, parents routinely exposed their children to the mumps, measles, or chickenpox of their siblings or next-door neighbor. They felt that it was better to have the disease as a child than as an adult. Very few people today are familiar with the way their great-grandparents inoculated children by deliberately exposing them to childhood illnesses, and even if they are, it's likely that they would dismiss the method as old-fashioned. It is, but it works. Often remedies and advice passed down from one generation to the next provide the most effective cures for illnesses. In years past, doctors would routinely treat their patients with herbs and plants. They proved that a poisonous plant could also be used to cure a person who had been poisoned by it, since the plant also acted as an antidote. This is the same principle in vaccines, such as those for polio and smallpox. A small amount of the disease is injected, and as the body reacts to this foreign substance, it finds the strength to combat the disease's future attempts to invade. This is the basis of homeopathy, a medical practice that believes in the Law of Similars—or "like treats like." This isn't as strange as it sounds; in fact, homeopathic physicians have treated the royal family of England for many generations.

Thimerosal

Thimerosal is viewed as a possible causative factor because prior to having received the MMR jab, an unusually high number of children who had been perfectly healthy and developing normally began to regress within days or weeks of the shot. Researchers noted that, as opposed to the triple dose, the single vaccines for each illness of the MMR vaccination did not contain thimerosal. Adding to the overall puzzle of autism and the controversy about vaccines is that some doctors believe the MMR jab is responsible for autism but that thimerosal has nothing to do with it.

This is probably the most talked-about subject of our time, with one side of the medical community insisting that mercury is the culprit and the other stating that it is not. In America, due to public outcry, thimerosal was removed from animal vaccines over a decade ago and from contact lens solutions in 1998—yet it remains in some human flu vaccines today, although these vaccines are never given to infants. All vaccines in Canada are thimerosal-free.

Mercury

The body breaks down thimerosal into methyl-mercury, which is known to cause neurodevelopmental abnormalities. High doses can cause kidney disease. Mercury is one of the most toxic substances on earth and can pass through the blood-brain barrier of children. It travels throughout the body, damaging the kidneys, central nervous system, and brain, and has the potential to be passed on to offspring through pregnant women. The Environmental Protection Agency (EPA) standard of safety for methyl-mercury, usually obtained from eating fish, such as tuna, is 0.1 micrograms. During most of the 1990s, many six-month-old babies in the United States had been given 187.5 micrograms through vaccinations.

Even if we don't eat fish, we probably have mercury in our bodies. It's in our drinking water, which is another reason to use distilled water. It is used in amalgam dental fillings, and almost everyone has at least one filling that's leaking mercury into their body. In 2005, the Norwegian Directorate of Health and Social Welfare recommended that dentists in that country not use amalgam in their practices.

Stem Cells

There is probably nothing more controversial in medical discoveries today than the harvesting and use of stem cells. This is not unexpected because all discoveries are initially met with suspicion, cynicism, and doubt as to how practical, affordable, and effective they will be. In the case of stem cells, the arguments focus on religious or moral beliefs.

Stem cells are cells that have the remarkable potential to develop into many different cell types in the body. Serving as a sort of repair system for the body, they can theoretically divide without limit to replenish other cells for as long as the person or animal is still alive. When a stem cell divides, each "daughter" cell has the potential either to remain a stem cell or to become another type of cell with a more specialized function, such as a muscle cell, a red blood cell, or a brain cell.

Research into stem cells is providing promising results and speculation that they might be used to rebuild tissue, cells, and neuropathways in the brain. Stem cells don't migrate to mature cells, only to those that seem to be lacking something in their own cells. This is potentially one of the most important advances in research into disease and neurological disorders. There is evidence that stem cells can grow new tissue in the liver, gut, and skin. It used to be thought that only stem cells found in the bone marrow could make new blood cells.

It had been previously known that bone marrow cells can enter the brains of mice and form new neurons. However, a study by Eva Mezey, MD, (along with S. Key, G. Vogelsang, I. Szalayova, G.D. Lange, and B. Crain) at the National Institutes of Health (NIH)/National Institute of Neurological Disorders and Stroke (NINDS), concluded that adult human bone marrow cells can enter the brain and generate neurons just as rodent cells do. Apparently, mature stem cells do not create new cells, but instead merge with existing cells. Although this study did not focus on autism, it does prove that cells migrate and form neurons and brain tissue. This is encouraging news, as this could potentially be used to prevent the development or progression of neurodegenerative disorders or to repair brain tissue damaged by trauma or incomplete neural tubes.

Stem cells are being investigated as treatment for Parkinson's disease and autism, since they migrate to areas of the body that are in need of repair. The statistics for success and failure will continue to grow as research and use of stem cells increase. Research and use of stem cells is still in its infancy, especially as it relates to autism. One can only speculate that with the encouraging results so far, stem cells hold much promise for a variety of diseases and disabilities.

There is probably nothing more controversial in medical discoveries today than the harvesting and use of stem cells.

SUMMARY

There are many theories about the causes of autism and many therapies that offer help in various areas. A multi-modality approach, or one that includes medicine, arts, nutrition, and other therapies, is usually most effective in treating the whole child.

Children on the Autism Spectrum should receive therapy as soon as they are diagnosed. The benefits of an integrative approach should not be underestimated. Your child might show signs of improvement that wouldn't be noted if only one modality, or style of therapy, were used.

Your physician may decide to use several means of physically treating your child, such as nutrition and chelation, while therapists will address your child's artistic sensitivities. With this combined approach, your child's three-fold nature of body, mind, and spirit will be stimulated in a way that encourages wholeness.

The next chapter helps to clarify some of the "mystery" surrounding autism. You'll learn that you're not alone in your search for answers, and you will no doubt find that your child shows some of the characteristics that are listed. In fact, you may relate to the case studies that are included. There is also quite a bit of information about the brain written in an easy-to-understand way. Since it's your child's brain that is affected, this is something you'll want to study. The chapter concludes with the fascinating story of Temple Grandin, who is the "poster child" for autism. Her success story is uplifting and shows the potential of each child with autism.

CHAPTER 3

Autism
Putting the Pieces Together

Autistic babies frighten and confuse young parents who had expected to hold a happy, gurgling infant in their arms. Instead, their baby may arch his back and scream when he's being bathed or changed as if the touch of clothes, water, or another person is unbearable. The average baby will smile and wriggle in anticipation as his parents approach the crib or playpen. He will raise his arms, waiting to be picked up. An autistic child, however, ignores the presence of other people and, in fact, generally appears oblivious to his environment.

Since they have no noticeable physical disabilities, the bizarre behavior and frequent tantrums of older autistic children are less apt to be tolerated by family and strangers. They may race through grocery stores, toppling displays in their wake, remove their clothing and urinate or defecate in the aisle. The anguished mother not only has to locate and subdue her child, she also feels obligated to apologize and explain the problem to clerks and shoppers who believe her son or daughter is an incorrigible brat who needs discipline.

We do know that children with autism are individuals in their own right. They may share certain characteristics—some are hyperactive and some are withdrawn. One may feel pain acutely while another appears impervious to it. Some are non-verbal while others are relatively fluent and high functioning—and may actually have Asperger's Syndrome.

Many researchers maintain that the major identifiable difference between Asperger's Syndrome and autism is that Asperger kids are quite verbal and articulate while autistics are not. They claim that "high-functioning autism" is an oxymoron and either a child is autistic or he isn't. Still more maintain an autistic child can be very verbal. Because some children don't fit all of the criteria for this disorder, they may be given an incorrect diagnosis. When the general public becomes educated about the neurodevelopmental disorders on the Autism Spectrum, they will be able to recognize the signs of autism, Asperger's, and ADD. Knowing what characteristics to look for is helpful and is discussed in this chapter.

The goal of this chapter is to help you identify signs of autism that may have caused concern about your child. The earlier you notice these symptoms, the sooner you can begin therapy to bring him into balance. If your child is older—ten to twelve years of age—and has the need for perfection, two case studies describe a method of alleviating this obsession. In this chapter you will discover interesting facts about the functions of the brain, how it produces new cells, and how stress reduces production of these cells. That may sound very complicated and intimidating, but it's written in an easy-to-understand way that ties it all together.

If you are like most parents, you have experienced moments of frustration and despair in dealing with your child. The last few pages of this chapter will lift your spirits and give you hope as you read about an amazing autistic woman who had supportive parents and a school mentor. A true success story, she is now a professor at Colorado State University.

EARLY SIGNS OF AUTISM

Although there may be no indication of abnormality during pregnancy, mothers often sense something is "not quite right" because a child with autism is generally less active in the womb. When they deliver an apparently normal, healthy baby, their fears dissolve, only to resurface later as their child fails to respond with age-appropriate behavior. As infants, they may have feeding and sleeping problems, and by the time a baby is one year old, a mother may worry there is something wrong with her toddler. Parents may notice he doesn't look at them or that he *perseverates* (repeats an activity endlessly)—spinning beads on the floor, for instance, or moving his fingers before his eyes as if he's mesmerized.

Periodic examinations by the family doctor or pediatrician may ease parents' anxiety by pronouncing their baby in perfect physical condition. However, as mothers tend to compare children of the same age, the difference in development and behavior of autistic children becomes obvious between eighteen and twenty-four months, when certain marked characteristics are noticeable. Even as early as one year, autistic children show signs of the disorder.

Dr. Geraldine Dawson of the University of Washington's Center for Human Development and Disability, director of the Autism Center, initiated a video-taped study of children who were celebrating their first birthday party. Dr. Dawson and her colleagues were looking for specific behaviors that are indicative of autism. They were able to spot early signs of autism in ten of eleven children who were later diagnosed with this disorder. Her study concluded that "infants with autism were found to have poor visual attention, require more prompts to respond to their name, excessively mouth objects and more frequently show aversion to social touch." The results were published in the *Journal of Autism and Developmental Disorders*.

As a baby goes through normal stages of walking and talking, parents may be unaware of minor changes that occur gradually until it's unmistakable that there is something very wrong with their child. In other cases, the change is dramatic, as their child suddenly stops interacting, or loses speech and eye contact.

Up to 90 percent of person-to-person communication is non-verbal, and much of that information is received from body language and facial cues. However, since people with autism-related disorders can't read face or body language, they miss most of what is being said or conveyed. Dr. Fred Volkmar of the Yale-LDA Social Learning Disabilities Project designed a study using modern technology to try to find out what prevents people with autism from establishing and maintaining relationships. Using cameras that tracked eye movements as two adult males (one with autism and one who was "cognitively able") watched the movie *Who's Afraid of Virginia Woolf?*, Volkmar and colleagues discovered that the man with autism looked at the mouths of speakers instead of the eyes and mouths as most of us do. (This study was published in the June 2002 issue of the *American Journal of Psychiatry*.) Moving their eyes back and forth from the eyes to mouths gives neurotypical children and adults facial cues in conversation that people with autism miss.

When a baby develops normally, he looks into his parents' eyes as they talk to him. The eyes and voice communicate intentions, love, and feelings to an infant. It is not until later that children with autism-related disorders switch their focus to the speaker's mouth. This switch could be one of the first signs that alert parents to Asperger's or autism.

Many parents associated changes such as loss of eye contact with a recent MMR (measles, mumps, rubella) injection and state the child was perfectly normal before the vaccination. (There is much anecdotal evidence to support this claim, although most researchers and physicians dispute it.) It is important to know what to look for in diagnosing autism.

CRITERIA AND CHARACTERISTICS

Autism was commonly diagnosed as schizophrenia until 1943 when Dr. Leo Kanner published his first paper identifying autistic children by their behavior and mannerisms. We now know that the Autism Spectrum is a group of neurodevelopmental diseases that affect the brain, gastrointestinal system, and immune system. Neurodevelopmental diseases are defined as those affecting the neurological system and development. As yet there is no biological test to diagnose autism; instead a determination is made by observation and interviews with parents. A child must meet certain criteria to be labeled autistic, but the list of characteristics continues to grow.

Criteria

The criteria for diagnosing autism are based on how the child interacts with others; how he communicates; and the presence of repetitive stereo-typical activities—repeating the same physical movement, or perseveration. These three major categories are further broken down into sub-categories that may include the following characteristics.

Characteristics

Here are some characteristics found in children with autism:

- Develops normally until between eighteen months and two-and-a-half years, when he stops and regresses
- Resists change
- Is hypersensitive—avoids being touched or touching things
- Is hyposensitive—feels no pain and may rush headlong into a wall for stimulation
- Complains that his clothes hurt
- Is sensitive to smells
- Has problems with muscle tone and coordination
- Is impulsive
- Has no fear of danger—runs into traffic, climbs tall trees and structures
- Points, pulls, and grunts to tell you what he wants
- Is not a cuddly child—doesn't want to be hugged
- Is overly active
- Is lethargic, uninterested
- Likes to line up objects
- Walks on tip toes
- Flaps his arms
- Rocks back and forth on heels
- Engages in little or no eye contact—looks between your eyes or off to one side
- Has attachments to objects, like a spoon
- Perseverates—repeats words or actions for long periods of time
- Engages in odd, nonsensical play
- Laughs inappropriately
- Needs perfection
- Is aggressive
- Is self-injurious—bites and picks at self
- Displays aloof attitude
- Counts objects like telephone poles when riding in car
- Is electivly mute—talks when he wants to
- Is electivly deaf—hears when he wants to
- Has difficulty sleeping

- Displays obsessive behavior like opening and closing drawers

- Doesn't like loud noises such as trucks, vacuums, flushing toilet

- Cries or screams for no apparent reason

- Has difficulty playing with others

- Is echolalic—repeats your words instead of answering questions

- Resists learning

- Throws temper tantrums

- Spins or runs in circles

- Has eating problems

- Frequently covers his ears

Some of these behaviors may be exhibited by children with other disorders on the Spectrum that are more in the middle of the bar. They include a large category of Pervasive Developmental Disorders—Not Otherwise Specified (PDD–NOS). Children with this diagnosis have a wide range of verbal skills, from nonexistent to normal language development. They may also appear to have a mild form of some autistic characteristics but don't fit the criteria necessary for that specific diagnosis; therefore, they are "not otherwise specified."

In addition to the characteristics listed above, parents should be alert for periods of brief loss of attention or consciousness, since one out of every four children with autism develops epilepsy, often as a toddler. These seizures are caused by abnormal electric impulses in the brain that may cause convulsions, a momentary loss of consciousness, or simply staring into space. There often is no warning, and a child will collapse on the floor for a few seconds, then pick himself up and continue with what he was doing. Some have hundreds of small seizures a day, the majority of which are detected only by an EEG (electroencephalogram). These episodes are so brief they are usually overlooked, but when detected can be controlled with medication.

THE NEED FOR PERFECTION

There are some characteristics of autism that overlap with typical behaviors listed under Obsessive-Compulsive Disorder (OCD). One of those is the need for perfection. It is more than a desire to be neat, but rather an absolute necessity. Following are two unorthodox methods I have used for helping children overcome this drive.

Laura

A ten-year-old girl, Laura was chatty and eagerly entered into any activity I suggested. We talked constantly while working, although her part of the dialogue was not always understandable. Her need for perfection was typical of children with autism. She was a very tactile child who touched and smelled everything that caught her eye as she circled the room prior to starting her session.

Our routine included coloring in coloring books as a preliminary step to watercolors. We would lie on the floor opposite each other, each coloring in a book. After upending a box of crayons, she had to line them up in a row, and as she finished using each, it was replaced in its spot.

One day, as I finished with a crayon, I placed it at an angle, and she immediately lined it up. After two weeks of this preparation, I casually tossed the crayon about eighteen inches from us. Laura would look at me and put the crayon back in the row she had created. Two weeks later I tossed the next crayon about six feet away, and she was shocked. I said, "You don't have to be perfect, Laura." She stared at me for a moment and asked, "I don't?" I assured her that she didn't and suggested she toss the crayon she was holding far away from her. It was interesting and moving to watch her inward struggle as she made the motion of throwing it but couldn't actually let go of the crayon. On the fifth or sixth attempt, she did, and the crayon landed beyond mine. This was a major achievement, and I was as excited as she was. Then I went briefly into the next room and heard her saying, "I don't have to be perfect! I don't have to be perfect!" When I returned she was happily throwing crayons all over the room.

From then on when she emptied the box of crayons, they fell in a jumble and she apparently felt she had been given permission not to be perfect when coloring, because they were never lined up again. However, as she matured, this need for perfection returned in the form of Obsessive-Compulsive Disorder, which is not unusual in children and adults with autism.

Ryan

A similar method was used with twelve-year-old Ryan. When he was finished drawing on sheets of paper, he would place them on the arm of a chair, the piano bench, the seat of another chair, and a table, making sure they were perfectly aligned.

One day I deliberately walked past one stack and brushed against it, throwing it out of alignment. He was watching me, as he always did, and immediately straightened the papers. We repeated that five or six times until I said, "Ryan, your pictures don't have to be lined up perfectly. It's okay if they're a little crooked." He looked at me in disbelief but walked with me to each stack of papers and watched as I pushed them to one side. Then I straightened and suggested he do the same.

As with Laura, he had an inward struggle and made a few half-hearted attempts, but finally did move them slightly. We practiced that a few times, and soon he was able to tolerate papers that were not neatly stacked. Soon he began putting them all in one stack and he no longer felt the need to make sure they were all lined up.

Those who work with children have to be perceptive, observant, intuitive, spontaneous, and unorthodox in their methods. Had I simply acknowledged that both Laura and Ryan liked to line up their crayons and papers, the moment for modeling and assurance would not have happened. Sometimes you have to use a method that is not in the books. It was the first step; however, it was no guarantee that they would overcome their need for perfection in other areas of their lives while at home.

Simply telling children they don't need to be perfect makes no sense to those driven to perfection. But seeing that nothing disastrous will happen if crayons or papers are not lined up and being assured that they do not have to be perfect, they can take control of a small but powerful part of their lives. It can be the first step of many towards a better way of perceiving the world.

As they mature, children may lose some of the behaviors that originally identified them as autistic, and other ones may appear. One of the most common is OCD or Obsessive-Compulsive Disorder. This is certainly not a condition known only to people with autism, but it is often seen in autistic teens and adults.

OBSESSIVE-COMPULSIVE DISORDER (OCD)

OCD in children is not as rare as one might think and is probably being recognized more frequently because of the intense research into autism and related disorders. According to the National Institutes of Health (NIH), OCD occurs in 1 in every 200 children with autism. As teens, they may reduce or eliminate some of their characteristics that are replaced by more debilitating OCD behaviors that may be very difficult for the entire family to deal with.

Children with odd, repetitive behavior are now often classified as having OCD, which was unheard of in young people several years ago. Some cases are mild and easily escape recognition; others are severe enough to interfere with a normal life. In some cases, children also have Tourette's Syndrome, which is characterized by facial and motor tics, OCD, and lack of ability to focus on tasks. They have a hard time in school because other kids tease them. This may result in physical and emotional problems that will get only worse if left untreated.

As children mature, their behavior may change in the areas of social interaction, communication skills, and ritualistic behavior. However, it is important to realize that not all changes in deportment are the result of OCD.

Characteristics

Obsessive Compulsive Disorder (OCD) can manifest as either obsessions or compulsions. People with OCD may have obsessions or worries and fears that can take over their lives. They become obsessed with fears that are out of proportion to the reality of a situation, and although they are aware the thoughts are not coming from something around them, they are unable to stop fixating on their concerns.

Compulsions are repetitive actions. People do things they feel they have to do. For example, Matilda may feel compelled to say the same three words seven times before an exam. Tommy may need to open and close the door five times before getting out of the car. People with OCD will say they know what they are doing is irrational but can't stop themselves from doing it. Young adults with autism often have obsessions and compulsions.

There is reason to believe that OCD has a genetic component, according to well-known doctors. Dr. Yin Yao Shugart of the Johns Hopkins Bloomberg School of Public Health states that OCD was originally thought to be psychological, but growing evidence indicates that it may be genetic.

Dr. Jack Samuels, an epidemiologist and assistant professor of psychiatry at Johns Hopkins School of Medicine, states that rather than being caused by a single gene, "OCD probably is associated with several different genes." His findings are reported in the March 2007 *American Journal of Psychiatry*.

Dr. Joseph Pevin, Director of the North Carolina Neurodevelopmental Disorders Research Center at University of North Carolina-Chapel Hill, explains that clinical diagnosis of OCD happens through examining the history of and interviewing the patient in order to understand his main behavioral characteristics. The cause of particular brain patterns is not known. While OCD is genetic, it is "not an all or none phenomenon." All cases of OCD cannot be attributed to any specific cause.

The list of OCD rituals is almost endless. The following are examples of how OCD affects various people's lives. Do any of these sound familiar?

- Annie has a fear of germs and believes she's surrounded with them.

- Billy likes to stare at himself in the mirror for hours.

- Caroline carefully avoids stepping on a spot on the carpet because she's afraid of it.

- Danny has to line up his crayons in a straight line.

- Elaine has to do everything twice.

- Freddie likes orange juice diluted with water, but they must be in two separate glasses.

- Gina collects dead bugs.

- Howard won't eat anything green.

- Isabel has to touch a certain tree before entering the building for her session.

- Jack won't eat anything if it is touching another food on his plate.

- Kerri will use an entire roll of toilet paper after using the toilet.

- Leo will write and erase the same letter or word a dozen or more times.

- Michelle takes jigsaw puzzle pieces out of the box and replaces them, repeating the process endlessly.

- Noel always plays the same CD, although he has an extensive collection of music, and it has to be turned just so in the stack.

- Ophelia likes to scrub the kitchen sink. Over and over.

- Peter walks on the sides of his feet, afraid to have his foot planted firmly on the floor.

- Quanda has certain phrases that she repeats continually throughout the day as a protection.

- Roger washes the family car every few hours, using several rolls of paper towels in the process.

Adults with severe OCD are often housebound, overwhelmed by fear of what might be found waiting for them outside their door. They have no social life and are unable to work. To say their lives are complicated is a major understatement. Antidepressants may be prescribed for this disorder.

There are several relatively rare disorders that have a neurological basis and may initially be diagnosed as autism. They have some characteristics similar to those of autism, but they are plainly separate disabilities. Because they are on the Spectrum and of interest, three of these rare disorders are listed below.

LESS-COMMON SPECTRUM DISORDERS

Fragile X Syndrome

Fragile X is the most common inherited cause of mental impairment, with an estimated 1 in 2,000 boys and 1 in 4,000 girls affected. One out of 260 women is a carrier. It affects 2–5 percent of children on the Spectrum, and there's a one in two chance boys born to the same family will have it. Since it is genetic, it is important for parents to be checked for Fragile X if they plan on having more children. Blood tests can find Fragile X.

Children with Fragile X and autistic children have similar reactions to sound and touch. They avoid social interaction and are reserved. This disorder is a result of an abnormal X chromosome that shuts down a brain protein necessary for cognitive development.

Landau-Kleffner Syndrome (LKS)

Growth is normal in children affected with Landau-Kleffner Syndrome (LKS) until the onset of this disorder between the ages of three and seven. Children stop developing and have symptoms similar to those of autism. Epilepsy is not uncommon and often disappears in adult years. Children with LKS have a severe language disorder that may improve with age. It's often helped with drugs and controversial brain surgery.

Rett Syndrome (RS)

First described by Dr. Andreas Rett, Rett Syndrome (RS) affects girls almost exclusively. They develop normally until between six and eighteen months of age, when they either stop developing or regress. Children with Rett Syndrome have stereotypical hand movements and difficulty walking, and the growth of their head slows considerably. Most girls with the disorder do not crawl as babies but scoot on their bottom or propel themselves with their forearms. Some begin to talk before they lose this ability.

If we were to place these three neurological disorders on our invisible line that represents the Autism Spectrum, they would be on the far right side with classic autism. Children with Fragile X, Landau Kleffner, or Rett Syndromes are noted either by symptoms that change as they get older or by blood tests. Although it is important to recognize a potential problem as early as possible, it is just as important not to label a child until everyone is sure of the correct diagnosis.

LABELS CAN BE CONFUSING There is no universal agreement as to whether children with autism should be known as "autistics," as they are widely known by parents, physicians, and themselves; or whether children with Asperger's Syndrome should be known as "Aspies," as they affectionately call themselves. It shouldn't matter if some people think those are disparaging nicknames as long as the kids themselves like them and their parents are not offended. Confusion may exist when a child is labeled autistic when he really has Asperger's Syndrome, or vice versa.

Autistics are speaking out about having autism. One boy with autism said that autistic children don't know why people insist on saying they're "suffering" from a disorder when most people with autism don't feel that way at all. They don't feel disabled, just "put together differently" from most people. This assertion brought immediate arguments that the boy had to have Asperger's Syndrome, not autism, because he was able to speak so coherently.

Some parents and professionals maintain that if an autistic child is able to write a letter or appear before a government committee to plead for services, he doesn't have autism because autistics aren't that articulate. Perhaps the problem lies with labels. We are a country that loves labels, and every year or so new ones are created and descriptive wording is changed. For example, "high-functioning autism" differentiates between children who are verbal and those who aren't. But are they autistic or are they Asperger's with some autistic tendencies?

There is also no universal agreement on some of the disorders that have been diagnosed since Kanner first named this condition. Because of an increasing number of children with unusual characteristics that have an autistic flavor, the term "Autism Spectrum" was created as a folder of sorts for a number of disorders that don't fit anyplace else.

Although labels are necessary for record keeping, we should not be so dependent on naming "what" a child is or "what" he is called. They are children, foremost, who are different for some unknown reason. Future generations will probably think it was absurd of us to have had arguments about whether a child should be called an Aspie or an autistic. By that time, children we now label as being on the Autism Spectrum may well be the norm, and the labels will be obsolete.

CHANGING OUR PERCEPTION

Although autistic children may never completely outgrow some of the characteristics of autism, recent advances in nutrition and therapy help many improve such that they no longer test—or are viewed—as autistic. This is an exciting breakthrough for parents who, until a few short years ago, were told that nothing could be done for their child. Worse than that was the disparaging statement by psychologist Bruno Bettelheim, who said that autism was the result of frigid mothers. It was a difficult period for parents who saw no light at the end of the tunnel because of a devastating diagnosis and the accompanying guilt imposed on them.

Most people find it difficult to believe that autistic children have intelligence, simply because they may be non-verbal or non-responsive. We tend to equate intelligence with book learning instead of an innate state of mind. Because of this, parents may feel—or be told—that since their child is unable to keep up with his peers, he is stupid or incapable of learning. On the contrary—he is learning all the time. An autistic child learns how others view him from the comments of his parents to family, friends, doctors, teachers, and therapists. Detrimental remarks, ridiculing or mimicking by peers, and even a lack of affection from family members are understood and felt deeply by the child. He may not comprehend all of the words, but the looks, energy, and tone of voice have an impact on his feelings of worth and his sensitive nature.

Anyone who thinks autistics are unaware of what is going on around them would have changed their mind during my session with Joshua, a ten-year-old non-verbal, non-responsive boy.

Joshua

Before music CDs became popular, music was mostly on two-sided vinyl albums. During one session, music was playing as Joshua and I were lying on the floor painting. I continued to talk with him and he maintained his stoic silence. I didn't notice that the record had stopped playing, but Josh did. He painted on his sheet of paper, "TURN OVER."

This silent boy who irritated his mother by ignoring her harsh words brought my attention to the fact that the music had stopped and that it continued on the other side. He demonstrated humor and intelligence, which should not be underestimated in autistic children.

Children with this disorder have an almost regal air about them; they are mysterious and attractive. One has the feeling that they know exactly what is going on around them even if they appear deaf or unaware. Because of this, those charged with the care and nurturing of children with this disorder should be conscious of their choice of words. They should never talk about children as if they weren't there. The child's spiritual essence is always there and aware.

It is not surprising that things sometimes go wrong with our brains. What is surprising is that more people don't have problems. To understand more clearly this amazing part of our body, some background information would be helpful.

THE INCREDIBLE GROWING BRAIN

A popular, long-standing belief held that we are born with a certain number of brain cells that exist and then eventually die (long before the body itself dies), never to be recovered or replaced. There is research, however, that makes it necessary for us to rethink that position. We know from experiments done at Rockefeller University in New York that it is possible to grow new brain cells. Doctors injected two tracer chemicals into the brains of mice, one of which would identify mature cells and the other of which would, they hoped, find new cells. The researchers found what they were looking for: new brain cells in the animals' hippocampus, thousands of which were being made each day.

Forty years ago, a Purdue University scientist found that during their entire lives, rats continued to make new brain cells in the hippocampus and the olfactory bulb, the area that detects smells. When this study took place in the 1960s, it was dismissed by the scientific community, which scoffed at the idea that making new brain cells was possible.

In spite of this rebuff, other researchers did their own studies that showed new brain cells in mice and rats were created throughout life— 5,000 to 10,000 each hour in the hippocampus and olfactory bulb. Again, despite the results of these studies, many ridiculed the idea that it could be possible to create new brain cells, and certainly, it was thought, not in the area of the hippocampus. Today, research has once again concluded what had been presented in the 1960s and finally accepted years later.

We can assume that the brain replenishes cells and tissues when it's damaged by trauma or illness. However, scar tissue interferes with the production of new brain cells and reconnection of circuits. Stroke victims, for example, retain the new brain cells, but these new cells are unable to connect to the nerves that influence memory. In autistic children, there's generally no scar tissue to interfere with the building of brain cells, nothing that prevents them from remembering. They are missing neuropathways and synapses that are necessary for communication and cognition. However, with proper remedial therapies and the reduction of stress, these missing links can be fashioned out of new brain cells that flow into the brain by the thousands every hour.

New brain cells are created in the hippocampus, where memories are stored. In a right-handed person, the right hippocampus is involved in visual memory, while the left side is involved in verbal memory. The hippocampus not only stores memories but also connects them with previous memories and forms sequential relationships between the new and the old. In other words, this part of the brain allows us to remember something and then to trace it back to previous memories. Thousands of new cells are made each day, but tests show that when a person is under stress, the hippocampus shrinks within one hour of the stressful incident.

The Role of Stress

Since stress reduces the number of brain cells produced, the logical solution is to flood the brain with calming, relaxing, and pleasurable activities and thoughts. It is difficult to contemplate a more stressful life than that of children with autism, Asperger's Syndrome, or ADHD, who know they are "different," who have no control over their disorders, who are aware of taunts by their peers, and whose parents may talk about them as if they are deaf.

These special children and adults are frustrated, hurt, and angered but unable to verbalize their emotions rationally, so the negativity builds, stress is a constant, and the hippocampus shrinks, decreasing the number of brain cells—which are needed to form new neuropathways and synapses necessary for communication. It becomes a cycle of futility.

It is difficult to contemplate a more stressful life than that of children with autism, Asperger's Syndrome, or ADHD, who know they are "different."

With constant stress that is almost always made worse by drugs, poor nutrition and environment, and the inborn infraction in the brain, it is understandable that autistic children cannot relate to the world in which they find themselves. In addition, children on the Spectrum are not fully integrated into their body, and when the body, mind, and spirit are not in sync and working in conjunction with the autonomic nervous system, the result is a fractured child who is clearly a puzzle with a missing piece.

Manufacturing New Brain Cells

Artistic therapies of music, art, speech, sculpture, sensory integration, and massage reduce stress and stimulate the growth of new brain cells.

We now know that new brain cells are created every hour of every day, and that cognitive experiences can help them grow faster and in greater quantities. Therefore, remedial therapies should be started as early as possible to keep the brain stimulated. The key to reaching and teaching a child on the Spectrum is to keep his mind constantly stimulated with new objects, words, images, activities, and music.

It is not enough just to keep a young child occupied for a half hour or so by painting. Whoever spends the most time with him must keep his mind busy by moving from one project to another in rapid succession before his attention begins to wander. He will usually give some indication that this is about to happen, and an observant adult will quickly switch his focus.

Artistic therapies of music, art, speech, sculpture, sensory integration, and massage reduce stress and stimulate the growth of new brain cells. They encourage the development of new neuropathways that may have never connected due to the infraction that occurred, most likely during the third month of development. However, if this remedial work isn't started before the age of twelve, it's more difficult—perhaps impossible—for this reconnection to take place. As a result of the recent research into autism, a diagnosis can now be made much earlier because physicians are becoming more familiar with the symptoms of this neurological disorder.

The development of an infant's brain is highly dependent on stimulation of his senses. There are several stages in brain development when a child needs sensory input, and if it isn't provided during this window of opportunity it will be almost impossible to achieve later. Parents have a wonderful opportunity at each of these stages of their child's development to help form his brain through repeated stimulation of cooing, talking, singing, touching, and loving. Today, it is common knowledge that a child needs nurturing to develop skills necessary to grow into a healthy body.

The obvious solution is for parents and caregivers to provide this sensory stimulation continually so the brain will develop at these optimum times in the various developmental stages. The tendency for autistic children's brains to be larger than those of typical children is testament that autistic children are different from other children and that perhaps there is some evolutionary process at work that is unknown to us at this time.

What Can I Do?

There are many things you can do to help stimulate your child, and that can help encourage the creation of new brain cells. For example:

- Read to your baby and toddler.
- Visually delight him.
- Take him for walks; describe the trees and sky in colorful language.
- Do not talk baby talk.
- Give him the respect of talking to him like a person.
- Use proper terminology even for body parts.

When you work with your older child, it is important to move from one location in the room to another. For example, begin at a large table for big projects and continue to move to other parts of the room as his interest begins to wane. Alternate between the following:

- Easel for dynamic drawing
- Floor for water colors
- Small table for projects such as miniature dolls
- Chair, couch, or futon for reading stories
- Large table for fingerpainting
- Open space for throwing, rolling, and catching a large ball

These activities can be in any order as long as the child's perception is new and visually different. With each change of location, he will use different eye and limb muscles.

Therapists, parents, and the entire family should constantly talk with a child to excite his mind. He's intelligent enough to want more than idle chitchat. Respect that intelligence by talking about interesting subjects with many images that can be created in his mind. This stimulation aids in the production of brain cells that help to create new brain tissue, and consequently the child becomes more aware of his surroundings, and more verbal, curious, and responsive.

HOW THE BRAIN WORKS

The brain is a very complex organ that, in today's high-tech world of computers, could be called a "mother board." All sensory input must go through this intricate piece of equipment. But to understand how the brain affects a child with autism, we need a working knowledge of its basic form and function.

To learn how and why the brain is affected by toxins and other influences at certain stages of development, we need to discover a few things about this remarkable organ that starts out as a cluster of cells. As it develops, this cluster expands to 10 billion cells called neurons. Each neuron consists of a nucleus, axons, dendrites, and synapses. The cells know where they have to go and begin moving early in fetal development to form the hippocampus, cerebral cortex, and cerebellum.

In a brain that works properly, a neuron "fires" a message and the axons send an electrical signal. (Think of a telegraph operator sending a message.) Dendrites then receive these signals from other cells. (The operator on the other end.) Synapses are the gaps between adjacent dendrites. (If the wires are down for some reason, the message doesn't get through.)

Children with psycho-neuro disorders often have an incomplete connection between axons, which send signals to dendrites, which receive the

The Second Womb

We can't begin to imagine what it's like to be living inside autism while existing in the world. Children with this disorder were enveloped during gestation in the womb and are now, metaphorically, in another womb where they are isolated, protected, nourished, and seemingly unaware of activity that surrounds them.

We don't know how the typical child's brain and mind work—much less that of a child with autism. We do know that they continue to learn, like other children, but unlike others, they may be unable to express their feelings or emotions. It must be very frustrating for a child to be unable to speak and tell us if she doesn't feel well, is in pain, hungry, scared, or angry. No wonder autistic children cry or scream for seemingly no reason. There is a reason; they just can't articulate it. They are extremely sensitive to noise, and a drip-

ping faucet may sound like a clanging cymbal to their delicate nervous system, so they hold their hands over their ears to protect themselves from an audible assault. This is not simply another odd behavior; it is a matter of survival in a harsh environment. The neurologically impaired child is a dichotomy: fragile in one respect but strong enough to live and grow in a very difficult world that is foreign to him.

We are discovering a lot about autism as more and more children are emerging from this "womb" to tell us their experiences. Some children have learned to type, and their poems and revelations are as beautiful as they are fascinating. With the right remedial therapies, you can give your child an opportunity to bring fresh insights from deep within the cocoon of childhood autism.

signals in various parts of the brain. Even at the tender age of nine or ten weeks after conception, cells and neurons know exactly what they're doing when they send electrical impulses through the nervous system in a very precise way. If they didn't, our brain would be a jumble of crossed wires creating havoc.

The brain builds billions of synapses, or bridges, over which a neuron sends its message to the dendrites. In autistic children, there's an infraction in the tissue or neuropathways that has to be repaired. Messages have to pass from neurons to cells by way of synapses. If those synapses, or connectors, are damaged, the information doesn't get passed on and may be unintelligible or, more likely, simply isn't received at all.

Building new brain tissue with medical, nutritional, and remedial measures that balance and stimulate the hemispheres of the brain can restore neurotransmitters and synapses. In the future, stem cells will probably be available as a treatment option, migrating to the areas of the brain that need repair. (See page 40 for more information on stem cells.)

Functions of the Brain

Fortunately, you don't have to be a brain surgeon to know the basics of how a brain works. There is a striking difference between the brains of autistic children and those without neurological disorders. For example, a "minicolumn" is a group of 80 to 100 brain cells, and we have millions of them. A study found that autistic children have smaller minicolumns, and more of them, than children without autism. The areas associated with emotions and memory in the brain's limbic system, the amygdala and hippocampus, are unusually small and more tightly packed together. Also, they appear not to be fully developed.

What does this tell us? That the composition of the brain of an autistic child is different. This causes different behavior and neurological development. But it doesn't tell us why. It leads to conjecture that since autistic children have so many more minicolumns than typical children, this difference might result in their brains working overtime, so they have little inhibition and a tendency to withdraw into their own world. More minicolumns with infractions make it even harder and require even more "communication."

The brain is actually two brains, or hemispheres, that are joined together by the corpus callosum. They have different functions, and although they appear to be identical, their purposes are vastly different. The left brain houses the intellect and the factual world, while the right brain is focused on the arts and intuition, and is more geared toward dreams than harsh, real things. When we think about what goes on in the

> The brain builds billions of synapses, or bridges, over which a neuron sends its message to the dendrites. In autistic children, there's an infraction in the tissue or neuropathways that has to be repaired.

left brain and how intellectual our lives are in a high-tech society, it's easy to see how we can become unbalanced and very "mental." On the other hand, right-brained people who live only in the arts with their intuition and dreams are just as out of touch with the real world around them. As in all areas of life, we need a balance.

The hemispheres communicate with each other through the corpus callosum. Information is first received by the right side and then transferred to the left. If this link is severed for some reason, the two sides can't communicate. If a person is handed a book, he immediately knows both the name—that it is a book (left brain)—and the purpose—that this is something to read (right brain)—of the book. If one hemisphere is missing, he will be able to know only the name or the purpose, not both.

Purpose of the Hemispheres

Each side of the brain has separate and distinct functions. In the past decade there have been books and articles written about working with the right side of the brain, or how to be more imaginative and creative. This is important, but we have to be balanced with the linear intellect (left side of the brain) to be a whole person. Table 3.1 outlines the various elements of the left and right hemispheres of the brain.

TABLE 3.1. LEFT AND RIGHT SIDES OF THE BRAIN

Attribute	Left	Right
Thinking	Abstract, linear, analytic	Concrete, holistic
Cognitive style	Rational, logical	Intuitive, artistic
Language	Rich vocabulary, good grammar	Poor grammar and vocabulary
Functions	Reading, writing, arithmetic, sensory motor skills	Music, rich dream imagery, good face recognition
Spatial orientation	Relatively poor	Superior, also for geometric shapes

With all this in mind, you will find yourself observing your child and gaining a better understanding of the hemispheric activity of his brain. It is important for therapists to know if a child is stronger in one area than the other so remedial and creative therapies can be designed to strengthen the weaker side. Combined with proper nutrition and medical treatment, if necessary, your child will be making giant steps towards realization of his three-fold nature of body, mind, and spirit.

Dr. Temple Grandin is one of the most well-known adults with autism. She earned her master's degree in animal science from Arizona State University and her PhD in animal science at the University of Illinois. Now she is professor of animal sciences at Colorado State University. An acclaimed designer of livestock-handling facilities, she is able to visualize the completed project without step-by-step instructions. She sees the finished construction as a video in her mind and can run test simulations in her imagination of how the systems would work with different-sized cattle. She has designed cattle chutes for meat-packing plants throughout the world, and almost half of North American cattle are handled in a center track restrainer system that she designed for meat plants.

INSPIRATION OF TEMPLE GRANDIN

We can learn a great deal about autism from Temple Grandin. Hers is the most well-known and documented case of autism in both children and adults, and she now writes and speaks eloquently about her experiences. She describes her hearing as having a sound amplifier set on maximum loudness. She can either shut out the sound completely and hear nothing or leave it on and get bombarded with sounds that are extremely painful to her ears.

She can't modulate incoming auditory stimulation, and her hearing has tested normal. One of her ears hears sounds before the other, and this can be over a one-second difference. Because of this some people think she's not going to respond when they talk to her, and she finds it difficult to know when to break into a conversation. She does very little socializing. It is like talking to someone on the phone who is watching the same television show that you are, but due to the time delay of the sound through the phone, you hear everything twice with a slight time delay.

Dr. Grandin says that the worst part of autism as a child was not being able to speak. She knew what was being said to her but couldn't get the words out to respond and instead could only scream. In school, when the teacher aimed the pointer in her direction, she screamed because she wanted to tell the teacher that at home the rule was not to point things at people.

She still can't sing with other people, and can't clap in time to music with others. Because a lack of rhythm is seen in most autistic people, music and movement in the early years are important to their development.

Sudden noises hurt her ears like a dentist's drill, and she said that it's the fear of noises that causes many bad behaviors and tantrums in autistics. They're afraid of what's going to happen and are constantly surrounded by noise from crying babies, barking dogs, cars, trucks, sirens, vacuums, telephones—even the sound of running water can be painful.

We say that autistic children live in their own worlds, and Dr. Grandin's experience and ability to verbalize her sensations helps us to understand that they're retreating into these worlds for self-protection and self-preservation. Autistic people generally don't want to be touched, and they often shy away from hugs. Temple said she pulled away because a touch sent a tidal wave of stimulation throughout her body. Even though she wanted to be held, she found the effect on her nervous system to be overwhelming. She now wonders whether she would be less nervous as an adult if people had stroked her when she screamed at someone's touch when she was a baby. It's important to hug your child even if he seems not to want to be touched.

Knowing these things from an articulate, intelligent autistic adult is extremely important to people who work with children on the Spectrum, as well as for parents and therapists who must care for them. Many parents are confused by their baby's screaming when they try to pick him up to feed or change him. They think they're hurting him, which they truly are, so they leave him alone in the crib or playpen, and he loses that human touch that bonds him with other people.

Hypersensitivity to touch can be reduced by firmly but gently stroking the child's skin with different-textured materials. A very light touch excites the nervous system and too firm a touch is painful, so it has to be a "happy medium." Autistic children like firm pressure on their bodies, and being wrapped in a mat has a calming effect. Temple used to lie under the sofa cushions and wanted her sister to sit on them.

Autism Statistics

Autism statistics change on a daily basis, the variance due to either an increase or a decrease in the number of autism cases. Reductions probably occur because more children being identified with one of the other disorders on the Autism Spectrum. The Internet is an excellent source for up-to-date statistics on autism and other Spectrum Disorders. Many websites provide a wealth of information that will keep you knowledgeable of all the relevant topics.

Dr. Raymond F. Palmer, of the University of Texas Health Science Center at San Antonio, stated in the *American Journal of Public Health* that children in low-income school districts aren't being diagnosed or provided with services as readily as those in higher-income brackets. This would mean that the number of cases of autism is much more prevalent than figures now suggest. Higher-income, better-educated parents are more apt to be familiar with autism and recognize symptoms earlier. They may be more articulate in stating their needs and concerns to physicians, school districts, and committees. It doesn't mean that there are fewer cases in low-income areas.

After reading Temple Grandin's story, you will be convinced that statistics are only numbers and not a predictor of a child's ability to attain a full and productive life.

When she entered puberty, she had severe problems with anxiety, nervousness, and sensitivity to touch and sound. The anxiety felt like a constant state of unjustifiable stage fright. She says that on the worst days she felt like she was "being stalked by a gunman."

Temple's parents insisted she sit at the table with them during meals, her mother read to her, and she had a therapist. She credits them with keeping her focused and helping her to live a relatively normal life. The only thing she regrets is that she has no emotional complexity. She's replaced it with intellectual complexity and describes watching people interacting on an emotional level as looking at people from a different planet, because she can't relate.

When Temple was eighteen, she visited her aunt's ranch in Arizona and saw how cattle calmed down when they were placed in a chute. She built for herself what she calls "a squeeze machine" lined with foam rubber that allowed her to control the amount of pressure applied over large parts of her body. Her over-sensitivity was gradually reduced, and what had once been painful now became pleasurable. She was able to tolerate another person touching her, and her anxiety was reduced. Several of these squeeze machines are now in use in sensory integration clinics in the United States.

Dr. Grandin is a remarkable case of an autistic child becoming self-sufficient and able to continue her education to the point of obtaining degrees and a teaching position. Her story is extraordinary because this all happened more than two decades ago, and with the ensuing advances in research, medicine, and remedial therapies, her success story will be much more common in the future.

SUMMARY

We continue to learn about—and from—children with autism. Mysterious and fascinating, they truly are a puzzle waiting to be solved. When we keep in mind a child's whole being of body, mind, and spirit, we more fully understand the need for an appreciation of his innate intelligence.

Although labels may be necessary at present to obtain proper therapy, care must be taken that children not be incorrectly identified on the basis of only a few noticeable characteristics. Carefully try to label the illness, the disorder, or the condition, but not the child!

You have learned some basic facts about the brain and how it works in order to understand autism better. As you read about Temple Grandin, your spirits may have soared to think that your child, given the proper therapies, has the ability to reach his fullest potential, whatever it might be. You know that you can take a proactive role in understanding your child, his uniqueness, his care, and his ultimate development.

Although labels may be necessary at present to obtain proper therapy, care must be taken that children not be incorrectly identified on the basis of only a few noticeable characteristics.

Attention Deficit Disorder (ADD) is the mildest disorder found on the Autism Spectrum, but it is debated whether it should be included at all, since kids with ADD exhibit few, if any, characteristics of autism or Asperger's other than a highly sensitive feeling nature, some allergies, and intelligence. You will learn about ADD and ADHD in the following chapter.

CHAPTER 4

Attention Deficit Disorder
Recognizing a Gifted Child

Attention Deficit Disorder (ADD) and Attention Deficit Hyperactivity Disorder (ADHD) are very common conditions in young children. Attention Deficit Disorder means, by definition, a child is deficient in the ability to pay attention. Ironically, when a child with ADD is interested in something, she can be very focused, which may give the impression that she is daydreaming or simply not listening the rest of the time. This is frustrating for teachers and parents, and their frustration is puzzling to the child. Children with ADHD have the added distinguishing characteristic of being hyperactive. However, the "average" young child is usually very active. It would be abnormal for a healthy youngster to be lethargic and morose.

There have always been boys and girls whose attention span is shorter than that of their peers, but until the past couple of decades, they were not classified as having a disorder. In fact, there is controversy about whether ADD and ADHD belong on the Autism Spectrum at all. If they do, they are at the very mild end, so far down the scale as to be almost off the Spectrum entirely.

However, there are similarities to other Spectrum Disorders. For example, most children with ADD have allergies, as do children with autism. Many have parents with some form of ADD. In fact, parents as well as their children may be on medication to control their inability to focus on tasks. Another similarity to children with autism and Asperger's Syndrome is their intelligence. Some children are less articulate than other children with ADD, but nevertheless they are aware, absorbing, and learning all the time.

Children with ADD are typically pleasant, often gifted, and frequently hard to discipline. They often "sass" their parents, are disruptive in the classroom, and on the playground usually want to be the leader. We see this more often in boys, probably because there are six times more boys than girls with ADD. The figure may be as high as ten boys per girl with ADD, depending on the published statistics.

Boys and girls with ADD are so intent on their inner life that everyday routines are usually overlooked. They lose school supplies, forget things, and their rooms are usually a disaster. These children need help and encouragement to integrate their inner and outer lives so they can do their best at home and in school. In addition to various therapies and nutritional guidance, they need someone to show them how to get organized.

In this chapter, you may discover that your hyperactive child who flits like a butterfly from one thing to another may, in fact, be gifted. She may actually be collecting many interesting tidbits of information like a bee collects pollen from dozens of flowers. In other words, there is a purpose to her apparent lack of attention to what you are saying. She is constantly researching, thinking, and forming graphic images. As you read, you will learn the signs of ADD and ADHD and find that some fit your child and others don't.

Although every child is unique, almost every child with ADD is unorganized and her room is cluttered, which doesn't bother her at all. However, an unorganized room shows an unorganized mind and that creates problems. You will learn how to help cultivate an organized mind with simple techniques. Are you told your child needs Ritalin? Do you think you may have ADD? This chapter provides food for thought for both of these questions.

Throughout this chapter and this book, the closely related conditions known as ADD and ADHD are frequently lumped together as "ADD" to avoid long and awkward phrasing of sentences. References to ADD are not meant to exclude ADHD unless specifically noted.

SEGMENTING A BRAIN

For some unknown reason, the brains of children with ADD or ADHD are smaller than those of neurotypical children, but that does not mean they are any less intelligent. There are many theories about how the brain of a child with ADD works, but nobody knows for sure. Here is one that is very unscientific and very visual.

Picture the brain as a circle divided into twelve equal segments, like a clock. Each segment has the capacity to hold infinite bits of intelligence, like a computer hard drive. An average person may have two segments that store interesting ideas, facts, and fantasies. It's fairly easy to think about two things at a time and to focus on one of them.

Children with ADD may have eight or ten or all twelve segments filled with things of interest that are learned or inherent. Instead of switching between two subjects, her mind races around the "clock," touching first on one segment to explore all of the bits and pieces, then another and another. She is so fascinated by her thoughts and inspirations that she appears to be daydreaming and distracted, which she is. Yet, those times in which she is searching her brain are the most fruitful of her waking hours.

The Multitasking Brain

The ability to multitask seems to be typical of children with ADD. Chad was a twelve-year-old boy with ADD who refused to take his Ritalin because he didn't like the way it made his head feel. During a tutoring session he was involved in a complex math problem when, still writing and calculating, he asked a rather deep question: "Tell me, Janet. Do you think graffiti is art or vandalism?" His mind was working full speed in at least two of the segments of his brain, and he had obviously thought of many things before even asking the question.

> The minds of children with ADD are constantly at work, and everything interests them.

The minds of children with ADD are constantly at work, and everything interests them. Sometimes it is hard for parents to keep up with their children who want answers to their questions and will not be satisfied until they have learned something new. It is not unusual for children as young as three or four to ask questions that surprise their parents, who don't always know the answers.

Insatiable Questioning

When children with ADD ask questions, they want details, not patronizing answers. As they walked into the office for her remedial arts session, six-year-old Justine and her father were having a serious discussion about heavy water. Not many adults have even heard of heavy water but Justine's father was intelligent and patient—and he had the answers for her inquiring mind.

He was responsible for driving his daughter to all of her after-school activities, and their time in the car was filled with dialogue that was far beyond her chronological years. She was given all of the information she needed to satisfy her curiosity about whatever subject she found most interesting that day.

This is not unusual for children with ADD. Their questions are more than a toddler's persistent, "Why?" They truly want detailed answers and are capable of understanding explanations without having them "dumbed down" too much. We are seeing a generation of "wonder kids" who continually surprise and amaze us. Traditional schools have a hard time

Many children with
ADD are brilliant,
constantly exploring
ideas that interest them.

keeping up with these students who challenge teachers and the system. Their need for something more has prompted school districts to add classes for gifted students, and many schools for advanced students have been created, especially for the arts.

Many children with ADD are brilliant, constantly exploring ideas that interest them. It isn't surprising that they're scolded for daydreaming in class when they are inwardly focused on things they feel are important and fascinating. If they're not paying attention to a book being read by the teacher, they may be solving a highly complex math problem or thinking about social issues in another country. Although this is impressive, they still need to learn to pay attention in class!

CLASSROOM ANTICS

Teachers are usually the first to notice that a child has ADD because they see the same symptoms frequently throughout the school years. They may suggest a meeting with parents and therapists to explore how they can all work together to help the child best. This meeting is not the time or place to label a child as having ADD or any other condition. However, based on experience, teachers and therapists will probably offer suggestions to parents about having their child tested for the source of her inappropriate behavior.

Perceptive teachers will be aware that children who throw things when frustrated, drop their books and pencils on the floor, or squirm in their seats may not necessarily have ADD. They may be ill, tired, hungry, or bored. ADD kids are very sensitive to criticism and when pressured to perform at school, they may become stressed, belligerent, rebellious, and disruptive. But at the same time, children should know that there are consequences for unacceptable behavior at home and school and clearly understand that there are no exceptions.

If children with ADD can't write legibly, they may refuse to do their homework as they are afraid of being ridiculed by other kids or scolded by the teacher. They soon refuse to try. Understanding teachers may allow such children to print rather than write their homework, because it may be easier for them. It is not uncommon for children with ADD never to complete in-class assignments or homework. They may write and erase the same word a dozen times because it is not exactly the way they want it to look. As a result, they wear a hole in the paper, don't get their work done, and receive a failing grade.

Teachers who are aware that kids with ADD think differently know how important it is to keep all instructions to a minimum and to assign only one task at a time. Adults often mistakenly believe that all children hear instructions in the same way, but we've learned that this isn't the case. If instructions aren't understood, ADD kids are reluctant to ask the teacher in class to repeat what she said or to ask for help. When a child is working on a project in school, the teacher should frequently check her progress and give sincere verbal support.

It is important for parents to learn about the four temperaments (see Chapter 8) because the disposition of a child and that of her teacher may be at odds. If you think this is a possibility, you may want to help the teacher understand the four innate and unchanging temperaments with which people are born. It is not uncommon for a teacher and a few students to clash while the rest of the class thinks she's great.

POINTS TO PONDER

When we examine ADD, Asperger's, and autism, we need to ask if a child with ADD really belongs in this group. Does she really have a disorder or simply a different kind of wiring in her brain? She may be disorderly in her chores or keeping her room clean, but many kids are. She may forget to take out the trash, but most kids have to be told more than once. She has to be reminded to listen to the teacher, but maybe the teacher needs to be saying something of greater interest to these brilliant little people.

ADD kids can focus on anything they feel is important. Their minds race ahead of things they feel are boring or inconsequential, and then focus on one thing that interests them. However, when that one thing is not what the teacher is talking about, they are said to have an Attention Deficit Disorder.

Do not be too quick to find an answer to your child's behavior issues. Although ADD, Asperger's, or autism might not be the easy answer, it could simply be a quick answer. With more attention being focused on these areas, it is easy to opt to take some "bad" news rather than no news. To include children in this group just for the sake of a category and a possible solution is as much a disservice as ignoring the fact that they might truly be different.

To say a gifted child who focuses on subjects of interest rather than things that have no relevance to her has an attention deficit disorder is an oxymoron, a contradiction in terms. If she is able to focus on things that interest her but ignores what she feels is unimportant or boring, how can she have a deficit of attention? The problem—if it is a problem—is that she appears to have too great a capacity to focus on what is important to her. She needs to be challenged in school or she will forever have a label of ADD.

Today's children are raised to multitask. It is not a concept that they even need to learn. They play in-depth computer or video games while listening to music and talking to a friend on the phone. Their generation has developed the ability to use different segments of their brain to perform different tasks at the same time. Twenty years ago, one of the most difficult skills for the young video game fighter pilot to learn was the use of an ocular device that fed information to one eye while she scanned the horizon with her other eye. Today most first-person participant games overlay maps and other information over the actual "view" of the player.

We, as adults, are trying to learn this multitasking that our children seem to be born with; however, we find it more difficult to drive and converse on the cell phone. Our children are one step ahead of us, and perhaps we want to slow them down to conform to our "normal" standards.

Children with ADD often show a sense of humor like Stephen, who, at the age of five, frequently said very funny things to get a reaction. Here is a conversation we had during a session after he returned from a lengthy vacation with his affluent family:

Janet: "Did you catch any fish?"

Stephen: "Yes."

Tammy: A Success Story

Six-year-old Tammy was a child who agonized over her printing. Her mother brought her homework assignment to our first session. It required her to read a short paragraph to someone. She began reading but when she came to an unfamiliar word she was not content to continue after being told what it was. She started over at the beginning—every time. Obviously she was not going to get her homework done at that rate. She was frustrated and cried that she couldn't do it, she didn't know how to read, and she wasn't going to do her homework.

I placed a one-minute hourglass on the table and asked if she thought she could read her homework before the sand ran out. She thought it would be fun, and just as the last few grains dropped to the bottom she finished her assignment. She still had times when she was stumped by a word, but didn't feel the need to repeat the paragraph from the beginning. Tammy knew she was capable of reading, which was a great morale boost.

Two weeks later, her homework was to print her name at the top of the paper and copy three words: "dog," "cat," and "car." She never got past her name because it wasn't neat enough for her. She wrote and erased it a dozen times and finally tore the paper. At that point she put down her pencil and calmly announced, "I don't want to do this. I'll do it tomorrow."

Tammy was like so many children who learn and remember from logical and honest explanations. She was told that as she got older there were going to be things that would have to be done "right now." I asked what she thought would happen if a boy broke his arm and was taken to the emergency room, where the doctor looked at it and said, "I don't want to do it now. I'll do it tomorrow." She laughed and understood the message.

Kids with ADD and Asperger's love to hear about personal examples and to receive explanations that are non-judgmental. They appreciate straightforward communication from one intelligent person to another. They often readily respond to that approach, while they may simply tune out lectures, irritated voices, or any other forms of condescension or impatience.

Janet: "What kind of fish?"

Stephen: "Smoked salmon."

If your child has ADD, you probably have had similar experiences that surprise and delight you. Or, you may be concerned if she is as aggressive and acquisitive as Erin (see inset on page 73). However, there are other things a professional will look for when attempting to determine if your child has Attention Deficit Disorder or Attention Deficit Hyperactivity Disorder.

CRITERIA FOR AN ADD/ADHD DIAGNOSIS

According to the *Diagnostic and Statistical Manual of Mental Disorders (DSM)* there are certain requirements that must be met for a diagnosis of ADD or ADHD. For either diagnosis, symptoms have to have been present for at least six months. Some symptoms have to have been noticed in the child before the age of seven. Symptoms should be the same even when the child is in different settings (for example, both at home and in school).

Characteristics

For a diagnosis of Attention Deficit Disorder, at least six of the following nine characteristics and behaviors should be present:

- Doesn't pay attention to details an makes careless mistakes in school work
- Doesn't follow through on instructions
- Doesn't like tasks that require a period of time to complete
- Doesn't respond when spoken to directly
- Is easily distracted
- Is forgetful
- Has limited attention span when playing or doing a task
- Loses possessions
- Is unorganized

For a diagnosis of Attention Deficit Hyperactivity Disorder, at least six of the following nine characteristics and behaviors should be present:

- Is always in motion, acts as if driven by a motor
- Blurts out answers before questions have been completed
- Can't remain seated for any length of time; gets up and walks about
- Fidgets and squirms
- Has difficulty waiting her turn
- Interrupts conversations or games of others
- Runs about, climbs excessively
- Talks excessively
- Is unable to play quietly

Below are other common characteristics and behaviors found in kids with ADD or ADHD, in addition to those listed by the *DSM*. Not all children will necessarily show every one of these signs, but all will show some of them:

- Acts silly to get attention
- Can't slow down on orders
- Can't tell right from left
- Doesn't finish what she's started, e.g. a painting
- Has trouble making and keeping friends
- Is frequently touching things or breaking things—especially onto and into other things
- Has constant runny nose
- Has red cheeks
- Has red ears
- Is imaginative
- Is impatient
- Is impulsive

- Has limited fine motor control: trouble with coloring, tying shoelaces, buttons, balance, using scissors, throwing or catching a ball
- Is hyperactive when playing with hyper child
- Displays excellence in one academ-ic area, incompetence in others
- Has low self-esteem
- Has poor coordination
- Is persistent and intense
- Has poor planning and judgment
- Stood and walked early
- Has dark circles under her eyes

An increasing number of people want to know if there actually have been more cases of children with ADD and ADHD in the past few years, or if this label has become a pigeonhole where children with a natural curiosity and allergies are increasingly being filed. While the National Institutes of Health states there are no accurate statistics for this disorder, it estimates that between 3 and 5 percent of children have ADD/ADHD, or approximately 2 million children in the United States. Other figures are much higher, between 3 and 5 million.

CAUSES AND THEORIES

There apparently is no single cause of ADD, but instead a cluster of triggers such as trauma, nutrition, environment, pesticides, brain damage, or other stresses. Genetics is likely to be involved, since most people with ADD can identify similar characteristics among members of their family. Some children react to dyes in food coloring and others don't. Some become hyperactive when given a combination of colorings but a single color doesn't bother them at all.

Although many symptoms of ADD are the result of allergies, we can't jump to the conclusion that if dairy products—the most common allergens—are eliminated, a child's ADD or ADHD will immediately disappear. A check-up by the family physician is important to identify all potential or existing causes and will probably include an elimination diet. This involves removing a suspected food, such as dairy products, for two or three weeks, then gradually adding it back to the child's diet to observe reactions, if any. Parents who have a "hunch" that a certain food triggers a burst of hyperactive behavior but are not sure how to prove it should do this.

Erin: An Unrecognized Gifted Child

Erin was one of the thousands of children who are not recognized as gifted. Instead, they are often considered foolish, spoiled, demanding, and artistic. At the age of six, Erin was given everything she wanted. Because she was a beautiful child, she was doted on, and she resented the time her parents had to spend with her two-year-old brother. She became manipulative, and her tantrums were legendary.

Because she was never corrected or disciplined, Erin did not know how else to behave. She was constantly in trouble at school because she bit, punched, kicked, screamed, and refused to do her schoolwork. Her report cards consistently stated she needed improvement, and her parents were told that if Erin didn't improve, she would have to leave the school. Naturally, her parents were concerned and confused about what was causing such a problem.

It was obvious to me at our first session, from her behavior and telltale runny nose and red cheeks, that she probably was allergic to dairy products. Although they were skeptical, her parents agreed to remove all dairy and substitute soy products in her diet for a few weeks.

Erin's heightened senses kept her in a state of constant physical and mental activity that was barely noticeable to the eye. She was an acquisitive child who grabbed whatever she wanted at the moment from another child. Often children with ADD need to be startled before a lesson can be learned, and it worked with Erin. When she grabbed a crayon I was using, I pretended it didn't bother me and used another one. A few minutes later, as she was clutching all of the crayons in her hand while coloring with the other hand, I reached out and grabbed the fistful of crayons. She was startled and speechless.

I asked, "Erin, did you like it when I grabbed your crayons?" She said, "No," and I was able to help her realize that nobody likes to have their crayons taken away from them. She understood the suggestion of, "May I please use your purple crayon?" and learned a valuable lesson. Except for forgetting "please" two or three times, she never again grabbed toys or crayons from anyone.

Within two weeks of eliminating dairy products, Erin's runny nose and red cheeks and ears disappeared. At the same time, her behavior improved and she was given more challenging assignments in school that required two people to complete. Erin and her new friend shared crayons, paper, and scissors with no grabbing or squabbles. After two months of weekly creative arts sessions and a lot of interesting dialogue, her grades skyrocketed. Erin was finally recognized as gifted and her school announced they were going to begin a class for gifted children.

Allergies

Casein is a protein, found in milk and other foods, that is easily broken down by the digestive system and assimilated by most people. However, in some people, mostly those on the Autism Spectrum, this process isn't complete and the result is an effect on the body similar to that of opiates or morphine-like drugs. A search of labels on food packages will often show casein as an ingredient. For children on a casein-free diet, even a small amount may cause an allergic reaction. According to Frank A. Oski, MD, chief of Pediatrics at Johns Hopkins School of Medicine, at least 50 percent of all children are allergic to cow's milk.

Milk, eggs, cheese, and other products containing casein are usually removed from the child's diet as soon as her pediatrician suspects ADD, and many symptoms are reduced or eliminated within a few days or weeks. Parents often say their child's runny nose and circles under her eyes disappear almost immediately. They are usually surprised because they had thought their child had constant colds.

It seems no mere coincidence that the growing number of children with ADHD appears to go hand-in-hand with the large increase in junk food in the diets of the American family. Most snacks and processed foods contain sugar, dyes, preservatives, and flavorings that cause an allergic

---

Maybe It Isn't Hyperactivity

Not all active children are necessarily "hyperactive." When a child is exhibiting unusual behavior, we should not immediately assume that she has ADD or ADHD and needs to be medicated. There could be a number of other factors involved. These include:

- Abuse—physical, sexual, verbal, or emotional
- Allergies
- Anxiety
- Bullies in school or on the bus
- Depression
- Disturbing arguments between parent
- Hearing loss

- Embarrassment at not keeping up with or understanding the teacher
- Frequent change of home and school
- Petit mal seizures
- Unknown chronic illness
- Unspoken fears
- Visual impairment

A physician, allergist, eye specialist, hearing specialist, speech specialist, and psychologist should ideally test children suspected of having ADD or ADHD before a clear determination is made.

reaction in many people, including those without any kind of disorder or previous history of allergies. Although some doctors dismiss the idea that sugar plays a part in hyperactivity, most parents dispute that. They maintain that it takes only one forbidden cookie to send their child into a frenzy of activity.

In 1973, Ben F. Feingold, MD, focused new attention on the effect of certain foods on behavior in children diagnosed with hyperactivity. His groundbreaking book, *Why Your Child Is Hyperactive*, startled the medical profession with statements that children reacted to food coloring. Although his work had its share of critics, parents praised his discovery, as their children's behavior changed dramatically when coloring was eliminated from their diets. Today, over thirty years later, research is being done on the same theory with the same results. The diet of a child with ADD should be closely monitored, because if she is allergic to an ingredient in her favorite snack, one treat might cause a burst of over-stimulation.

Common Food Contributors to Hyperactivity

Children on the Autism Spectrum are sensitive to a number of things in their environment, including what they eat and drink. In addition to the most well-known food allergies—those to dairy products and wheat—your child may have a reaction to other items in your kitchen. The following is a list of possible dietary contributors to hyperactivity:

- Additives such as MSG
- Artificial coloring and flavorings
- Caffeine in soda
- Chicken and beef (from animals fed antibiotics or given steroids, which we then eat)
- Chocolate
- Mercury in fish
- Peanuts and cashews
- Preservatives in dried fruit
- Preservatives in baked goods
- Sugar and honey
- Wax on fruits and vegetables

As you begin to search your kitchen cabinets, you may be surprised at the additives, preservatives, and dyes used in your child's favorite food. Red, yellow, blue, and green dyes are common in food marketed to children for an obvious reason: They are attracted to the bright colors. You should make it a habit to read labels on everything you eat and use in the house.

You can easily substitute other, healthy foods for these problematic foods. You will find ideas for doing this in Chapter 6. But food isn't the only thing to think about. There are other potentially harmful elements to consider when reevaluating your home and lifestyle with your child in mind.

Environment

Our environment is a constant source of toxins and allergens. You probably won't be able to protect your child from all of the threats that surround us in our environment, but at least you can be aware of the possible results of over-exposure. You should be advised of some suspected dangers in your own home so that you can eliminate, or at least significantly reduce, your child's exposure to as many as possible. The following is a list of everyday objects that pose potential dangers to your child:

- Computers
- Electric blankets
- Fluorescent lighting—known to cause seizures in susceptible people
- Carpet fumes
- Cleaning substances
- Gas appliances
- Hair spray
- Laundry detergent
- Paint fumes
- Pesticides
- Perfume
- Scented tissues and toilet paper
- Second-hand smoke
- Video games
- Allergens in the air
- Automobile exhaust
- Leaf blowers and lawn mowers
- Power lines

Television

Television is listed as a separate category because children are almost constantly exposed to it. It is identified as a potential cause of ADD since during commercials, many different images and music flood the brain in a few seconds, causing confusion and overload of the senses.

According to a study of children between the ages of one and three led by Dr. Dimitri A. Christakis, director of the Child Health Institute at Children's Hospital and Regional Medical Center, Seattle, Washington, children who watch a lot of TV are more apt to have ADD. Those who watched only one hour a day had a 10 percent greater chance of developing ADD by the age of seven than kids who never watched television. Watching three hours a day increased the risks to 30 percent to 40 percent over those who never watched television. The results were published in the April 2004 issue of the journal *Pediatrics*. Dr. Christakis concluded that watching television "rewires" a child's brain.

Is this a cause or an effect? Kids with shorter attention spans, such as those with ADD, generally prefer fast-paced television to books, so do parents give in and allow more television just to get some moments of peace and quiet while their child is occupied?

Schools

In addition to the emotional distress children may experience at school, there is also the possibility of unintentional physical harm. Schools are often blamed as sources of illness and ADD, since sealed windows prevent fresh air from circulating. New furniture and carpeting are made with chemicals that give off fumes that can cause illness, and there's no way to clear the environment of them.

This is particularly noticeable when school starts in the fall and the rooms have been prepared for the new school year. Mold and spores multiply in air-conditioning and heating ducts, sending allergens throughout the building. When people began complaining of headaches and nausea in their workplaces years ago, the cause was quickly determined and labeled as "sick building syndrome." The solution was to clean all ductwork throughout the building thoroughly. We still hear about sick building syndrome every so often in the news.

Stress

If your child has ADD or ADHD and you're stressed, you are not alone. A lot of adults are stressed, and, strange as it may seem, very young children are as well. As adults, we expect babies to be gurgling, toddlers to be happy, and older children to be carefree all the time unless they're obviously sick. This isn't realistic, and when kids are grouchy, well-meaning parents may try to suppress their feelings of irritation or failure. Young children usually can't describe how they feel, and the only way they can tell us is through moodiness, crying, anger, rebelliousness, or withdrawal.

> If your child has ADD or ADHD and you're stressed, you are not alone.

As adults, we feel we are the only ones in the family who could possibly be stressed. After all, advertising never mentions a pill for children who are stressed, so it doesn't exist in the minds of most people. Grown-ups have to pay bills, and they may have problems with their boss or working conditions, but they're not alone.

Young people with ADD have their own sources of stress. One of the most stressful is the time spent in school. Classes can be especially difficult, since they are surrounded by the noise of children, bells, and the general activities of a school day. They may be concerned about failing a test or not having their homework done. They may have to face a bully on the bus and refuse to go to school without any explanation.

At home, there may not be enough money for them to buy new clothes or to buy lunch like their classmates. As a result, they may be teased about wearing out-of-style clothes or having to bring their lunch to school. There may be a father in the home who says, "Big boys don't cry," so they try to hide their feelings of anger, hurt, and maybe even physical pain.

Perhaps there is frequent loud arguing between parents. This is very stressful for children because they often feel they are the cause of disagreements. They may have fears for a member of the family who is fighting a war halfway around the world. They may have an unreasonable fear of thunderstorms that is ridiculed by other family members. A storm is a small thing for most adults, but for children it can be a major cause of fear that telling them to "grow up" does not help.

All of these are potential sources of stress, some of which you can help your child deal with. Helping a young child relieve stress isn't much different from working with an older child. The causes of stress may differ, but the methods of helping are similar. See "How You Can Help" (see page 79) for some tips on easing your child's stress, whatever the source.

When stress is a constant in the home, everyone is affected by harsh words and strident voices. Children are particularly affected because of their sensitive nature. If you feel yourself getting angry and stressed because your child seems to ignore you and never follows through when you ask her to do something, perhaps it's time for reorganization.

GETTING ORGANIZED

Often both a child and her parents need some assistance. Therapists can help by explaining ADD to the parents and emphasizing how common it is so they don't unduly blame the child or themselves.

Parents may complain that their child forgets to do her chores, and teachers may complain that she forgets her homework. A child with untreated ADD can't help it. She's not trying to irritate her parents and teachers; she just has a hard time living by their rules. Yelling, scolding, or punishing have no effect except to reduce her self-esteem and increase her resistance.

Like a child with Asperger's Syndrome, she has good intentions, but on the way to get her homework for school, she finds a dollar bill on the floor, picks it up, and thinks of all the things she can buy with it. Her homework is forgotten. She looks for her notebook and pens and her mother yells that she hasn't taken out the trash and the bus is coming. She goes to school without paper and pens, but at least she's taken out the trash.

Often both a child and her parents need some assistance. Therapists can help by explaining ADD to the parents and emphasizing how common it is so they don't unduly blame the child or themselves. Being shown how to set up an organizational chart, parents and their child will be reminded of schedules, time constraints, and the reality of expectations and accomplishments.

Charts are made up of chores and activities that a child must do—homework, feed the dog, take out the trash. These are placed on a grid with the days of the week across the top. Chores and activities appear in the boxes of the grid for each day. As each chore or activity is done, a check is placed in the corresponding box. If Mom has a meeting after work or Dad has to go to the dentist, the appropriate boxes could also be marked. This really works, but it works only if people look at it.

A marker board is great for keeping track of chores. The days of the week and the grid can be printed with permanent marker, with chores and activities written with a dry-erase marker. The list can include as many things as you like, such as accomplishments like "Didn't fight on the bus" or "Made a new friend."

How You Can Help

Here are a few suggestions for things you can do to help your child overcome physical and emotional stress:

- Be sure she has plenty of sleep at night.

- Be sure she starts her day with a nutritious breakfast.

- Look at her drawings or paintings for signs of a problem she won't talk about.

- Listen to her because she will give clues about what is bothering her.

- Tell both girls and boys that it's okay to cry, and that men cry, too.

- Have her body, including eyes, ears, and teeth, checked for problems.

- If she's afraid of war or other current events, let her talk out her fears and try to put her mind at ease.

- Don't let her watch television programs that may increase her fears, especially before bedtime.

- Monitor her diet—some foods increase aggression and cause intestinal discomfort.

- If there is a bully on the bus, talk with the driver and/or principal about it.

- If she doesn't have her homework done, ask if you can help, but don't make a habit of it.

Your child may sometimes have a fear of something that may seem irrational to most people. However, many other children and even adults might also share the same fear. For example, if she's afraid of thunderstorms (and maybe so are you), make an effort to be with her and play a game when it storms. Explain to her that she can tell how close a lightning strike is by counting the seconds between the thunder and the lightning. Four seconds equal one mile of distance. This game can help reduce the fears of both parent and child and is something she will remember as an adult every time it storms.

Orderly Thought

Children with ADD need sincere words of encouragement for their progress.

Orderly thinking is the result of an orderly life, just as unorganized thinking and work reflect a haphazard and unorganized life. If a child with ADD is taught to be neat with her toys, clothes, and books, she will be more orderly in her thinking. The facts she has learned will fall neatly and easily into place, making a sensible whole. When they keep their books in a certain place, in alphabetical order, children can go immediately to a particular volume without having to search through two dozen books for one necessary reference. This is particularly important for ADD kids because they like to read and research, but may give up if they can't find what they're looking for. For example, orderliness will be very important as a person puts facts together in a logical and comprehensive way to develop an essay or report. What children learn now, about orderliness or anything else, can influence the rest of their lives.

ADD children who are orderly will rarely act impulsively on their emotions because they will instantaneously be able to see the cause and effect of their actions. They have the capacity to be observant, perceptive, and independent thinkers because of their innate intelligence and quick mind.

It sometimes becomes easier for parents to pick up after their children than to remind them constantly to pick up after themselves, because kids with ADD often start the job and don't finish it. But, when Mom cleans the child's room herself, she's not really solving a problem, because it hinders the development of a sense of responsibility, which is necessary if a child is to be successful in whatever she chooses to do in life, even cleaning her room.

Children with ADD need sincere words of encouragement for their progress. They don't need rewards of candy or money for doing their homework or picking up their clothes. Honest praise runs deeper than candy; it affects the inner nature of the child and encourages her to do better than she thought she could.

Learning the Art of Debate

Children with ADD have fine minds that, like a garden, have to be cultivated. When they learn about logic and reason, they will see the logic behind any situation. They won't accept something outlandish or harmful just because someone says it's true.

A good way to develop logic is through dialogue and discussion. Young children with ADD love to debate, which isn't surprising to parents who've tried to tell them to do something. The child wants to see both sides of a situation and wants to know "Why?" This can be frustrating for Mom, who just wants her child to take off those muddy shoes!

Teachers can encourage this quality of logic by having age-appropriate mini-debates in class on such subjects as, "Should we sit in the sun?" One side may say, "Yes, because the sun gives us Vitamin D, and if someone lives in a climate with long winters, they might get depressed from not getting enough sunlight." The other side might argue, "That may be true but sitting in the hot sun isn't good for your skin. People should sit outside in the morning and not at noon."

They will eventually see that both sides are right, neither is wrong, and there can be a meeting ground that's acceptable to both sides. This is logic.

In order to debate or even speak intelligently, a child has to know what she is talking about and how to articulate her thoughts. A simple subject—pro and con—can encourage debate around the dinner table. The key is "debate," not argument. A child with ADD will learn critical thinking by seeing flaws in other people's arguments or statements. When she can do that, she will be more discriminating in her choice of friends and activities as a child, teen, and adult.

Debates are not just for grownups. Children like them because they give them a chance to "argue" with their parents in a respectful way. Having original thoughts occurs only through original thinking. Children with ADD have the potential to be great thinkers because they have a natural intelligence that grasps facts quickly and "sees" the outcome of a situation.

The Need for Quiet Time

It is important for children with ADD or ADHD to have a quiet time and place where they can read, listen to classical music, daydream, draw, write in their journal, paint, and maybe even write poetry or a science fiction story. Unless they have quiet times, they can never get in touch with their spiritual and creative nature because their attention is constantly switching from one activity or sound to another. It is for this reason that Ritalin is often recommended.

Unfortunately, not all parents ask their doctor or check for information on this drug before giving it to her. Parents often find their child has changed from an imaginative bright child to one who seems to have lost interest in things that had previously intrigued her. Other parents and teachers find Ritalin to be a lifesaver for the rest of the family or the class. However, there are two sides to every story, and Ritalin is no exception.

RITALIN—THE CONTROVERSY

When a child is disruptive in school, her teacher may suggest the prescription drug Ritalin to calm her down. Ritalin is the most well-known medication for Attention Deficit Disorder and is one of a group of central nervous system stimulants known as methylphenidate, or amphetamines.

According to the Mayo Clinic's website, Ritalin works to treat ADD and ADHD by increasing attention and decreasing restlessness in children and adults who are overactive, cannot concentrate for very long, or are easily distracted or impulsive.

It makes the teacher's job easier when none of the children speak out of turn or wander around the room. It makes for a more pleasant home environment, too, when there isn't constant friction between parents and their ADD child. But critics of Ritalin ask if we are too quick to prescribe a drug that the Drug Enforcement Administration (DEA) has classified as a Schedule II substance, comparable to cocaine.

What Exactly Is Ritalin?

There is a lot of controversy about this drug, which is taken by so many children throughout the world. For accuracy, here is what the Greater Dallas Council on Alcohol & Drug Abuse has to say:

Ritalin (methylphenidate) is a central nervous system stimulant, similar to amphetamines in the nature and duration of its effects. It is believed that it works by activating the brain stem arousal system and cortex. Pharmacologically, it works on the neurotransmitter dopamine, and in that respect resembles the stimulant characteristics of cocaine.

Short-term effects can include:

- Abdominal pain
- Anxiety
- Convulsions
- Dizziness
- Headaches (may be severe)
- Excessive repetition of movements and meaningless tasks

High doses of stimulants produce a predictable set of symptoms that may include the following long-term effects:

- Insomnia
- Irregular heartbeat and respiration (may be profound and life threatening)
- Nausea and vomiting
- Paranoia
- Restlessness
- Skin rashes and itching
- Weight loss
- Loss of appetite (may cause serious malnutrition)

According to the Drug Enforcement Administration, the number of prescriptions written for stimulant medications to treat ADD has increased by 500 percent since 1991. About 80 percent of all the 11 million prescriptions doctors write each year are for Ritalin.

Ritalin is the most well-known and popular drug of this kind, but others are also routinely prescribed—Cyclert, Pamelor, Tofrnil, Norpramin. With over 11 million prescriptions written for Ritalin every year to counteract ADD, it is now the drug of choice among teens and adults. Ritalin and other similar drugs are known for their ability to calm a child who is thought to have ADD or ADHD. Amphetamines energize adults and, for some reason, subdue energetic children, making Ritalin popular among a diverse group of people. Teens and young adults take Ritalin to stay awake for tests or business meetings and to increase brain activity.

According to the Genetic Science Learning Center at the University of Utah's online site, Ritalin is very much like cocaine in its effect. Like cocaine, Ritalin may cause brain damage if taken longer than is necessary to treat a specific problem. It is the drug of choice among teenagers because it is inexpensive and easy to get. Ritalin is often considered a "gateway drug," since many people who use it as a recreational drug often move on to more addictive drugs. Young people who have taken Ritalin for ADD/ADHD, however, seldom follow this course.

Naturally, some parents question the safety of a drug that has known side effects, and they often claim that children who had a natural zest for life are being drugged into submission as a result of the drug. Others are very grateful for anything that calms their child and reduces constant hyperactive behavior. Ritalin helps children complete their homework and do their chores at home. Despite the benefits of medication, some doctors are concerned because we don't know all of the long-term effects of Ritalin.

Many children who are being treated with psychotropic drugs like Ritalin don't have ADD, and many children who meet the criteria for ADD aren't being treated. In some states, parents aren't allowed to enroll their son or daughter in school if they refuse to give their active child Ritalin. In some cases, parents who refused to medicate their children have been reported to Child Protective Services for neglect.

There are children who need medication, but it doesn't necessarily have to be a drug with known side effects. Health food stores now have safe natural remedies that can be effective for kids with ADD. Homeopathic and naturopathic physicians can prescribe other remedies that aren't available in stores and are made from natural sources, such as plants and flowers. Before the advent of the drug industry, plants and flowers were the only medicines known to our ancestors, so this isn't as strange as may sound.

There are children who need medication, but it does not necessarily have to be a drug with known side effects. Health food stores now have safe natural remedies that can be effective for kids with ADD.

ADULT ADD/ADHD

The characteristics of an adult with ADD or ADHD are similar, if not identical, to those of children. Parents may not realize that they also have the disorder, only that their children should be better organized and not continually losing things.

You may have ADD if you always have a lot of energy and can't sit still in a meeting. Do you twirl your hair, spin your pencil, tap your foot, and doodle instead of taking notes? Even worse, are you always late for appointments and completely unorganized at work and at home? Do you become irritated at little things? Maybe get bored with a project and tell yourself you'll finish it tomorrow—or just forget about it?

Like children with ADD, adults often have low self-esteem and are reluctant to enter into new situations, whether business or social. While talking with someone, their mind may wander until they come back to the conversation and realize they've missed half of what was said. The ease of being distracted is a sign of ADD, although it occasionally happens to everyone.

If you can identify with the above, it doesn't mean there is anything wrong with you or even that you have ADD. But if you do, you will appreciate knowing that adults with ADD are very creative, artistic, intelligent, observant, perceptive, and sensitive. Does that sound familiar? You probably were all of those things as a child, only now you fidget in meetings instead of in class. You are no longer scolded by your teacher for fidgeting or by your parents for not taking out the garbage. But perhaps your boss makes a remark about your not finishing a report that was needed yesterday, and the constant clicking of your pen drives your coworkers to distraction.

If you have adult ADD, you are in good company. Thomas Edison's teachers didn't have a very high opinion of him and said he wasn't capable of learning anything. Winston Churchill failed sixth grade, and Beethoven's teacher said he was hopeless as a composer.

Apparently Einstein had a "problem" as well. He didn't speak until he was four years old and didn't read until he was seven. He spent his time building complex structures with building blocks and putting together puzzles. He was expelled from school for being "mentally slow, unsociable and adrift in his foolish dreams." He later stated, "It's not that I'm so smart. It's just that I stay with problems longer."

Both Einstein and Edison are thought to have had either ADD or Asperger's Syndrome. However, we have no way of knowing for sure. Fortunately for us, these great talents believed in themselves and didn't give up when they were criticized.

SUMMARY

Children with ADD are a challenge and a delight. Because they are so articulate and imaginative, they often surprise us with their observations that seem to come out of the blue. But, as you've learned, these kids are capable of thinking about more than one thing at a time. For children who are said to have an "attention deficit," they have a remarkable ability to focus on something that intrigues them. Debating an interesting subject is something that comes easily to children with ADD. Their rapid-fire mind can see many varied viewpoints, and they will continue debating until they feel they have completed their thoughts—or until they're bored.

The list of ADD/ADHD characteristics is long, but with proper diet, creative therapies, and your understanding, your child's behavior will noticeably improve. Similarly, there is a long list of possible causes, but your diligence when buying food or household products will eliminate many of them. All of the suggestions for helping your child with ADD or ADHD are also appropriate for the disorder known as Asperger's Syndrome. You will read more about Asperger's in the next chapter and will learn how to identify these brilliant children by a few major signposts.

CHAPTER 5

*A*sperger's Syndrome
The Middle of the Bar

Do you have a child who would rather play by himself than in a group? Does he get angry easily and have a fiery temper? Does he spend too much time playing with a robot toy or focusing on obscure facts? As a very young child, could he discuss complex subjects with you that were far beyond his age? Has your doctor dismissed your concerns with, "He's just like every other little boy?" If you have answered "yes" to more than one of these questions, your child may have undiagnosed Asperger's Syndrome.

Asperger's Syndrome (AS) is a neurological disorder that falls midway on the Autism Spectrum between mild ADD and severe autism and affects four times as many boys as girls. It is not usually discovered until a child begins school and teachers notice behavior that is obviously inappropriate. Until then, a boy's obsessions and outbursts of anger are often explained away as, "He's all boy."

This disorder was named after Hans Asperger, an Austrian pediatrician who first published a paper in 1944 about the large number of children he was seeing with unusual symptoms. He named this set of characteristics, "Autistic Psychopathy." Coincidentally, he made his discovery in Austria a year after Leo Kanner identified autism in Baltimore, Maryland, never knowing of Dr. Kanner's work.

Decades later, physicians began to notice an increase of behaviors that didn't fit any criteria other than those written about by Dr. Asperger. In 1981, a year after his death, this disorder was named after the Austrian doctor, but it wasn't until the 1990s that physicians were beginning to see a large number of children with the symptoms Hans Asperger had detected in the 1940s.

Parents are relieved that the behavior of their child has a name and a category for identification. We need to be sure, however, that children aren't labeled with something that really isn't their condition. Confusion can result in diagnosing your child because children with Asperger's Syndrome—or Aspies—often have some characteristics of autism and some of ADD. A common complaint of parents today is that their child's doctor failed to recognize the signs of AS or misdiagnosed it and gave their child a variety of psychotropic drugs hoping that one of them would work. Since some medical professionals are not familiar with Asperger's Syndrome, they may incorrectly label a child as having a different disorder.

PERSONAL CHALLENGES OF ASPIES

Because symptoms can be so easily misunderstood, children with Asperger's Syndrome are usually considered troublemakers, undisciplined, rebellious, or strange. As adults, they may be called eccentric. When parents learn about the characteristics of AS, they often make connections to the odd behavior of relatives that have been amusing or puzzling the family for years.

> Because symptoms can be so easily misunderstood, children with Asperger's Syndrome are usually considered troublemakers, strange, undisciplined, or rebellious. As adults, they may be called eccentric.

Children with Asperger's Syndrome can vacillate between being charming and humorous and being belligerent and threatening. They don't like criticism and don't accept defeat in any undertaking. Instead they thrive on praise. As they mature, they either outgrow or learn how to deal with their behaviors, but at the same time, they are more aware that they are different from other kids and blame themselves. As one boy said, "I'm so stupid. There's something wrong with my head!" Another declared, "I'm angry with God for making me this way!"

This awareness leads to frustration and anger, but that can be channeled into constructive physical activities, such as karate. This form of martial arts is good exercise and an outlet for pent-up emotions. AS children are usually not interested in team sports, and if they play, they do so grudgingly and not very skillfully. As a rule, they would rather not take part in competition, because it involves socialization, but there are exceptions. (Some boys enjoy team sports such as basketball, which contradicts the prevailing thought that all Aspies would rather play by themselves.)

Children are frequently very resistant to change and to new events, but this will decrease as they become more balanced through therapy. Like children with autism, most AS kids like routine and become agitated if it is changed in the slightest. This inflexibility is often seen in their activities and focus on repeating the same routine when drawing, putting a puzzle together, writing, or reading.

It helps to prepare a child several hours, days, or even weeks in advance of a change in schedule or plans so he can become accustomed to it. We don't want to take away from his gifted nature, but rather to enhance it so he can share it with others. We also need to know how Asperger's differs in boys and girls and how it is similar in both sexes.

DIFFERENCES BETWEEN ASPIE BOYS AND ASPIE GIRLS

Asperger's Syndrome affects both boys and girls—although boys are much more likely to have it—but there are noticeable differences in the way AS symptoms are perceived for each. What may be seen as negative traits in a boy may be viewed as positive in a girl. Consider the following generalizations, which, although not universal rules, are popularly supported in society:

- If a boy does not like sports, he is considered odd, but if a girl does not like frilly dolls, it's okay.

- If a boy does not join his peers in their interests, there is something wrong with him, but if a girl does the same thing, she "has original ways of doing things."

- Boys are more aggressive and often call attention to themselves.

- Girls tend to have fewer behavior problems at home and at school.

- Boys have outbursts of temper; girls are more passive by nature.

- Passive behaviors in a boy are unacceptable but they are okay in girls.

- Girls may be quieter and, therefore, may not be identified as having Asperger's Syndrome.

- Boys may be fascinated by bus schedules, which can seem odd, while girls may be just as fascinated with details of recipes because cooking is a "girl thing."

- Daydreaming is considered negative in boys but not as much in girls.

- Girls are more rules-oriented, so they don't get into trouble as much as boys.

- Girls are more interested in pleasing people; boys are more interested in talking about their interests.

- Boys tend to get angry at things that irritate them; girls have better coping skills.

- When quiet, boys may be considered sullen and girls are thought just to be shy.

It is easy to see why Asperger's is frequently overlooked in girls, since their innate behavior is different from boys'. However, they can be alike in some ways. The following are similarities among Aspie boys and girls, who usually:

- are loners

- frequently appear rude

- have better eye contact than children with autism, but don't like being stared at

- can be very charming

- are verbal and articulate

- are creative

- have a good sense of humor

- would rather choose a partner to work with on a project instead of being assigned one by the teacher

- are sexually naive and easily taken advantage of

SOCIAL SKILLS

Aspies have undeveloped social skills that may remain characteristics into adulthood. They have difficulty reading faces or body language, and fleeting telltale signs of interest or boredom are lost on them. Consequently, Aspies tend to ramble about things of interest to them without comprehending why kids wander off to find friends they can talk with instead of being talked to. Others can carry on a lengthy conversation with someone who shares his interest. Still others have trouble understanding what people are saying. They may still be processing a response to a question when another is asked or something is added to what was just said. This can be confusing to Aspies, who may be carefully considering an answer but apparently aren't quick enough to respond verbally.

Children with Asperger's have an excellent memory, as six-year-old Kurt showed a reporter who was doing a story about this disorder. When I mentioned that Kurt had a good memory, the boy said, "I sure do! I remember the time my Mom and Dad had a big fight and..." The reporter was writing it all down, and I said that I wasn't sure Kurt's parents would want everybody to know about that. Like most children, Aspies do not think about the consequences of what they say, but unlike other children his age, Kurt couldn't read the cues on his mother's face as she tried to tell him non-verbally not to talk about the argument that had taken place.

AS kids are socially awkward and tend to play with younger children, who readily accept them without judgment. They may have one close friend, perhaps with a form of autism. They are often teased by other kids, who target them because they are vulnerable and unable to defend themselves. Often the butt of practical jokes, Aspies are deeply hurt once they realize what has happened to them. Most Asperger's children have no guile; they see no ulterior motives in others, and in their innocence, they are easily bullied by older children who taunt them. They are still too young to realize that they are often strong in other areas in which bullies are not.

Aspies have undeveloped social skills that may remain characteristics into adulthood.

DELIGHTFUL ASPIES

Aspies often have an unusual and delightful way of expressing themselves. Parents often see unintentional moments of humor in their literal Aspies. Some of the things we say they visualize literally, and have to be seen through their eyes to help us understand their confusion when they hear a puzzling statement. For example:

- A mother told her Aspie son to keep an eye on his little sister while she ran to the bathroom. When she came back into the room, her son had his head pressed against the baby's arm. He was literally keeping his eye on the baby.

- I once told eight-year-old Jefferson a story about a helicopter. He was shocked and said, "Don't say that!" I asked, "Don't say what?" and he replied, "The thing you said has two 'L's. You know, 'H-E-blank-blank.' That's a bad word." When I said, "Helicopter only has one 'L' so it isn't a bad word," he said, "Oh. Okay then."

- A father was driving when he commented on a road sign that said, "Stop ahead." His son insisted he stop the car so they could find the head.

- A visiting aunt was telling a boy's mother that a coworker "rolled her eyes." The confused child took it literally.

- At his first practice game, Lionel's baseball coach told him to "cover third base." He ran over and laid down on it.

There are other things we say that confuse Aspies, who take our words literally. Because they try to picture what is said, it is totally confusing to them. Put yourself in their place when you hear the following common phrases:

• Take a seat.	• He's such a road hog.
• Get a move on.	• The sun is in my eyes.
• Has the cat got your tongue?	• Hit the road.
• I changed my mind.	• It's driving me crazy.

You can probably think of others.

I asked the following question of an Aspie: "When things are loud, do you cover your ears or just not listen?" He answered, "When a friend and I were bullied we listened to the wind in our ears instead of what he was saying."

They are very observant, as a four-year old showed when he walked into my living room and asked, "Did you vacuum?" I had before he arrived. Most children his age either would not have noticed or would not have asked the question.

Aspies frequently show great sensitivity and maturity. Simon was upset when he came home from school to find his pet mouse had died. He was inconsolable and traumatized because the mouse was his one good friend and confidant. His mother suggested he call me, which he did. He talked and cried for a few minutes, and I asked if he was going to get another mouse. He said, "Yes. When the pain is gone."

Jarrod

Like kids with autism, they may improve to the degree that they are no longer considered to have Asperger's Syndrome, but there will probably always be some minor difficulties in their social interactions.

Six-year-old Jarrod was a delightful child who would obsess about different things that captured his attention. One day he went to the bathroom and saw a spot-remover tool that was plugged in and recharging. He asked what it was and I told him, and I then asked if he wanted to see how it worked. Of course, he did. I found a spot on the carpet and removed it. He was fascinated and wanted to clean one, which he did. This captivated him and every week after that he would carefully examine the carpet for spots and insist on cleaning them. Only then could we begin our sessions.

He loved all of the art and physical activities and was a pleasure to work with for several months. On his last day in the program I told him he could do anything he wanted, thinking he might like to paint on a huge piece of paper or go outside and play kickball. Instead he said, "Remove spots" and pointed to two that were barely visible. He cleaned them and was satisfied with a job well done.

DIAGNOSING ASPERGER'S SYNDROME

Asperger's Syndrome is identified by symptoms, behaviors, deficits, and strengths. Aspies outgrow many of their initial characteristics and usually learn to channel their behaviors into more acceptable and productive activities. For example, a child who is obsessed with computer games may be very successful in a field of high technology or medical research. Or, adults who as children had AS may empathize with Aspie children and decide to become a psychologist or teacher to help them with challenges or difficulties.

As they mature, Aspies learn to control their anger through techniques they may have developed, such as counting to three before responding to what they perceive to be an insensitive or insulting remark. Like kids with autism, they may improve to the degree that they are no longer considered to have Asperger's Syndrome, but there will probably always be some minor difficulties in their social interactions.

Characteristics

Asperger's has its own spectrum, as you can see from the following list of characteristics. Children may have a number of symptoms or only enough for diagnosis. Explosive temper, poor social skills, and obsessions are the three signposts most often found in all children with Asperger's, but they may have an assortment of the following traits and behaviors:

- Is artistic
- Blames himself for being "stupid"
- Cannot or will not engage in small talk
- Cannot take criticism
- Is clumsy
- Is compulsive
- Is creative
- Has difficulty maintaining friendships
- Is distractible
- Does not know how to lie— tells it like he sees it
- Is easily angered
- Has explosive temper
- Frequently appears unhappy
- Frequently announces that nobody likes him
- Has good vocabulary
- Hates to lose
- Is highly intelligent but scores below average in performance abilities
- Is unable to focus on a task
- Likes to read
- Likes TV and computer games
- Has limited range of facial expressions
- Has good math skills
- Has hyperlexia (see below)
- Needs praise
- Has obsessions
- Has poor social skills
- Is resistant to change
- Is self-centered
- Is tactilely defensive (does not like to touch or be touched)
- Is teased or bullied by others
- Threatens to kill himself or other people
- Is very literal
- Has voice lacking intonation

In addition to these signposts, some children have an amazing ability to read at an early age.

Hyperlexia

Some children read beyond their years but their comprehension is limited. They may complain that they like to read but do not understand or remember much of what they have read. These children may have hyperlexia.

Children with hyperlexia are self-taught readers who are able to read books at a very young age, although there is little or no comprehension of the material. They usually have a fascination with numbers and letters and share a few similarities to children with autism, such as echolalia (automatically repeating or echoing what was just said) and irritation when their routines are altered.

The mental activity of a child with hyperlexia needs to be balanced with creativity. When working with a child who has this ability, we need to alternate artistic activities with those that include reading. You can finger paint at the easel, and then read to him from a book you've chosen while listening to classics. Then you can model and sculpt at the table and finally sit together in a chair or on the couch as he reads to you from his favorite book. These children need a change of position and activities to help them adjust to inevitable changes in their lives. All of these activities should be varied during the time you work with your child so they don't become a routine.

IN THE CLASSROOM

AS kids are impatient and unfamiliar with social rules of conduct or rules of the classroom. A child with Asperger's is often clearly a fiery manager (see Chapter 8 for more information on this and other temperaments). An obvious similarity is that most Asperger's kids and children who are fiery managers have a penchant for punching other kids, although their motives may differ. This makes it doubly difficult for a teacher who may be unfa-

Asperger's: The "Geek Syndrome"?

Steve Silverman, who wrote an article for the December 2001 issue of *Wired* magazine, coined the phrase, "Geek Syndrome." He described the increasing number of children being diagnosed with Asperger's Syndrome in California's high-tech Silicon Valley. It was suggested that many computer programmers, mathematicians, and scientists who live and work in this area have Asperger's, which has been passed on to their children. Since many men and women with the same interests often marry and may carry a genetic link to Asperger's Syndrome, their children may have a substantially greater chance of having it as well. They also will likely have a greater sensitivity to toxins and environmental pollutants. There is no proof for this supposition; however, it is true that peo-

ple with Asperger's are usually very intelligent, interested in electronics, and capable of sustained focus when involved in a subject that is of great interest. In our culture and society, "geek" is often the label given to kids and adults who typically gravitate towards high-tech industries. We see the stereotypical adult "geek" on television shows with several ballpoint pens in a plastic protector in his white shirt pocket, letting us know that this man is analytical, fastidious, and "dorky."

Although some would say there is no connection with Asperger's and those in high-tech industries, it is noteworthy that, according to the *Wired* article, Bill Gates provides insurance for Microsoft employees who have to pay for therapy for their children with Asperger's Syndrome.

miliar with either a child's innate disposition or Autism Spectrum Disorders. Knowledge of both will make the teacher's job much easier. It certainly will help parents understand why their child behaves as he does.

An Aspie in the classroom can be a challenge in many ways. Such children tend to wander about the room or yell out the answer to a question without raising their hand first, both of which are annoying to the teacher and other students. If someone stares at them, they are apt to punch the child who is looking at them. (The difference between this action and that of a fiery manager is that a fiery manager doesn't need an excuse.) If someone angers them, Aspies are apt to threaten to kill him, and if they think everyone is picking on them, they are apt to threaten to kill themselves. Although this is unlikely to happen, the anger that accompanies this threat is frightening to everyone.

On the other hand, teachers may tell parents that their child is well behaved in school, while parents say their child is unruly and often violent at home. Perhaps emotions are pent up during the day and the child knows he should not create a scene in school. When he gets home, it is another story, and he explodes with a force that surprises even himself. Temper tantrums are common when a child is trying to verbalize a thought and nobody understands him at school or at home.

As stated, Aspies often yell out the answer to a question without raising their hand and waiting to be called upon. Naturally, this creates a disruption, but teachers can help by pointing out to an Aspie what the class is doing. For example, tell him to copy what the other kids do when the teacher asks a question. It may take some time but he will eventually learn the routine.

> You, a parent, can help your child control his anger by recognizing things that trigger the outburst.

Teachers can educate the other children in the class by being a role model. If they have learned the behaviors of ADD, autism, and Asperger's, they are more understanding of how children may react to sounds or being touched by other students. A simple statement that "Jimmy does not like to be touched. Remember when we talked about that a few weeks ago?" may prevent potential outbursts and animosity.

Recognizing Triggers

Aspies recognize something in themselves that is different from other kids in school and may confide in a therapist that they do not know what causes them to get angry and have no idea how to control it. You, a parent, can help your child control his anger by recognizing things that trigger the outburst. It could be allergies to food or the environment, where new carpeting, furniture, and paint can cause reactions. His emotional response to a minor problem may erupt into a major meltdown, which can scare parents, siblings, teachers, and kids at school.

Some things can be changed and some things cannot, in which case the child's reactions have to be changed. For example, when he feels his temper rising, tell him to count mentally to ten. This does an excellent job of diffusing the situation. Some children find that a small rubber ball in their pocket can be squeezed until the tension disappears. Another tactile method is a "worry stone." These are small, highly polished stones with an indentation for the thumb to "massage" the surface when he feels worried or tense.

The problem with anything tangible is the very real possibility that he will lose the ball or stone. This happened with Aaron, who lost a ball that he kept in his pocket. He then was given a stone to rub when he felt irritated, and it calmed him almost immediately. He began to rely on it, and when it was lost he was terrified that he wouldn't be able to control his temper and would hurt someone. When it was suggested that he tell himself, "I can do this myself and don't need a stone," it worked wonders.

When children have a meltdown in the classroom, it is often caused by something that has startled them. Some things are predictable, such as the bell ringing at the end of the period. In this case, the teacher can tell students that the bell will be ringing in less than one minute so they can prepare themselves. Other loud sounds, such as a student dropping a book that lands with a bang, are unavoidable. An outburst can be diffused by the teacher saying softly, "Oh, boy! That was loud, wasn't it? I think we were all startled by it, weren't we?" The AS child will learn that everyone was affected, not just him, and it will help him to regain his stability.

Parents are often called to school to take their child home after an episode of anger (as previously mentioned, the child is usually a son). It doesn't help that an angry and frustrated mother (it is usually the mother who is called) has to leave her job—again—to get her son. Maybe her boss does not understand the problem and her job is in jeopardy. She doesn't always understand it either, so the stress is compounded by fears that her child is always going to be causing trouble at home and at school. She feels

Luke: A Simple Success Story

Eight-year-old Luke would fly into a rage when someone stared at him because he believed, as he said, "they don't like me." I said that maybe they were looking at him because they liked him, not because they didn't. Or maybe the girls were looking at him because they thought he was cute. He looked dubious but didn't say anything. I suggested that he smile at them and tell himself, "They're looking at me because they like me." That might not have always been the case, but it worked, and he was able to transform potential outbursts. In addition, it helped his self-image because the boys and girls smiled back.

unable to cope with it. Parents may say that their child is better behaved at home than at school, while teachers may say the opposite. Perhaps both teachers and parents are trying to squeeze the child into a mold of conformity, while he is trying to be an individual.

Teachers

Teachers may notice that a child does not fit the patterns of ADD, ADHD, or autism, but since less is known about Asperger's Syndrome, they may begin to feel a child is simply misbehaving. Since teachers are usually among the first to see a child's behavior as developmentally inappropriate, it would be helpful to parents, physicians, and therapists if schools had information available to help identify AS characteristics. This could also show parents that how their children behave in school may be very different from the way they behave at home. It may be possible to identify situations that trigger certain behaviors such as hitting, yelling, or wandering about the classroom. The school would share this information with parents, along with the suggestion that their child be seen and tested by a Developmental Pediatrician.

A questionnaire may be an immeasurable help in determining where a child fits on the Autism Spectrum—or if he belongs on it at all. It is not up to the teacher to make that determination, but a therapist, counselor, or school psychologist could suggest more complete and professional testing. One of the first questions should be whether parents have noticed other family members—siblings, nieces, nephews, cousins, aunts, uncles, or grandparents—with some of the characteristics of Asperger's. The genetic component is becoming more of a factor in the diagnosis of this disorder. When an accurate diagnosis is confirmed, a list of treatment options is given to the parents, who may opt for conventional treatment, alternative therapies, or an integrative approach that utilizes both.

Although some early behavior is dismissed as childish, boyish, boisterous play, or as normal activity, some of it may need to be taken into consideration when forming an opinion or making a diagnosis. Everyone involved in the child's well-being should have working knowledge of the four temperaments. This can help in differentiating a fiery manager from a child who has a neurological disorder. (See Chapter 8 for more on temperaments.)

PARENTS AND ASPIES

We are all still learning about Asperger's Syndrome. Mothers and fathers often feel guilty about their child's behavior, believing it reflects on their parenting skills. They don't understand why their child doesn't listen or do what he is told. Although AS children may appear just like any other

> Parents may say that their child is better behaved at home than at school, while teachers may say the opposite. Perhaps both teachers and parents are trying to squeeze the child into a mold of conformity, while he is trying to be an individual.

child, they aren't. They are quite different, and like kids with ADD, they are easily distracted. They may start on a project, such as feeding the dog, and be intrigued by a random thought and completely forget the dog. They are not being rebellious—they just don't function mentally like most other children, a characteristic shared by children with ADD.

They may excel at one subject such as math, reading, science, or music, and therefore it is easy to think that they are as capable as, or more capable than, your friends' children or the rest of the kids in their class. Most young AS kids feel on a par with other students until they suddenly realize their classmates have surpassed them academically and experienced a shift in interests as they matured. For example, a formerly shared interest in plane schedules may no longer appeal to a neurotypical teen, who is now interested in girls. This realization at first puzzles, and then saddens,

Famous Aspies

As AS children recognize their differences from other kids, it is important for Aspies to know that they are not crazy or "retarded." Depending on his age, stability, and need to know, a child can be told he has Asperger's. Some children readily accept it, and others feel even more different from other children. Knowing about all of the famous, creative, successful people who are thought to have had Asperger's Syndrome is very helpful in letting Aspies know that being different can be really good. Here are just a few, many of whom could be a great subject of research as a child matures:

- Jane Austen, 1775–1817, English novelist
- Ludwig van Beethoven, 1770–1827, composer
- Alexander Graham Bell, 1847–1922, inventor of the telephone
- Henry Cavendish, 1731–1810, scientist who discovered the composition of air and water
- Emily Dickinson, 1830–1886, poet
- Thomas Edison, 1847–1931, inventor
- Albert Einstein, 1879–1955, theoretical physicist
- Henry Ford, 1863–1947, industrialist
- Thomas Jefferson, 1743–1826, politician
- Carl Jung, 1875–1961, psychoanalyst
- Gustav Mahler, 1860–1911, composer
- Wolfgang Amadeus Mozart, 1756–1791, composer
- Isaac Newton, 1642–1727, mathematician and physicist
- Friedrich Nietzsche, 1844–1900, philosopher
- Bertrand Russell, 1872–1970, logician
- George Bernard Shaw, 1856–1950, playwright
- Richard Strauss, 1864–1949, composer
- Nikola Tesla, 1856–1943, engineer, inventor of electric motors
- Mark Twain, 1835–1910, humorist
- Vincent Van Gogh, 1853–1890, painter
- Andy Warhol, 1928–1987, artist

Aspies, as they once again experience feelings of being alone and different in a world that does not understand them.

Aspies are very sensitive to their environment. If it is filled with hostility, anger, and rejection, a child with Asperger's will be guilt-ridden, thinking he was the cause. At home, it is not unusual to find sibling rivalry and relatives who are unfamiliar with Asperger's and unyielding in their belief that the mother's and the father's parenting skills need improving. Asperger's Syndrome is not as simple as black and white. It is a very complex disorder that intensifies when Aspies know they are "different" and that there is "something wrong" with them. They need complete understanding from their entire family—or all the therapy they receive in school or at home will not bring them into wholeness.

Once parents become familiar with the signs of Asperger's Syndrome and learn how they can become a part of their child's therapy, they are generally eager to participate fully in the home. This has many benefits for the entire family, including, of course, their child whose social skills improve as he is recognized as a very intelligent person who is finally given the recognition and respect he craves.

> Aspies need complete understanding from their entire family—or all the therapy they receive in school or at home will not bring them into wholeness.

Proactive Parenting

Many suggestions for parenting children on the Autism Spectrum are appropriate for ADD, autism, and Asperger's. First and foremost, respect your child. Don't simply tell him you love and respect him. Show him by example. Children learn from what role models do, not necessarily what they say. Talk *with* your child, not *at* him. He will enjoy a stimulating and pleasant conversation, and so will you.

Aspies are often capable of sustained dialogue on a variety of topics other than their obsessive interests. They are eager to learn. Morals and ethics are easily understood when included in conversations; sitting them down to teach them a lesson is less effective. The former shows respect; the latter may tell him you know best and he is wrong.

It is unfair to compare an Aspie child with his neurotypical sibling. This is especially true if he is a twin. They may look alike, but they aren't. All children are individuals and should be allowed to express their uniqueness and personality instead of being expected to be like everyone else.

It takes more time for a child with Asperger's to process information and to respond to queries or directions. This is why you should speak in short sentences when giving instructions and not ask him to do more than one or two things at a time. Some parents find it works to ask their child if he understood what was said and then have him repeat it.

If you don't know how to communicate with your child, try understanding him with your heart, not just your head. Your goal as a parent is to nourish the whole child. This includes healthy and nourishing foods and activities that feed the body, mind, and spirit. If a person is malnourished, he is unable to work up to his capacity, regardless of how great that might be. (See Chapter 6 for suggestions on a healthy diet.) His mind and body will be sluggish and will not respond as quickly as they should.

Since your child is your responsibility, it is important that you take a firm stance on participating in his therapy. Ask his therapist to show you some of the methods used in sessions so you can use them at home. Continuing the work the therapist has started will keep the momentum going, and your child will improve that much faster. Your child's therapist will be pleased to know that you care enough to implement such techniques in your home.

If your child does not qualify for services that cover other neurological disorders because he functions at a higher level, and you are unable to afford private treatment, this lack of therapy may result in a lifelong struggle to maintain a position in a society that has no patience, compassion, or understanding for anyone who doesn't fit the norm. Keep trying and do what is necessary to get remedial therapies for your child. It is important to get the therapeutic services he needs.

CAUSES AND THEORIES

It is not easy to pinpoint the cause of Asperger's Syndrome other than to recognize the fact that it is a neurological disorder. Since AS is on the Autism Spectrum, many of the causal factors of autism are suspected in

Jason

Jason's mother gave him a twenty-minute deadline to pick up everything on the floor of his room, organize his toys and books, and hang up his clothes. He didn't even come close to getting it done because he began to read the first book he picked up. His mother had threatened to throw out everything left on the floor at the end of twenty minutes, which she did. His clothes, toys, and books were scooped up into a trash bag and thrown in the dumpster. Jason was devastated because she threw out his favorite cup. He didn't care about the other things that were tossed out with the trash, but the cup meant everything to him. His mother dismissed it by saying it was "only a cup" and that she would buy him another one.

In addition to having no understanding of how a person with Asperger's, especially a seven-year-old boy, processes information, she effectively told Jason that his feelings were worthless and so was his favorite cup. When this was explained to her, she was chagrined. She said she would talk with Jason and retrieve his cup from the trash.

Asperger's Syndrome—genetics, the environment, nutrition, toxins, and an infraction, or gap, in the brain during fetal development. Unlike autism, AS has never been connected to MMR vaccinations, but does appear to have a genetic link: Families of children with Asperger's have a higher incidence of phobias, depression, and poor social skills.

Although there is no clear-cut correlation between our genes and our behavior, it appears that Asperger's does have a genetic basis. Older relatives of an Aspie may have always been considered eccentric with amusing and obsessive behavior, such as collecting old newspapers. Other family members may be nervous, always in motion, or have fears of new places.

The huge increase in the number of children with Asperger's is partly because of earlier recognition of this disorder and partly because there are more children with AS. The possible influence of vaccines, genetics, and heavy metals in the system, combined with the possibility of the herpes simplex virus—which may be transmitted through the infected mother and causes autism-like tendencies—can yield a complex set of symptoms. Some researchers feel there is a defect in the development of the neural tube, which is the beginning of the brain itself. Like children with autism, Aspies have a psycho-neuro basis for their disorder and are unable to process input or to cross the mid-pole so the right and left hemispheres of the brain can talk with each other. And like autism, this improves with remedial therapies that balance the child's three-fold nature.

When we consider the three-fold nature of children, it is logical to investigate causal factors on three different levels: organic, psychological, and spiritual. It is illogical to ignore the importance of the spiritual nature in the treatment and totality of the child.

Strategies, Therapies, and Treatment

Treatment for a child with Asperger's is similar to that for children with autism, with a few variations. Aspies enjoy music and art, but often also have a wide range of interests. Like autistics, they are highly intelligent and personable, but are easier to communicate with since children with Asperger's are quite verbal and articulate.

There are numerous therapies that have claimed great success rates. The truth is that some methods work with some children and don't with others. There is no reason a variety of therapies cannot be used in tandem as long as the philosophies and methods of treatment don't conflict.

Speak to a child with Asperger's with absolute conviction. When he senses that you know exactly what you are talking about, he will listen. Never talk down to a child. At some level, he may be more educated, more knowledgeable, and more compassionate than you are. He knows if you

Speak to a child with Asperger's with absolute conviction. When he senses that you know exactly what you are talking about, he will listen. Never talk down to a child.

respect him—in which case he will return your respect—or if you are being condescending, in which case he will probably ignore you. To increase the effectiveness of any treatment plan, especially those of the creative arts, a relationship needs to be established with the child. This is done through communication, dialogue, mutual respect, sincerity, trust, and more dialogue.

Therapy without sincere and constant dialogue is only partially effective. Aspies appreciate our understanding of their struggle and challenges. They are quick to learn lessons, ethics, and morals from our honest desire to help them. Talking is one of the greatest therapies for Asperger's, but only if the parent or therapist is imparting lessons or useful information. Idle chat is not very productive unless it is interspersed with a conscious act of teaching. Aspies will quickly understand an example of personal experience that teaches a lesson or solves a problem.

All of the therapies described in this book are appropriate for Aspies, but there are a few that are particularly effective. These include:

• Artistic therapies	• Nutritional guidance
• Massage	• Sensory integration
• Mental stimulation	• Sound and speech

You will find details on all of these treatment modes in later chapters.

Aspies' paintings are often remarkable for their texture and combination of media. A picture might include acrylics, watercolors, and pencil, all in vibrant colors. Most children with AS like classical music and know the works of various composers. They like to play music when they're reading out loud or being massaged. They may have a favorite piece, but seem to enjoy them all.

AS kids need movement to give their gross motor muscles a workout. Because most are clumsy, dancing and twirling with scarves is probably not the best routine for them at first. Instead, use a combination of music, movement, and calisthenics.

Many children with Asperger's think puppets are for little kids, with the exception of finger puppets, which intrigue them. However, they like to build things, and making puppets is fun. Puppets are also great for role play, in which children may reveal themselves to observant parents and therapists. As adults we may still have a childlike love of puppets. Talking with a counselor or in a support group through puppets is often very helpful to adults with Asperger's Syndrome, too.

As a child progresses through his treatment plan and matures, he will become increasingly aware of his lack of friends. He sees other kids in his class sitting together before school or during after-school activities and wants to join in, but is rebuffed by others as "weird." He cannot simply walk up to one of the groups and join in the conversation because he is socially awkward, cannot keep up with what they are saying, and in many cases doesn't understand their jargon. Sadly, they have no common ground, but a support group of Aspies provides the opportunity to share feelings in a non-judgmental environment, which may not be possible in any other setting.

Support Groups

There are many support groups for children, teens, and adults with AS that were not in existence a few short years ago. This is especially true on Internet message boards where Aspies, and parents of Aspies, feel free to talk about their feelings and ask questions in an anonymous, non-judgmental environment. Virtually all parents need support in some form. Many adults with Asperger's need support groups, but with earlier intervention, as AS children age, their symptoms may decrease or be controlled.

Just as ADD may continue into a person's adult years, so do some earlier behaviors exhibited in Asperger kids. When adults learn they have this disorder and identify with some of the characteristics, they are usually relieved to know that there are others who think, talk, and act as they do. For this reason, support groups are a great help to Aspies of all ages who feel—finally—that they are not being observed or judged. They can be themselves without the presence of "NTs"—or neurotypical people—who are not on the Spectrum. Both male and female adults with Asperger's Syndrome will generally say they have few friends, problems with organization, and frequent tantrums.

ASPIE ADULTS

The characteristics typically found in adults with Asperger's are not necessarily the same signs that are found in children. The adults may have sustained eye contact and a good sense of humor. Adults may have remnants of the poor social skills that were obvious as children, but with early remedial therapies and constant personal effort, they will learn to adjust to their environment not only to survive, but to prosper.

You can help your child prepare for a productive life as an adult by:

- Providing proper therapy when first diagnosed
- Suggesting techniques to control his anger
- Encouraging him to focus on projects rather than train schedules
- Helping him acquire social skills through meeting with a support group
- Helping him find employment that suits his needs and abilities

Many adults work very hard to overcome some of their behaviors. Once we are familiar with the characteristics of Asperger's, we realize that there have been many people over the years who may have been Aspies. They all have one obvious thing in common: They were people who did not conform to societal rules, and instead were individuals with original ideas.

Vocations

People with Asperger's vary in their abilities and areas of strength just as we all do, but their interest and focus are more extreme. An adult with AS tends to do well in a position that requires great skill in one particular area, as long as he does not need to have much social interaction with other people. For example, careers in fields such as computer science, library science, programming, and research would suit Aspie adults.

In general, Aspie adults have good jobs and are quite difficult to spot in a group. Many have done very well without therapy because they had no idea there was anything "wrong" with them and naturally gravitated to vocations that fit their interests and abilities. They have learned to redirect their younger fascinations with robots or train schedules to activities or occupations that require concentrated effort.

Despite the label of "Geek Syndrome," not all people with Asperger's are in high-tech, computer fields. Because of their intense focus on subjects that interest them, adults would probably do well in any chosen field. By the time they reach their twenties and thirties, most, if they are fortunate, will have learned how to control their anger and to channel their thoughts into positive, constructive ones instead of negative, destructive ones.

Dyslexia is common in people with Asperger's, and adults with this disorder are often very good in science or math and in problem solving, since many think in three dimensions. They are able to see the end product and work towards it, much as Temple Grandin does with the equipment she designs. (See page 61 for Temple Grandin's story.) No matter what kind of a position an adult Aspie has, it is important that his employer know of his limitations and abilities so there is no problem or misunderstanding on the job.

Older teens and adults might benefit from occupational therapy to help them find jobs they will be good at and comfortable in. Because of their discomfort with socializing, Aspies often find a vocation that provides individual cubicles where they can work at their own pace without pressures from others ideal. No matter what kind of a position an adult Aspie has, it is important that his employer know of his limitations and abilities so there is no problem or misunderstanding on the job.

For example, an adult Aspie, as is often the case, felt great compassion and empathy for children with Asperger's and earned a degree as a psychologist. Throughout her schooling she worked to overcome her lack of social skills and involuntary movements or "tics." She found that, by focusing intently on the eyes and mouth of her clients, and with great effort, she could control her movements and engage in fluid dialogue. In conversation it was almost impossible to identify any Asperger's traits, but if, for some reason, she became uncomfortable or distracted, her entire body would jerk slightly. Fortunately, coworkers were accustomed to this mannerism, and strangers gave it little, if any, thought, since it was so brief and slight as to be almost unnoticeable.

SUMMARY

Children with Asperger's are delightful, irritating, amusing, and puzzling, just like other children. The difference is that most Aspies are socially awkward, have a fiery temper, and have obsessions with mechanical and electronic objects. Unfortunately, children with Asperger's Syndrome or autism aren't given credit for their intelligence, which is often outstanding. AS kids are fun to be with because you never know what will pop up in your conversation with them. They have a delightful sense of humor that takes you by surprise, and sometimes they say things that are unintentionally funny. Therapists enjoy working with Aspies because they are such a challenge.

There are four times as many boys as girls with Asperger's, and they are not usually diagnosed until the age of six or seven. Teachers are increasingly able to spot developmentally inappropriate behavior in their students and may bring it to your attention when your child enters school. Therapy for AS is similar to therapy provided for autism, except that therapy for Aspies accounts for the fact that they are much more articulate and can hold intelligent conversations on many topics. Kids with Asperger's are also very literal. They mean what they say and they say what they mean.

Now that you have learned about ADD, ADHD, autism, and Asperger's, you can begin your search for remedial and creative therapies. The strategies described in the following chapters are designed to help you— the parent, therapist, or teacher—to recognize the latent abilities and spiritual reality within each child. Then you will be best able to help him grow safely into a healthy life. But before beginning to use music, color, and art, anyone working with children on the Spectrum must understand the necessity of good nutrition, the subject of the following chapter.

> Children with Asperger's are fun to be with because you never know what will pop up in your conversation with them. Therapists enjoy working with Aspies because they are such a challenge.

CHAPTER 6

Nutrition

Eating With Consciousness

L ike most parents, you probably have times when you think your
child's diet could be healthier but don't know what to do or where to
start. Perhaps you think it would be too much work, it would upset the
rest of the family, or that your child will outgrow her crying and complaints about pains in her head and stomach. Maybe she is hyper or the
reverse, lethargic, and you think a pill or shot is all she needs.

If your child does not have proper nutrition as a base, the therapies
described in this book will not be as effective as they could be. If she is
lethargic, she will not participate in the program or she will enter into it
listlessly. If she is hyperactive, she won't be able to sit still long enough to
do any of the exercises.

This chapter will help you understand the importance of good nutrition and will give simple suggestions for improving the diet of your whole
family. Children may receive different kinds of therapies, but if they have
a poor diet they are in danger of being malnourished. As a result, their
spirit as well as their body and brain will be affected and sluggish. Nothing will operate at capacity, and a destructive cycle begins as children feel
ill, are seen by a doctor, are possibly prescribed medication that subdues
symptoms of irritability, become more sluggish, go to a doctor, and the
cycle continues.

Our spiritual nature is the most important element of our three-fold
constitution of body, mind, and spirit. With reduced spiritual influence,
the body will continue to live and the mind will function to a degree, but
the fullest potential will never be realized. Every human being needs to be
nourished on all three levels to attain and maintain a healthy balance. Parents need to be aware of the fact that a feeling of fullness is not the same
thing as being nourished. A child may eat three meals a day, but unless the
food is the right kind, she is not being nourished as well as she could be.
It is a fallacy that the more we eat, the healthier we are. Obese children are
seen everywhere and soon become obese teens and adults as eating pat-

Nutrition plays a large role in the development of consciousness, in addition to building a healthy body.

terns are established. Obesity is a national concern because of the immediate and potential health threats. Overall, we eat things we don't need and do not eat the things we should.

No discussion of nutrition and the Autism Spectrum would be complete without suggestions for healthy eating that also apply to the entire family—vitamins, protein, food preparation, and sugar. Everyone's body has to be nourished for the mind and spiritual nature to work at optimum levels.

EATING WITH AWARENESS

Nutrition plays a large role in the development of consciousness, in addition to building a healthy body. Animals eat only when they are hungry, whereas most people eat because something strikes their fancy—for example, a television commercial for popcorn or pizza. They eat with no consciousness regarding what is best for their body, and the result is an undernourished body, mind, and vital force. We are learning more about the body-mind connection, yet rarely consider how food affects our spiritual nature.

Adults need to (and can) learn to eat what they need, not only what they want; but children don't have the knowledge or will power, so they often crave things that may create an allergic reaction. Food sensitivity is another name for an allergy. For example, a child may like a certain kind of sugar-filled cookie that has been made more attractive by the addition of food coloring and preservatives. Soon after she eats it, she's climbing on the counters and in general showing obvious hyperactive behavior that slowly wears off. She doesn't realize that her craving for the cookie is creating an allergic reaction, only that it tastes good and that she wants more.

Most children on the Autism Spectrum have allergies that may be traced to their mother. Everything the mother eats, drinks, or otherwise places in or on her body affects her unborn child. One of the most common causes of illness and dysfunction are allergies, which may be tied to something the mother had a fondness for—peanuts, for example. Children may develop cravings for cheese, milk, butter, sugar, peanuts, rice, corn, oats, preservatives, artificial coloring, and additives. They may also develop allergies to these foods.

Nutrition is a prime consideration in the treatment of children, especially those with psycho-neuro disorders. We tend to forget that they are very sensitive to everything they see, breathe, hear, and eat. Loving friends and relatives who give them treats are usually not around to see the meltdown that happens a couple of hours after they eat the food. Parents may have to deal with the consequences for several days. Education is an ongoing process for everyone who is involved in any way with a child who has ADD, autism, or Asperger's.

When children are undernourished, their brains cannot function up to capacity. They are sleepy, inattentive, and irritated, and may be misdiagnosed as having ADD. They may drink little juice or milk but consume great quantities of caffeine-laden soda. All stimulants rob something of our nervous structure and impair the passage of necessary nutrients to the brain. The first 25 percent of the nutrients from all food we eat goes directly to the brain, so it makes sense to eat our salad before the main meal, which is the way many restaurants serve their courses.

If you are a therapist, offering help for parents who don't know how to shop, prepare, and cook nutritious food may be an extra service you can provide to help your client. Some mothers simply do not know how to cook or don't like to. They often work outside the home and come back tired while the kids are busy with extracurricular activities and Dad is out of town on a business trip. So Mom doesn't cook and is relieved she doesn't have to. Everyone has fast food and snacks eaten on the run. Even when the average mom (or dad) does cook, she often uses canned foods, has no time to fix a salad, and has little knowledge of food combining and even less about the importance of its appearance. *Food combining* is a nutritional approach that emphasizes the importance of the relative timing of the consumption of different types of food. For example, some people with sensitive digestion find that combining starches with fruit creates feelings of fullness or even nausea. Fruit digests very quickly while starches take longer, and each uses a different enzyme, so they should be eaten separately to avoid discomfort. Eating well begins in the high chair.

Infants

Nutrition is directly tied in with a child's mental development, as the synergy begins at conception. When babies nurse, mother's milk is alive and rich in sugar, which is needed for brain development (however, consuming refined sugar found in processed food inhibits the ability to learn). Mother's milk, liquid life, is enjoyed by infants because before they were born they were intricately connected with the body that produces it—their mother's.

An infant shows pleasure throughout her entire body as she quivers and glows while at her mother's breast, whereas older children and adults have sensation only in their palates, which indicate only whether food tastes good. Infants also will stop nursing when they are full; many older children and adults continue to eat far beyond that point, which may result in obesity.

Babies need milk to grow, and if other foods are introduced at too young an age, they will intuitively rebel and may develop an allergy that will remain with them for the remainder of their lives. Some of the most common allergens that can create lifelong problems are cow's milk, tomatoes, and citrus fruit. These are frequently part of a toddler's diet and often included at an early age. Breast milk or fortified formula is all babies need until they are between four and six months of age. They don't need cereal in their bottles or mashed fruit and vegetables at this early age.

When toddlers begin to eat solid food, their kidneys and livers have not matured to the point where they can handle heavy proteins and heavy fats, yet these are a large part of children's diets. As a result, the body begins a process of acidosis, or becoming out of balance in terms of yin/yang, feminine/masculine, and alkaline/acid. These are extremes that have to be balanced in order to be holistically healthy. Human performance, whether mental or physical, depends primarily on what we eat.

ESSENTIAL NUTRIENTS FOR HEALTH

Our body needs four basic nutrients for optimum health: fat, carbohydrates, protein, and minerals.

The average person gets adequate fat in her diet without having to add more. Essential fatty acids (EFAs) are different from the fat in cooking oil, and as their name implies, they are essential. For more on EFAs, refer to Chapter 2.

Plants don't produce much fat, and since we need it for a healthy body, our own body takes it upon itself to produce fats from its reserves. Saliva and gastric juices turn the fat we eat into an entirely different kind of fat that is necessary for the body to function. We actually become a conscious builder of our own body. If a person doesn't take control of her inner body, she can't control her outer life.

Carbohydrates are also found in plants. We commonly think of potatoes as starch, but they are actually carbohydrates that are transformed into starch by our saliva. Our bodies need starch, but eating starchy food such as pasta is not necessary. As a final step in assimilation, these starches are turned into sugar, which we also need. We do not need additional sugar in or on our foods, but sugar inwardly supports us when it is eaten properly. Reading labels is eye-opening, since almost every product includes sugar in its list of ingredients. This is important to be aware of because juvenile diabetes, also known as Type I or insulin-dependent diabetes, is becoming more prevalent in our society.

Protein is found in plants as well as meat and dairy products. Surprisingly, seeds and legumes supply more energy than meat. They provide lasting strength rather than an immediate surge of energy that soon dissipates. Plant protein is known for its ability to maintain stamina even after strenuous activity.

If plants already have protein and they don't consume it, where does it come from? The fact is that they get it from the minerals in the earth, something human beings and animals cannot do. The quality of plant protein depends on how the vegetables are grown. Because plants are alive, they need proper nourishment that can come only from the soil. The soil itself has to be nourished with natural fertilizer—manure, for example. Once again we can look to our ancestors and farmers who lived long, healthy lives. Today many people think manure is old-fashioned and that modern chemicals are more effective in producing good crops. Organic farmers have proven otherwise, producing higher yields using manure as fertilizer and avoiding chemicals and pesticides. As our society gets weaker and sicker, there will, out of necessity, be a return to healthy and intuitive eating. In the meantime, organic produce is becoming more popular as people learn about nutrients and chemicals in their food.

> As our society gets weaker and sicker, there will, out of necessity, be a return to healthy and intuitive eating.

There is a symbiotic relationship between plants and humans, and neither could live without the other. In this mutual exchange, we exhale carbon dioxide (CO_2) that is absorbed by plants, and plants give out oxygen that we inhale. For a healthy body, we need another vital ingredient: chlorophyll. Although we exhale CO_2, we still have a lot of carbon in our body. Somehow chlorophyll, the vital sap of the plant, retains the carbon and releases the oxygen into the air. The entire process makes one wonder at the intricacy of this very elemental act of breathing.

Roots and Grains

Root vegetables have a high mineral content and should be part of everyone's daily diet. Today's soil is so depleted of minerals and vitamins, supplemental protein and minerals are often added to our daily vitamin intake. A child who is not developing normally and is not in good health usually has worms. But if she is physically fortified with nutrients—especially minerals—worms can't grow in the intestines. In later years, a child with untreated worms will be naturally weak-spirited as her vitality is sapped. Strange as it may seem, the simplest tactic for counteracting worms is to add carrots to the child's diet. This vegetable is the root of the plant that contains the minerals of the earth that are missing in our diets today. Other root vegetables are beets and radishes but, understandably, kids would rather munch on a carrot. Organic raw carrots are an excellent snack for people of all ages, especially for children who are in the process of forming a strong body.

If a child has no allergies to grains, she should alternately eat wheat, rye, barley, rice, and oats for breakfast. By baking our bread or cooking grains, we are adding warmth to our bodies that otherwise the body

Ideally, people would
eat instinctively,
choosing only what
their body needs.

would be forced to create. Whole grain cereals actually help the learning process, as they provide needed nutrients for the brain.

All raw food has to be changed through bodily functions into warmth before it can be digested. People who eat only raw foods have the mistaken idea that they are healthier than other people, but eventually the body will break down from the lack of warmth, which is gained through eating cooked foods. Animals eat their grains raw, but the human body needs inner warmth, and "uncivilized" man long ago learned to cook rice, rye, and other grains before eating them. Ideally, people would eat instinctively, choosing only what their body needs, just as animals do.

ALTERING OUR FOOD, CHANGING OUR BODIES

Numerous studies conclude that one's diet influences one's life. This is clearly seen in Eskimo, American Indian, and South African tribes, all of whom were healthy and without many illnesses until Europeans introduced problematic elements to their diet, at which time the previously healthy tribes began exhibiting signs of disease and malnutrition.

More surgery was needed and childbirth became more difficult with each generation. Obesity in adults and children increased, as did Type II diabetes. There could be only one conclusion: Something had changed in their diet or environment. Here are some examples of what we are doing to healthy foods to make them more palatable to "civilized society."

Rice is often polished to replace its natural brown shade with the nice, white color we are most familiar with. While this is more visually attractive to some people, vitamins that are found only in the hulls are lost in the process; as a result, we are robbed of nutrients for the sake of appearance. Brown rice has a slightly different consistency from and richer flavor than white rice, and is often mixed with wild rice for a robust taste. In a similar process, grains for bread and cereal are ground, which robs them of nutrients. The solution is to buy and eat brown rice and preservative-free, whole grain bread and cereal.

Many of us don't question additives in our food and eat it without considering the consequences. For example, while sulfur dioxide is used in the United States to increase the shelf life of dried fruit, some countries refuse to import treated fruit from the U.S. To be sure you aren't eating chemicals along with your treat, read the label. It is possible to buy fruit that is dried without sugar. Naturally, it's not as sweet, and the appearance is different, but the result is fruit that is dried naturally. Best of all, buy a dehydrator and dry your own. Dried apple, banana, and pear slices are wonderfully sweet and crunchy. You may not know that citrus fruit in produce departments is often picked before it is ripe, then dyed or subjected to gas treatment to produce color. If your orange smells like a carnation, you may want to change your mind about eating it. Organic fruit and vegetables are free of all additives. Unless you read labels, it is impossible to know if the food you are purchasing and eating has additives. Read the list of ingredients on the box of your favorite cereal to see if it lists artificial coloring and flavoring. That's easy to do, but additives are often hidden in products that don't have labels. For example, meat and fish that is dried, salted, or pickled may be injected with gelatin, chemicals, and

Aspartame: A Popular Poison

At the 1995 World Environmental Conference on Aspartame, specialists and physicians presented interesting and frightening information on this artificial sweetener that is also known as Nutra-Sweet, Equal, and Spoonful. They announced an epidemic of systemic lupus and multiple sclerosis in the United States stemming from this substance, and reported that people with lupus who drink only three or four cans of Diet Coke or Diet Pepsi aggravate their illness so much that it sometimes is life threatening.

The conference presented a total of ninety-two documented symptoms that are attributed to aspartame, including those of fibromyalgia. Here are some of them:

- shooting pains
- depression
- cramps
- anxiety attacks
- dizziness
- memory loss
- headaches
- manic depression
- joint pain
- rage

Aspartame and the Gulf War

The illness that has debilitated military troops who served during the Gulf War in the early 1990s has puzzled doctors, who have said it is probably caused by a sand flea. Returning men and women felt their illness was attributable to the vaccinations they had received. In truth, the symptoms are those of aspartame poisoning.

The World Environmental Conference report revealed how the wood alcohol in aspartame converts to formaldehyde when subjected to heat over 86°F. When this happens, there is a metabolic acidosis that causes symptoms similar to those of multiple sclerosis. Thousands of pallets of diet drinks were shipped (with good intentions) to the troops and were stored at 120°F. Some ill veterans have stated that their children, who were conceived after they returned to the United States, show the same symptoms they do.

On November 3, 1987, H.J. Roberts, MD, Director of the Palm Beach Institute for Medical Research, appeared before a U.S. Senate hearing of the Committee on Labor and Human Resources, in "NutraSweet: Health and Safety Concerns." A diabetic specialist and expert on aspartame, Dr. Roberts stated, "consuming aspartame at the time of conception can cause birth defects," which might account for many children exhibiting illnesses formerly seen only in adults, such as depression, anxiety, sleeplessness, and anger. If you are a therapist, you have a responsibility to inform the parents of your clients about the adverse consequences of foods that may be affecting their children.

Although the World Environmental Conference on Aspartame was held in 1995, the controversy over this substance continues today.

smoky flavoring to disguise the stringy meat of malnourished animals. It is now common knowledge among health-conscious people that to produce large animals, cattle and chickens are routinely injected with steroids, which we eat along with the antibiotics given to sick cows.

If your loaf of bread stays soft and "squeezable" for a month on your counter, it obviously has preservatives. If it doesn't mold or start going stale in three or four days, it is not natural, regardless of what the label says. Some labels state the contents are "healthy" or "natural." Don't be fooled by this, as some still contain artificial flavor and/or coloring.

FOOD FOR THE MIND

Children with ADD need to be challenged mentally more than the average child. These boys and girls are brilliant, above average, secure within themselves, restless, and usually bored. Most schools are not equipped to teach the challenging subjects they want, but there are things parents and therapists can do to challenge these bright children. They enjoy and crave mental stimulation, and reading a difficult book is just what they need to provide necessary nutrition to the brain. When we make an effort to understand a book's subject matter, the blood is vitalized in the brain.

Unfortunately, the average person does not want to be intellectually stimulated. Students want short reviews of one or two paragraphs that can be copied from the Internet and are content with knowing nothing more about the book. This lack of stimulation and resultant lack of intellectual curiosity is becoming more and more commonplace as people of all ages would rather watch a movie made from the book than read the book itself. Watching movies or plays infrequently requires effort, and as a result, the blood becomes thicker through lack of stimulation. People become lethargic, and the quick fix is a trip to the doctor or drugstore for a drug that will "pick them up."

A heavy diet with a lot of meat, starch, and carbohydrates often makes us drowsy and lethargic. We commonly see this after a large meal, such as on Thanksgiving, when people tend to overeat. It is a common misperception that protein can be found only in meat; there are many sources of protein. Some foods, especially meat, give us immediate strength, but when that surge is exhausted, for example by strong physical activity, the body weakens quickly. This isn't the case with plants in our diet. In fact, it is just the opposite. We are given strength, which the body retains by virtue of the carbohydrates we need. The truth is that it is generally healthier to eat a diet predominantly composed of fruits, vegetables, legumes, seeds, and nuts, which help to strengthen the immune system.

We Are What We Eat

Ludwig Andreas Feuerbach (1804–1872), a German philosopher, wrote, "A man is what he eats." He is, naturally, more than that, but Herr Feuerbach was referring to the benefits of a healthy diet and to the fact that the body is the instrument of the spirit. If we continually deny the body the attention it needs through healthy food, natural remedies, and physical activity, it will slowly degenerate and cease to function on anything more than a level of mere existence.

If we continue to eat as our society does today, we will eventually have a sickly and weak civilization. When we accept that as a probability, we can more easily understand how we can—and why we should—improve our physical, mental, emotional, and spiritual selves by living a healthy life through nutrition, which is simply one way of generating improved health. We owe that to those children on the Autism Spectrum who are resolute in their poor choices of food (hot dogs, fried chicken nuggets) or who have no options other than to eat what is given to them.

Many people are unable to act and think the way they should because of poor nutrition. If proper nutrients aren't eaten every day, the body can't perform in a healthy manner mentally, emotionally, spiritually, or physically. Animals know instinctively what to eat and what to avoid. Adults do a great disservice to developing children by offering them no choice but to eat food that will lead them astray from their healthy instinct for nourishment.

Raw foods should be encouraged whenever possible, since they are living plants that have absorbed the energy of the sun. They stimulate and maintain the nervous system. It might be said that the outer light of the sun has a direct bearing on the inner light of the child. It is this inner light that produces fats, starches, carbohydrates, and glucose. Simply eating food that tastes good or is filling, quick to buy, or easy to prepare doesn't necessarily nourish us. When we do that, there is no consciousness involved, and we become ill.

Although a vegetarian diet is beneficial, it is not always the best diet for every person. For people who are involved in strenuous labor and must be aggressive to perform their work, a meat diet is often necessary for heavy protein and substance.

We need only think of militant, warlike nations whose citizens tend to be heavy meat eaters. Other countries—India and Tibet, for example—are mainly vegetarian and historically more passive. This is not an absolute; however, it is true that people who eat mostly plants and vegetables are more apt to be less aggressive than those who eat a great deal of meat. Many meat eaters are changing to free-range beef and chickens that are fed naturally and without chemicals. Even so, it is a fact that fewer people are eating meat than in previous generations, as if they intuitively know the effects of a lighter diet that enhances their inner life.

PROTEIN SOURCES

If your child is on a casein-free diet, she will have to avoid dairy products, which are a common source of protein. In this case, she will need to obtain protein from other sources, the most readily available being soy products that can be found in all supermarkets and health food stores. Soy provides protein to the body, which is needed for muscle function; however, too much soy may build up in the body and result in a potentially dangerous accumulation of copper. It also has a natural estrogen-like substance and is therefore recommended as an alternative to estrogen, which had been widely prescribed. On the other hand, some doctors feel that boys should not eat soy for that very reason, which has created an ongoing controversy. If soy is not an option, rice products, legumes, nuts, and seeds are also sources of protein, and supplements are available in health food stores.

Our bodies need protein, and if your child refuses to eat meat or if you are a vegetarian family, the body may not be getting the protein you need. It is important for children on the Spectrum to have a healthy amount of protein in their diet, and they depend on their parents or guardians to provide it. Throughout the country, people are eating less red meat and more fish, poultry, and salads. Vegetarians eat no meat in any form, and vegans eliminate dairy products as well, which always brings up the question, "Where do you get your protein?" There are many sources of protein, but most of us are familiar with only two: meat and dairy products.

Other good sources are:

- Nuts (almonds, pecans, walnuts, pistachios)

- Nut butter (almond is best)

- Tofu and all soy products refrigerated or frozen in supermarkets

- Legumes, such as peas and beans

- Seeds, such as pumpkin and sunflower, which can be roasted for a snack

Read the labels on cans or packages of nuts. Some are honey coated, which taste great but are loaded with sugar. Some, like macadamia nuts, have a higher fat content than others.

Terrific Tofu

Tofu, once the mainstay of health food devotees and sold exclusively in specialty shops, is a soy product that is compressed into cake form and is now available in most supermarkets as well as health food stores. Although gaining in popularity, acceptance is slow, since people are generally reluctant to try unfamiliar foods and do not know how to prepare it. All soy products are great sources of protein, and many taste like meat. Children who refuse to eat anything other than real meat won't be able to tell the difference when they're given soy hot dogs or soy chicken nuggets.

Tofu is one of the most versatile foods available. It can be browned, marinated, and grilled, and is often used in shish kebabs. You can use it to make meatballs for your favorite spaghetti dish or meatloaf. It can be mashed and used as filling for lasagna and stuffed shells. Strange as it sounds, tofu can be made into mayonnaise, sour cream, and whipped cream. Tofu changes consistency when it is frozen and then thawed. From a soft composition, it becomes chewy and meat-like. Added to soups, salads, stir-fries, and casseroles, it provides extra protein, flavor, and texture.

Tofu will keep unopened for several weeks in the refrigerator. Once opened, the water should be changed daily; it will keep for a week or more. If it starts to smell slightly "off," simmer it in water for twenty minutes and it will be ready to use. Many of these ideas are included in *Tofu Cookery* by Louise Hagler, which is also a gold mine of recipes.

VITAMINS

Whether to take supplements is a personal and controversial subject. Some people feel that they get all the vitamins they need from their diet. This is unlikely for most people but would be the ideal situation and was probably true fifty years ago or more when our soil was rich in minerals and naturally fertilized. Today the soil is depleted and full of chemicals. Crops are sprayed, and, unless we buy organic produce, we are eating vegetables that are not as nutritious as they were generations ago.

If your diet is lacking a balance of green and yellow vegetables, fruit, protein, minerals, and trace elements, then a supplement should be considered, since everyone requires all of these to maintain a healthy body. Additionally, if you live in a polluted environment, as many people do, you may want to consider taking supplements, since pollutants affect your body's ability to absorb and utilize vitamins.

Three of the most common and important vitamins include vitamin B, vitamin C, and vitamin E. It is a good idea to know what foods are sources of these vitamins and the results of their deficiencies.

Whether to take supplements is a personal and controversial subject.

Vitamin B is destroyed by boiling vegetables, while very little is lost in steaming. If your body is lacking in this important vitamin, you may show signs of deficiency such as loss of appetite, weight loss, lack of energy, or constipation. To ensure having enough vitamin B in your diet, include an assortment of whole grain cereals, peas, beans, fruit, corn, cabbage, spinach, and honey each day.

Vitamin C is easily found in citrus fruits. If you are lacking this vitamin, you may find that you bruise easily, and have weight loss, gum problems, and shortness of breath, along with rapid respiration. Vitamin C is naturally found in green peppers, oranges, lemons, tomatoes, bananas, sprouted grains, potatoes, cabbage, and green leafy vegetables.

Vitamin E is a necessary lubricant that strengthens our cells. Lack of this vitamin shows up in the body as dry skin, hives, joint and muscle pain, and gall bladder and liver problems. To obtain vitamin E naturally, eat plenty of whole grain cereals, raw fruit, almonds, sunflower seeds, and spinach.

Fresh vegetables and fruit are the greatest source of vitamins, and while steaming and baking reduces the vitamin content of foods somewhat, boiling may almost eliminate it. Steaming vegetables is a good way to cook vegetables without losing too much nutritional value. Stainless steel steamers, which many consider a necessary kitchen utensil, are inexpensive and available in the housewares section of most stores.

Changing your family's diet may seem like an overwhelming impossibility, but it really is not that difficult once you discover your options.

WHAT CAN I DO?

A visually pleasing plate will entice a child at least to try something new. We need to feed our mind and spirit as well as our body.

As a parent, you can do a lot to make sure your child is properly nourished. In fact, you can do more than your doctor or therapist because you are the one who buys and cooks the food. This is a good time to mention color psychology. We are influenced by color every day in our environment, and food is no different. We eat with our eyes before we eat with our mouths. An attractively set table and eye-catching food set the stage for a relaxing meal. If a meal is monochromatic (such as containing carrots, squash, and yams), it is less appealing to the senses. Presentation is an important tool for chefs simply to add to the appeal of their creation, but it can also be a useful tool in getting children to try new or different foods. A visually pleasing plate will entice a child at least to try something new. We need to feed our mind and spirit as well as our body.

Parents who are told they have to change the diet of their child because of allergies or medical problems are often confused and frustrated. Patterns of eating are set in their own childhood and passed on to their children. For example, cereal laced with sugar is a given in most households, and for parents to be told by a physician that sugar is harmful to their child often creates chaos in the house, even beyond the kitchen. Adults grumble, children squabble, and the child with ADHD, autism, or Asperger's Syndrome is in the middle of it. Nobody should argue about our need for certain foods or supplements to maintain a healthy body.

If you have been told that you need to change your child's diet to one with no dairy, preservatives, chemicals, coloring, or sugar, it won't be easy, but it won't be impossible, either. If you are serious about changing your child's diet, the transition should be gradual, since habits are difficult to change and a sudden shift to a diet without sugar probably won't be welcomed with open arms. There may be a physical reaction if a person used to a heavy diet radically and suddenly changes her food intake, so moderation is the key.

A good place to start is by reducing salt in the family's diet. Salt can be very harmful, and is found in processed foods, fast foods, and canned foods. One serving of canned soup may have as much sodium as is recommended for a full day. The average person in the United States consumes a staggering twenty-six pounds of salt per year, much of it unknowingly. Herbs and sea salt, also known as Celtic salt, can be used instead for flavoring. This is pure sea salt with all of the vitamins and minerals intact, and is found in supermarkets and health food stores. A staple for people who want flavor, but no salt, is Bragg's Liquid Aminos. It is an alternative product found in health food stores that can be used in just about everything you prepare, from soups to salads.

Although some authorities reject the idea that sugar is a cause of hyperactivity, many mothers claim that when their children eat sugar, they become high strung and, at times, irrational with bizarre behavior. In fact, as people reduce their sugar intake and detoxify their bodies, they often

Benefits of Conjugated Linoleic Acid

We know that most children with autism have an abundance of heavy metals in their system that is stored in the fat in the liver. Rudolf Steiner stated, "A surplus of fat stands in the way of the unfolding of mental forces." By reducing fat in the entire body, including the liver, toxins will be reduced or eliminated. Conjugated Linoleic Acid (CLA) removes toxins in the liver that might be affecting the brain and digestive system of children with neurological disorders. It also lowers cholesterol and triglycerides, lowers insulin resistance, reduces food-induced allergic reactions, and enhances the immune system.

When toxins that are stored in the liver are not released through normal bodily functions, they build up and create poisons in the body. CLA is routinely taken for weight loss and may not be advertised as being of benefit to children on the Autism Spectrum, despite its potential positive effects. CLA is available in health food stores and is taken according to your physician's advice.

comment on the effects of sugar. One child said, "Sugar makes me grouchy." Another said, "It makes me feel poopy!"

Some children react strongly to sweets and soft drinks and say they feel "strange" or "weird," or have severe headaches. They complain of not thinking clearly or not functioning properly. One boy stated he felt as if he was drunk and walked into walls. Interestingly, most are aware it is a result of something they ate or drank because it conforms to a pattern.

While it is very difficult to eliminate all sugar from the diet, especially outside of the home where peer pressure or socialization affects our decisions, many people find that sugarless cookies and cakes can be delicious. In most recipes, honey can be used as a sugar substitute.

DELICIOUS AND NUTRITIOUS

There is no rule that says food that is good for you has to taste terrible. The truth is that as you begin to make changes in your kitchen, you will learn many ways to serve tasty, healthy drinks and snacks that everyone will enjoy.

Drinks

Children who are allergic to dairy products—and those with ADHD usually are—often can tolerate rice, soy, or goat's milk, all of which are fine substitutes for cow's milk. But for something different, try fresh carrot juice. Many people try the canned variety and swear off all carrot juice forever. There is no comparison, and no substitute, for fresh juice, which is sweet and satisfying.

Allison: Success Sabotaged

Allison was very hyperactive and, like most children, ate too much sugar. When the therapist suggested that sugar be reduced or eliminated from Allison's diet, her mother was eager to do anything to help her child, and it disappeared from the kitchen. Allison became obsessive, asking at every meal and every snack, "Does this have sugar in it?" Her father was irritated because he loved sugar in liberal amounts. He soon became angry at her constant asking and ordered that sugar be put back on the table and in his food.

Although Allison became less addicted to sugar and less hyperactive, she became intolerable to her father. It was a long time before she stopped asking about the sugar content and began eating it again with no comments or questions. Her father was happy, her mother was frustrated, her therapist and teachers were concerned, and Allison was once again hyper. Needless to say, family members—especially parents—must be willing to accept the dietary changes necessary to improve the health and behavior of a child on the Autism Spectrum.

Fresh apple juice has a flavor totally unlike any bottled juice, even the "natural" or thick drinks. Try different varieties of apples, since each has its own special flavor. Fresh fruit and vegetable juices have an abundance of vitamins, proteins, and minerals; however, don't confuse vegetable juicers with citrus fruit juicers, which extract the juice from oranges, grapefruit, and lemons. Vegetable juicers extract the juice from the whole vegetable or fruit, discarding the pulp and providing you with a juice that is surprisingly delicious. Vegetable juicers can be purchased in health food stores and in the housewares section of most large stores.

Children love blender drinks and they're good substitutes for the soda they may be used to drinking. Combine orange or apple juice with bananas or strawberries, whiz for a few seconds, and serve a thick, frothy drink to thirsty children. This is easily prepared by youngsters who can pour juice in the blender container, clean berries, and cut or break bananas into pieces. Children who are involved in the preparation of snacks and meals are usually more inclined to accept new drinks and foods.

For a warm drink in cool weather, nothing can beat apple juice or cider that has been heated and served with a cinnamon stick as a stirrer. These sticks are so flavorful, they can be used several times.

Watermelon makes great juice, and if we are to believe our ancestors, it's a sure cure for kidney problems. Watermelon tea was an old standby in Granny's kitchen. All melons juice well, although cantaloupe and honeydew have less water content, so they produce a thicker liquid and require more melon per glass.

Mineral water, such as Perrier, is a pleasant change and children like the bubbles. Perrier is available plain or with orange, lemon, or lime natural flavoring and is naturally carbonated, without the artificial carbonation that is found in most mineral water. A delicious combination is half Perrier and half grape juice.

Sun tea is easily made by children and enjoyed by the entire family. Place two herbal tea bags in a gallon of water, cover, and set in the sun for several hours, then chill. Be sure to read the labels, though—many herbal teas contain caffeine, and some may have more than coffee.

Snacks

For easy snacking, prepare a bowl of vegetable cubes and keep in the refrigerator. Not all vegetables lend themselves to this, since some are soft and watery. Use carrots, radishes, jícama, and celery, which is a good choice for hot weather since it is a source of potassium, which may be lost through perspiration. Kids love grabbing a handful of "veggie popcorn" as a snack, and many like it with dip.

There are many ways of nourishing our children, and although food is the most obvious, we also nourish their sense of morals, beauty, honesty, and all of the virtues we hope will become part of their character as they grow into adulthood.

Some of the best-tasting snacks are the best for you, and fun for the children to help prepare and eat. Fruit juice can be frozen in popsicle molds or ice cube trays and given as a treat instead of store-bought products, which have added sugar and coloring and are more expensive.

Buy grapes and berries when they're in season, plentiful, and inexpensive. Rinse and place in plastic bags or containers and freeze. These can be eaten by the handful and are as satisfying as other sweet treats.

Once you make your own raisins, you'll prefer them to store-bought ones. Wash plump, green grapes, spread them in a flat pan and cover with cheesecloth or other porous fabric. Place in the sun for several days until dried, but still slightly soft. Be sure to stir or shake the pan several times a day.

Children are fascinated with the transformation of one familiar fresh food into another familiar packaged one. These raisins can be frozen indefinitely, as they retain their moistness and flavor when packed in an airtight container.

The same drying process can be used with apples, pears, and apricots, which can be dried on skewers or threaded on a string between two hooks. With all fruit, be sure there is room between pieces for the air to circulate. The natural sugar in dried fruit gives needed energy to children on the Spectrum, but not enough for those with ADHD to react adversely.

Fresh fruit can be pureed and spread on a flat surface to dry, then cut or torn into pieces and stored in the refrigerator. This "fruit leather" is a great snack for children who may want something a little different.

If a child is able to tolerate dairy foods, plain yogurt contains protein, minerals, enzymes, and all known vitamins. It is digested and utilized twice as fast as milk and prevents putrefaction in the large intestine, which is the major cause of disease and premature aging. Yogurt is a natural antibiotic, with eight ounces providing the same amount as fourteen units of penicillin. The fewer manufactured drugs a child is given during childhood, the healthier she will be as a teen and adult. Yogurt with fruit may taste better than plain yogurt, but it contains either sugar or aspartame, which is reported to cause illness and/or unacceptable behavior. Plain yogurt can be easily sweetened by mixing it with either fresh fruit or all-natural jam, which is available in supermarkets.

Many parents give their children a handful of hazelnuts as they leave for school in the morning, since they are high in phosphorous, which is necessary for brain development. These nuts can also be ground and added to cereal or soup. Rich in iron, hazelnuts combat fatigue and poor concentration.

There are many ways of nourishing our children, and although food is the most obvious, we also nourish their sense of morals, beauty, honesty, and all of the virtues we hope will become part of their character as they grow into adulthood.

A Few Final Suggestions

Leave the television off while eating. It captures everyone's attention, reduces communication, and everyone might as well be sitting in front of the set, eating from TV trays, instead of at a table.

Soft music played during dinner is a good way to introduce children to the classics at an early age, in order to provide them with the opportunity to appreciate the music of the masters. The best part is that it helps calm hyperactive children.

Try to avoid arguments at the dinner table. Voices raised in anger pollute the emotional environment just as much as smoke or chemical leaks affect the physical atmosphere. Few people are willing to take responsibility for their words, yet verbal abuse is more common than physical or sexual abuse.

The key word is respect. Children are people, worthy of the respect we reserve for our adult friends. Respect for our children begins during infancy and is reciprocated as the child grows older. Parents who complain that they receive no respect from their grown children probably never gave them the respect they now demand.

Above all, we need to respect our children who have neurological disorders, such as those on the Autism Spectrum. It's easy to take kids for granted or to tolerate them. It's more difficult to try to understand them as people and to respect them as individuals who have, as we all do, a body, a mind, and a spirit.

SUMMARY

Proper nutrition is vital to the physical, mental, and spiritual health of a child on the Autism Spectrum. Children need food that builds their immune system, and this often means a dramatic change in established eating patterns for the entire family, as diets are modified to include fresh fruits and vegetables instead of canned or processed foods. It includes the elimination of junk food, fast food, and all processed foods as well as artificial colors, preservatives, dairy products, and foods that contain casein and wheat.

A change of diet may be the first thing you need to consider when trying to help your child. This is especially true with children who have ADD or ADHD. If a child is unable to sit and focus on what you are trying to accomplish through therapy because of the discomfort of allergies, nothing will be as effective as it could be. Once dairy (or other allergens) has been eliminated, it will then be time to move on to the creative, remedial, and artistic therapies of music, art, color, puppetry, and speech that you will find detailed in the following chapters.

CHAPTER 7

*T*he Spiritual Meaning of Art

A rt can be defined in many different ways, according to one's talent, appreciation, and understanding. It can be as simple as a finger-painting or as complex as a Monet. "The Arts" is a wide-reaching category that includes painting with various media, drawing, sculpture, music, poetry, dance, and drama. Painting and drawing are particularly effective activities for children with ADHD, autism, and Asperger's Syndrome.

With the proper remedial and creative therapies, a child with autism slowly awakens to the outside world from the inner realm in which he has spent most of his life, resistant to touch or sound. Art is non-competitive, and children are free to create what they want to without fear of being criticized. It is a great boost to their self-esteem to be able to paint something that is appreciated by others.

Children on the Autism Spectrum are innately attracted to all of the arts. The energy it takes to focus on a work of art, regardless of the art form, eventually affects all areas of their lives. Children who have little interest in their environment are stimulated through the arts and come alive inwardly. Their spiritual nature responds to the beauty of art in all forms, and care must be taken that the music played during a therapy session be of fine quality classical composition. The great musical masters wrote music that has the power to affect every level of a human being, and if we quiet ourselves enough to listen, we feel it.

Socrates wrote, "Education is the kindling of a flame, not the filling of a vessel." The true meaning of the word "educate" is to bring out what is within us or to evolve and grow. This is the goal of every therapist and should be the goal of every teacher and parent. We can substitute "art" for "education" in this quote as we ignite the spark of life within children through Artistic Therapy. When children are introduced to various art forms, their spiritual nature is energized, and they express their feelings and emotions through whatever medium they are using. Because children are still so close to their inner spiritual source, they paint what they sense, not what they see.

COLOR, SHAPES, AND THE JOY OF PAINTING

Children love pure art because they are still unsullied and untrained by lessons and absolute directions. Their rich fantasy life is experienced through their painting, drawing, music, and movement.

When children are allowed to paint what they feel, their work has a beauty that shines through the colors. One has a sense of figures, shapes, and sensations that are moving from within the colors to the surface. We can either let a child imitate us when he begins painting or let him experiment with color and shapes. Working with colors strengthens our sensory life and allows us to see the world around us more clearly. We become more aware of our surroundings and we think more coherently. Because of this, art is most beneficial to a child who is unable to relate to his environment. When a child is lethargic and loses interest in his life, the fundamental kernel of his existence—his spirit—responds to the colors of nature used in a painting.

When we look at a child's painting, we are tempted to analyze it. If we are doing a psychological assessment, this may be helpful, but when we are trying to help a child reconnect with his creative and spiritual nature through Artistic Therapy, it can be harmful. Your child's painting of a turtle may look like a pile of mud to grownups, but he has drawn something meaningful to him. When we dissect a child's picture, we are injuring the creative spark that was ignited, if only for a few minutes. Children with autism, ADD/ADHD, and Asperger's enjoy all forms of art and should be given the opportunity to experience each. We need to let it happen without comments or analysis, which can hamper or destroy the creative process.

People who paint for sheer joy do not care what other people think of their art. They paint for themselves and depict what they see and sense. When we draw or paint for someone's opinion, we are not calling on our innate gifts—we are trying to impress other people. Children love pure art because they are still unsullied and untrained by lessons and absolute directions. Their rich fantasy life is experienced through their painting, drawing, music, and movement. Children on the Autism Spectrum not only like the arts, but they *need* the arts for their spiritual development. Then, the rest of their lives will improve as well.

We Need Art

No one doubts that we need food to eat, water to drink, and oxygen to breathe, but most people do not realize that our spiritual body needs to be nourished as well. Many people rarely think of their spirit, much less talk about it; they are neglecting the most important and influential aspect of their lives. With a renewed interest in Artistic or Remedial Therapy, we are discovering how to help children improve the quality of their lives by addressing their three-fold nature. Boys and girls respond to the arts because they are given freedom that goes beyond the physical limitations of their body.

A major factor in our society's inability to recognize the spiritual aspect of art is the mistaken idea that it is not basic to life but is instead something that is simply added to everyday existence, like a painting bought to fill an empty wall. Art is—and always has been—important to civilizations. Early art included journals of hieroglyphs and petroglyphs that detailed day-to-day activities that are still visible in newly discovered tombs and in remote desert areas.

When art is beautiful, it is absorbed by our body, mind, and spirit.

The purpose of art is to connect with the beauty of spirit and bring it into the physical world for people to experience. When a child paints a beautiful picture, he is praised. One that is considered "ugly" is either met with silence or "What is that!?" But if the child is painting what he sees or senses, it is beautiful because it has sprung from some place deep within him. There are some children who have problems that are not talked about but they show in their paintings and drawings. For this reason, the vocation of Art Therapy was developed to help reveal the unspoken emotions of youngsters.

ART AS THERAPY

Art Therapy is based on the premise that people are able to express their unrecognized or subconscious feelings through painting or drawing. Children who are unable to communicate in traditional ways often produce exceptionally beautiful and thought-provoking art. They should be provided crayons, paints, and paper of different textures and allowed to draw, paint, or even scribble anything they choose. The object is not to create a Picasso, but to offer opportunities for young children to investigate—and be introduced to—the world of art and color.

For their children to continue the improvement that was initiated during therapy sessions, parents must be willing to purchase supplies such as crayons, coloring books, plain paper, watercolors, a blackboard, and marker board with a variety of colored markers. A parent once commented about his child, "I don't buy him crayons. He just scribbles." All children scribble at first, but most soon start using crayons and coloring books before moving on to paint. Their self-esteem grows with each painting that pleases them. Show them how proud you are by hanging their pictures on the refrigerator, even if they are "only scribbles." Better yet, frame them and hang them on the wall.

Art helps children communicate and inspires an attempt to control their movements. If they have poor motor skills, a large brush and a large sheet of paper attached to an easel provides an inviting and wide surface on which they can paint just as their peers do on smaller paper with a smaller brush. Paints in pots are preferable because the colors flow on the paper easily, creating shapes and forms as the paint moves across the paper.

Painting Is Revealing

Painting is a learning experience. When a child paints a tree, he may look for the green paint. But when you tell him that by mixing blue and yellow in a clean cup he will create green, his dismay turns to excitement at this discovery. A child learns about himself as he paints pictures of his family, dog, and the swing that hangs from the tree in the backyard. He experiences again the feelings of pleasure, enjoyment, fear, and/or anger as he paints what he remembers. Painting brings a child's unseen life to the surface of his consciousness, and it is through this revelation that an Art Therapist can begin his work.

When he learns to draw, a child wants to paint everything that is part of his life, usually his family. If one member of the family, for example a younger sister, is left out of his painting, it may be an oversight, or it may be a sign of problems within the family that should be addressed by the therapist or counselor. It may also mean he is simply angry with his little sister for throwing his puzzle pieces around the living room.

However, there may be more to it than the puzzle. He may feel that his parents spend too much time with his sister and ignore him. This may have a grain of truth, but children tend to exaggerate. In a week or so ask him to draw his family again. It is a good possibility that his sister will appear on the paper, but if not, ask if he has left something out of the picture. If he says "No" and denies having a sister, this needs to be explored further. A sensitive parent or therapist will encourage him to talk as he paints, and at some point he will confide his true feelings.

Remedial or Artistic Therapy

Remedial Therapy, often called Artistic Therapy, incorporates exercises that stimulate the child's entire three-fold nature, moving him ever closer to wholeness. Certain exercises help children become more outgoing and social who previously had shown little interest in their surroundings or other people. Many children on the Spectrum need structure in their lives, and art may provide the necessary guidelines for hyperactive youngsters who seem to have no boundaries in their own lives. A very simple exercise reduces hyperactive behavior. Still others help children to develop inner symmetry, in which they experience the interplay of inner and outer forces. Such exercises are explained in this book. For example, if a child has a breathing disturbance, he relaxes as he paints, and his breathing corrects itself to a natural rhythm as he paints to classical music. Obviously, the choice of music is an important element of all remedial therapies.

Painting also helps children who cannot relate to their environment. Applying color to paper has a grounding effect while at the same time stimulating his spiritual nature, which responds to beauty and color. Aspies often create beautiful multimedia pictures. They are very artistic and inventive and will often ask at an early age for paints, markers, and colored pencils to begin their projects.

Within every child's spiritual essence is a desire to participate in some aspect of art, and as he begins to trust you—the parent, teacher, or therapist—he is eager to improve. His sense of touch will become sharper. He no longer has to grind the crayon into the paper with what appears to be a death-like grip and unexpressed fury. He is beginning to chip away at the wall he has created and is beginning to trust not only you as his therapist, teacher, or parent, but also his environment. This is a significant achievement for a child. You will probably notice that eye contact improves as tactile defensiveness decreases, attention span increases as the need for perfection is reduced, and verbal and fine motor skills improve as perseveration decreases.

Children with autism and Asperger's Syndrome often have rigid patterns of behavior and react visibly to changes in their routine or environment. Painting softens this adherence to structure with colors that flow across the paper and into each other. Children who are left-brain dominant are usually very precise in their artwork, and their drawings show a lot of detail. They should be encouraged to use watercolors instead of markers, crayons, or pencils, since the paint will flow more easily and form its own patterns. Precision does not play a part in this type of expression; instead, it is almost a spontaneous act of abandonment that tends to balance their intellectual pursuits.

In all expressions of art, one uses many senses, and the sense of touch is prominent, especially in sculpture and fingerpainting. Be sure to use markers with delightful fragrances—but only those that are labeled as non-toxic, because autistic children like to taste things to learn about them.

Make a note of which color your child favors according to his disposition and physical condition at the time. Is it bright and cheery or dark and melancholy? Don't just "look" at his paintings. Observe whether they are drawn with borders or frames. This is usually an indication of feeling "hemmed in." When frames no longer surround his paintings, the child is making progress and is preparing to meet the world and his environment.

> Children with autism and Asperger's Syndrome often have rigid patterns of behavior and react visibly to changes in their routine or environment.

Remedial Therapies are different from traditional therapies because they incorporate the child's body, mind, and spirit into every individualized program. Changing times call for new methods of addressing children's neurological disorders.

ART IN CHANGING TIMES

It is interesting to look back through history and see how art has changed. For example, art in East Asia was known to be a gateway—or at least a source of insight—into the spiritual world. It was felt that art united heaven and Earth. Ancient teachings held that the good, the true, and the beautiful are inseparable. By substituting morality, science, and art, we can arrive at the same conclusion. This belief was also held by the West until the dawn of the Renaissance in the fourteenth century.

During the Renaissance, as the great universities were built in Europe and men became more mental, a painting became simply an object, a representation of a physical object. By the nineteenth century, this paralleled the beginning of a materialistic decline of Western spirituality that continues to this day. The good news is that we can see an upward swing of the pendulum as art is gaining recognition as the kindling that ignites the flame of creativity in a child with a neurological disorder.

It is difficult for us in the twenty-first century to understand the ancient Greek culture that honored the physical body or the warlike Roman influence that later changed beauty into competition. Greeks revered the body as a form through which spiritual beings expressed themselves in the arts. They regularly had games and competition to fine-tune their bodies because they felt the physical form was an instrument that needed to be healthy at all times and in all ways. Later, the Roman era lacked such reverence for art. People became more warlike, with cultural emphasis on physical strength rather than ephemeral beauty.

By the sixteenth century, as man became more focused on the material life, art was only a show of wealth and power. As a person becomes more material, he moves further away from his spiritual nature. We cannot have it both ways, and we cannot be exclusively in either world and still remain balanced. Today, man has to work hard to develop his spiritual nature because of his materialistic environment. Art lost a great deal of meaning when it was removed from a position of reverence in houses of worship and brought into homes, businesses, and exhibitions.

Art is no longer largely felt by the masses, and people paint from models rather than from their spiritual perception. In a society known for accumulating possessions, many people buy paintings for others to admire rather than for a sincere desire to own fine art, and there may be little appreciation involved, since the paintings are looked at, not experienced.

Art should be chosen for the feeling it conveys, not because the artist or style is currently in vogue.

It is very difficult for an artist who paints from a spiritual perspective to interest most people in his work, simply because it is different and does not conform to tradition. Yet it is this very "differentness" that affects the inner nature, or life force, of the person who really sees and feels what is represented. The essence of the artist, whether a musician, painter, photographer, poet, or sculptor, always shines through his work. This is because part of his entire being has penetrated his art, and it comes alive. The art of many creative autistic children is "different," and because it is not traditional, it is often too quickly dismissed.

The essence of the artist always shines through his work. The art of many creative autistic children is "different," and because it is not traditional, it is often too quickly dismissed.

The Needs of Our Time

As we learn about the increase in autism and the many courses of music and art therapies in major universities, we might ask if it is a mere coincidence that at the lowest point in the cyclic swing of the pendulum from spiritual to material and back to spiritual consciousness in our culture, all of the old art forms are making a comeback in the form of therapy. As we are experiencing a global phenomenon of autism, we are learning how to combat it with creative arts, nutrition, exercise, and alternative medicine. Times change, people change, concepts change, and needs change.

The needs of our time are to recognize the intrinsic benefits of art and to bring it back into our lives as a spiritual influence. As the spiritual begins to balance the material aspect of everyday experiences, it will once again join with the world of science. These two principles of polarity, or opposites (spiritual and material or art and science), are inextricably connected, although they have long been considered separate ideals. We see the same polarity in heart and head, or mind and body, which combine to develop an integrated person. These may sound like lofty goals, but they are not impossible ones, once we recognize how important music and color are to a healthy life.

COLOR YOUR STORIES, COLOR YOUR LIFE

If we cannot feel or see the beauty of the arts or a spectacular sunset, we will probably have a hard time stirring the imagination and inspiration of a child. We can learn by listening with our hearts to what children mean, not only what they say. Our goal as parents is to be part of our children's experience by working with them so we can reach and teach them by our example. It's important not to succumb to all of your child's requests for your help, especially when engaging in fun, but challenging, Remedial

By being very
descriptive when you
are talking with your
child, you encourage
him to create a
much more detailed
image in his mind.

Therapies. Your help is not always needed; it may just be a habit for the child. (See the inset on page 133 for more on this.)

If your child seems unable to paint a picture or is generally lethargic about the creative process, he needs to be stimulated by images. For example, you could tell him a story about a trip you took, or describe a picnic in the park with other children. Fill the story with visuals, such as: red birds, green grass, blue sky, white clouds, yellow flowers, children playing with an orange ball, a brown dog sleeping in the sun, and goldfish swimming in a pool of blue water. These images will implant themselves in a child's mind, and he may soon want to put them on paper. By being very descriptive when you are talking with your child, you encourage him to create a much more detailed image in his mind.

Children with autism, Asperger's, and ADD often enjoy spraying paper with water, then painting swaths of color, one below the other, and seeing how they flow into and around each other. They like to see objects or forms in paintings that seem "magically" to appear. This use of color has the effect of calming overly active children who are having a new experience of creating something they have never seen before. (See Chapter 11 for more information on color.)

As adults, we intuitively want to surround ourselves with color, whether it is in our clothing, home décor, or art. Maybe Joey cannot verbalize that blue is his favorite color, but he can show you by his desire always to wear a blue shirt. Having the pleasant experience of enjoying a preferred color is something we need, and if we can produce something we need, like a painting, we will feel satisfied and fulfilled. Children are no different. They are simply smaller and younger people with potential that has yet to be explored.

Painting is a powerful art form that helps children relate to their environment. When a child discovers the depth of colors, he begins to see color in his surroundings. He notices the red cardinal, the green tree in his front yard, and the colors of his toys and clothes. He looks at things with an artistic presence, and when painting a mountain, instead of simply outlining the shape, he might paint it with shades of green. When a child begins to paint, he has found a wonderful interest, as a new part of the world has been revealed. Once your child discovers colors, he will remember them always and will be a creator instead of an imitator. His spirit begins to shine through the colors with which he is filling his white paper, as he begins to participate more fully in the outer world.

Children on the Spectrum like art because it is non-competitive and each picture stands on its own merit. It is not compared to anyone else's, and every picture is a work of art. Often when a child is through painting or drawing, his faucet of inspiration suddenly turns off, and there is no doubt that he is finished. For example, he may be totally engrossed in painting a picture, as his attention span increases enormously while he is engaged in something of interest. When he completes what he is doing, he may suddenly put down his brush, stand up, and lose interest. He may begin to circle the room, touching everything, and need to be brought back to awareness.

When you sense your child is reaching this stage, it is time, quickly but smoothly, to transition to another project, like fingerpainting, before he has a chance to become restless and inattentive.

FINGERPAINTING

Although fingerpainting is not usually considered art, it is possible to create very beautiful and expressive paintings with this method. By intimately connecting a creative medium with the materiality of the paper, your child begins to balance the inner and outer aspects of his life. It cannot be too strongly emphasized that children on the Autism Spectrum are very intelligent, despite having such characteristics as not wanting to touch things or be touched.

Help Me!

Children often ask for help even though they don't need it. They're used to having someone do everything for them when they appear helpless. Many children can dress themselves or brush their teeth but say they need help.

When other people do everything for a child, he has no initiative or motivation to do things himself. When he's asked to do something in therapy—for example, to draw a line from point A to point B—he may say, "I can't." When it's obvious that he's capable of doing what he's asked to do, a conversation often goes like this:

"Billy, will you please draw a line from here to here?" (Therapist points to marked spots on board.)

"I can't."

"Sure, you can."

"I can't."

"I know you can."

"I need help."

"No, you don't, Billy. You can draw the line."

"You need to help me."

"No, I don't Billy, because I know you can draw the line. But I'm here in case you really, really need my help, okay?"

"Okay." (He feels secure and draws the line)

If a child is constantly helped when he says "I can't," he'll never be able to call fully upon his own forces to become part of his environment and realize his potential.

Children who are tactilely defensive may initially balk at fingerpainting and refuse to touch the paint, but if you matter-of-factly paint with enthusiasm and continue to chat about what you're doing, they will eventually overcome their feeling of repulsion. It may take a few weeks and a lot of patience, but autistic children will learn to create with fingerpaints as long as there are a basin of water and a lot of paper towels available so they can wash their hands often. For this activity, sitting opposite or next to each other on the floor with the water in between seems to be the best arrangement.

A Triumph Through Fingerpainting

Turner was ten years old and tactilely defensive. He had no eye contact and was non-verbal, but it was clear that he understood what I was saying to him. Despite Turner's mother's comments that he had no idea what was said to him and would never improve, I had a feeling she was wrong. I frequently told him that I knew he understood everything I said and I knew he was very intelligent. He would occasionally smile just a little, and then it was quickly gone.

His mother gave me a list of things not to "bother with because he won't touch them." On the list was paint, which I introduced in our first session. Because he was considered unreachable, Turner was given no chance at home to prove otherwise. He had no crayons, paints, clay, or anything else that could be used for artistic creations.

We rapidly established a mutual respect, and Turner was captivated by the paints I placed before him. He watched every movement of brush to water, to paint, to paper, and back to water for cleaning. His first efforts were streaks of one color, then two or more. We painted during every session for two months. Finally came the big day of fingerpainting. This would be a real challenge because he would be using his fingers instead of a brush. A strategy had to be devised and slowly introduced to Turner so that the idea of soiling his hands wouldn't repel him.

We began a nine-week process to desensitize Turner to the idea of touching paint. He eyed the containers of paint suspiciously but didn't clench his fists, which would have been a sign of nervousness or fear. For the first, short session, I explained what I was going to do and continued talking as I placed a dot each of red, yellow, and blue in different spots on the paper. I then drew designs with my index finger and washed it off in the basin of water that was between us on the floor. He observed every move, and at that point, I removed the paint, paper, and water.

The "secret" for some children is to intrigue them by presenting a certain exercise for only a short time at first and then removing it. This generates a desire to know more, and they will look forward to doing it again—instead of being over-saturated with one activity that can become tiring and boring.

Each week we advanced to another step, and Turner made some remarkable discoveries about his latent talent. Whenever the objective was reached, the paint, paper, and water were removed, and we began a new exercise that required a change of location and activity. The following is an outline of the slow but successful process:

Week 2: Each week a basin of water was placed between us as we sat opposite each other on the floor. I told him that he could wash his hands whenever he wanted to. I put the paint on the paper with a craft stick. I slowly made some lines and circles with my fingers and talked about things and places that were colorful. That process took only a few minutes, just long enough to arouse his interest. Then I rinsed the paint off my hands, dried them on a paper towel, and we began another exercise.

Week 3: I asked if he would like to put the paint on the paper. He was verbally unresponsive but again showed no sign of resistance. I put the paint on the craft stick and handed it to him. He touched the paper with the stick and quickly grasped how to transfer the paint to the paper. Even though he hadn't physically touched the paint, he washed and dried his hands.

Week 4: I asked if he would like to put the paint on the craft stick and then on the paper. He reached for the stick and gingerly held it between his thumb and index finger with the other fingers up in the air. Then, he dabbed the paper with paint without hesitation and quickly washed his hands even though, again, he hadn't touched the paint.

Week 5: I drew lines, circles, numbers, and letters with my index finger, and he was transfixed. There was no effort to include his participation in this exercise; it was designed to arouse his curiosity.

Week 6: I encouraged him just to touch the paint. He tentatively reached towards the red dab I had placed on the paper but drew back several times. With great inner effort, he did touch it—barely—and washed his hands.

Week 7: At the next session he not only touched the paint, but also drew circles and swirls with his index and middle fingers. Two fingers! This was an accomplishment.

Week 8: This time I put the paint directly on his index finger and he "drew" on the paper. He did this with all the colors, washing his hands between each.

Week 9: This was the day we had worked towards. I asked him to hold his palm up and showed him what I meant. I then put a large amount of paint in his palm. His initial reaction was to freeze and look at the horrible thing I had done to him. But for some reason, instead of washing his hand, he tried to get rid of the paint by pushing the palm of his hand on the paper. The effect was startling to him because he realized he had just created a piece of art. He did it again and again and stared at what he had done.

Several times he had moved towards the basin of water and I would say, "Just do a little more and then you can wash your hands," which he would do. It always amazed and saddened me to realize that this child was considered severely retarded and incapable of understanding anything. Turner clearly understood the suggestion of doing "a little more," and from then on, he fingerpainted during each session, to the amazement of his mother, who observed.

During a lecture and slide presentation to a group of physicians at the University of Arizona Medical School demonstrating art by autistic children, observers noticed one particularly compelling picture in shades of green that appeared to be spirals in an upward motion. One doctor maintained, "An autistic child who is tactilely defensive cannot paint like that!" The other doctors agreed. This was high praise and testament to the latent potential and wonderfully creative mind of a little boy named Turner.

Although Turner continued to paint with his fingers and brushes, he still liked to color in his favorite coloring book of circus scenes.

CRAYONS AND COLORING BOOKS

Don't be afraid to use crayons and coloring books. They are usually the first form of art and color a child experiences. Some Art Therapists are taught that a child should never use coloring books because they are too restrictive; however, when a child with autism or ADHD has no sense of boundaries, the short-term use of coloring books can be very helpful. When a child begins to create with crayons, his struggle, progress, and pleasure are obvious as he moves from scribbling across a page to seeing forms take shape on his paper as he stays within the lines and uses various colors. The process is one of containing his energy within a specified area, which has the effect of reducing hyperactive behavior.

Children are often overwhelmed by a large selection of crayons, so offer only three or four colors at first. They usually begin by scribbling with one color over the entire page as they gradually become aware of the pictures.

When this happens—as it will—you can help by asking, "What color would you like to make his hair?" or "What color would you like to make the trees?" You may have the impression that he had never thought of using a color other than his favorite—which is usually black or gray. If it looks like the trunk of a tree is going to be the same green as the leaves, you can quickly ask, "What color do you think the trunk of the tree should be?" This can work with everything else in the coloring book until he begins to choose various colors on his own.

Prompted by your gentle questions, he will soon complete a multi-colored picture that is partially—or completely—within the lines. After this accomplishment, you can then move on to watercolor and fingerpaints. This process could take several weeks or months, and each week's pictures should be labeled and dated. Unfortunately, not all children's colorful pictures are appreciated by some people, especially if they haven't accepted their child.

OBSERVATION AND PERCEPTION

Don't just "look" at your child's paintings. Observe and absorb them. Typically, the paintings of right-brain-dominant children are fluid and flowing instead of rigid and structured. These artistic children are attracted to color and the ability to create by blending two colors to make something new.

Hayden: An Unaccepted Child

A delightful nine-year-old boy with autism, Hayden was never accepted by his father. His younger brother was better at soccer and his grades were higher. Hayden was clumsy and his brother was nimble. Hayden had autism and his brother didn't.

I began Hayden's first session with a coloring book, and Hayden's picture was scribbled with a black crayon. Over a period of weeks with the gentle coaching question of "What color would you like to use for the ___?" he began to use different colors. He stayed fairly well inside the lines and soon was thinking about his choice of crayons before coloring in the shapes. One day, he did a great picture and colored the boy's hair red. All in all, it was a wonderful session—until his father came to pick him up. Hayden was excited and couldn't wait to show his father his masterpiece. The first thing his father said was, "Why is his hair red? You know it's supposed to be yellow." I knew both Hayden and his brother were blond, and so I said that it was a wonderful picture with many colors. I further pointed out that Hayden had stayed inside the lines, and that in addition, many children had red hair. His father could not tolerate anything less than perfection, which meant he could not tolerate Hayden, and despite his wife's pleas, his son was placed in a residential home for children with severe neurological disorders.

Because of his intolerance, Hayden's father was unable to see the good in his son. His rejection was rather extreme; most mothers and fathers are pleased with their child's progress. By being more observant, they can begin to see things they had previously overlooked in their children's art work.

When asked what their picture represents, they may describe their painting in vivid, graphic terms instead of simply identifying a person or dog.

It is not unusual for very young autistic children to grasp six or eight crayons, pointed-end down, and draw circles with them. They are fascinated with being able to produce so many colors at one time. Because autistics are so drawn to all of the arts, this is not surprising.

Do your child's paintings have many angles and straight lines? These are typically drawn by children who are left-brain-dominant. You can help to balance these children with Energetic Drawing (see page 140) and the exercises beginning on page 267 in Part Two.

Many angles in a picture seem to give needed support, and frames around pictures might show a child's feeling of being hemmed in. Children who are very rigid in their patterns find it difficult to draw curved lines, and their pictures usually consist of many angles. As their self-esteem improves and as their sense of security and sense of self-worth are enhanced, frames and angles are gradually eliminated from their pictures, replaced by swirls and flowing, free-form figures or swaths of color and figures. Art opens all of us up to new experiences and gives us a freedom to create without boundaries.

When a toddler is given a crayon, he scribbles across the page, but if your older child scribbles instead of drawing and shows no perception of the meaning of contours or boundaries, he feels little or no relationship with his own self. Just as the colors are scattered, so are his inner forces. When he begins to contain the colors and draw simple figures, he is showing signs of self-recognition and self-worth. If you are his therapist, he may become very attached to you because you have helped him in this process.

A child's inability to recreate an object in the conventional sense does not diminish his feelings of accomplishment or the fact that he has actually achieved something great. When he discovers that by combining two colors a third is produced, or that a blue dot on paper is his representation of a bird and a yellow one a butterfly, he has accomplished a piece of art. He has suddenly become a creator and wants to experiment with other combinations.

Many children will mix all the colors, thinking the result will be a rainbow, and are surprised to see they have produced a puddle of brown paint. This in itself is a lesson, as the child learns to restrain his impulse to mix more than two colors at a time. This lesson also carries over into other aspects of his life, when he learns that trying to mix too much of anything usually does not have a positive outcome.

Our goal as parents is to help our children develop their inner life, since their connection with the outer world is tenuous. Children daydream and have enviable imaginations that need to be encouraged. When a child begins to create, the struggle and progress are obvious as he moves from no artistic activities or interests to pleasure in seeing a form spring to life on his paper. When a painting is done that shows a child has an understanding of his environment, it stirs his desire to know more. He wants to paint more—many more—pictures. His demeanor and physical appearance change as he begins to release his dormant creative forces. He becomes more attuned to everything around him, including people.

The Awareness of Children

Young children are very perceptive. If a parent, teacher, or therapist says one thing but thinks the opposite, the child knows intuitively he is being lied to and will not trust this person who has the responsibility of educating him during the early years of his life. During a child's formative years—from birth to the change of teeth, around age six or seven—it is what teachers, therapists, and parents feel and think that is more important than what they do or say, because thoughts always precede physical or verbal acts.

There is always a communication when working with art that is often more meaningful than words. A touch, a slight smile, or a flash of eye contact are all wondrous signs that children enjoy the process and appreciate your support.

Because children on the Spectrum are bright and aware, you should talk with them constantly. Don't use baby talk or raise your voice. Neither is productive and both are an insult to their intelligence. Instead, be gentle, supportive, and generous with sincere praise. Talk about the colors they use and the beauty of the soft yellows, brilliant reds, and lovely blues. Tell them how pleased you are with their work and how graceful their flowing lines are.

Then, draw their attention to the beautiful classical music you have (ideally) been listening to and to certain instruments that are most noticeable in the piece. A deep horn is heard just once in Harrison's favorite album. When we painted, this non-verbal child knew when the horn was about to make its appearance and would laugh and say loudly, "Big horn!"

Be sure to document your child's improvement in all areas, including artistic ones such as coloring, sculpture, role playing with miniatures, and any creation from his first scribbles to his final painting. This will be helpful to his therapist, teachers, and physician, who will have a visual testimonial to the work you have done at home with your child.

As you begin this journey with your child, it will become obvious that both he and you are very aware of this development. The process of growth involves everyone who works with him; every person learns, evolves in his thinking, and changes his perception.

Changing a Child's Perception

Drawing and painting should be done in various positions and with different media. Move around the room and alternate your child's physical location and focus. For example, children should be encouraged first to draw circles or designs in the air. This frees the arm and gives a greater range of motion.

During part of one session, the child may be at a blackboard with chalk, then at an easel with tempera, at a table with smooth bond paper and watercolors, on the floor with construction paper and crayons, at the easel again with markers, and then back to the table with fingerpaints.

By changing position, paper, and media, he is strengthening his perception of color, texture, and body involvement, as each of these requires the use of different muscles, including those of the eyes and brain. If possible, all of these techniques should be part of one session, and each may last only a few minutes at first. Your own perception and observation will determine how long to spend on each project or whether to include it at all.

Working sessions should not be devoted entirely to art. Between these positioning changes you can play games, do puzzles, read a fairy tale, play pick-up sticks, stack blocks, or go outside (weather permitting) to walk or to kick a ball. Programs need to be rounded and balanced between active and passive activities. Once your child has learned and practiced many artistic activities, it is time to begin the process of developing spatial perception through various exercises known as Energetic Art.

ENERGETIC DRAWING AND SYMMETRY

The goal of the exercises presented in this book is to help children achieve symmetry of their three-fold nature of thinking, feeling, and willing through artistic means. Energetic Drawing is a process of seemingly simplistic exercises used to help children with psycho-neuro disorders improve academically, socially, physically, emotionally, and spiritually. It is one of the most effective forms of art for this purpose. Energetic Drawing is more than sketching figures or objects. Specific drawing techniques stimulate the brain cells and create new neuropathways in both the left brain and the right brain. These exercises avoid a hardening one-sidedness of the brain. The objective of this art form is to balance the hemispheres of the brain by engaging the child in spatial relationships.

The series of exercises in this section is helpful to all children, with or without disabilities. In "typical" children, the exercises are made gradually more complex and lead to understanding the science of geometry.

Lines are gracefully drawn in an up-and-down and in-and-out process. The rhythm corresponds to breathing—inhalation and exhala-

> The goal of the exercises presented in this book is to help children achieve symmetry of their three-fold nature of thinking, feeling, and willing through artistic means.

tion—so that the child's respiration becomes smooth and even, and he relaxes. Some children who are adverse to clay or other tactile substances are attracted to Energetic Drawing and have an inner rhythm that flows out on the paper. This process encompasses simple and complex art that may be beyond the capability of most children with psycho-neuro disorders, but that does not mean they cannot be introduced to basic forms.

To strengthen a child's memory, draw a straight line and say, "This is a straight line." Then draw a curved line and say, "This is a curved line." Ask him to draw each on the board or paper. At the next session, draw the same two lines and ask the child to name them. Then ask him to draw them while saying what they are. If the child is non-verbal, simply repeat the words—he will hear and absorb them.

The next step is a wavy line, which indicates motion. A straight line has no motion; it just is, while a wavy line always seems to be going to—or returning from—a destination. Wavy lines remind one of graceful movements such as those of a ballet dancer. It is a moving up and down or a drawing to or away from you in a rhythmic pattern. It's like a dance drawn on a board or paper. A wavy line depicts the cycles of up and down or back and forth, showing polarity—or opposites—at work. Just as everything in nature has a peak and a valley, an ebb and a flow of seasons and tides, so do we in our life cycles. Some days we feel great and other days we don't. It is difficult for a child with autism to duplicate a wavy line, in either direction, and this is a good exercise for moving between the right and left sides of the brain.

Spatial Relationships

Therapeutic drawing defines space. Many children cannot tell above from below, left from right, in from out, high from low, because they are unaware of the Law of Polarity, or the fact that everything has an opposite. Physicists might say that for every action there is an equal and opposite reaction. Techniques allow a child to see the differences in squares, triangles, and spatial qualities as he begins to understand the concept of opposites. Drawing, as with painting, can be done standing at an easel, seated at a table, or sitting on the floor.

Each position presents its unique perspective as the child sees his work from various vantage points. His perception of his art may vary a great deal as he sees it from different levels, and with each change, the muscles in his arm move slightly in a corresponding manner. For example, as his eyes move following the outline of a circle, there are minuscule but detectable movements in the muscles of his arm. As muscles are activated, they stimulate circulation, which also affects various organs of the body.

Spatial Relationship Exercises

You can help your child understand the concept of space and shape, both of which are difficult for some children to grasp. For example, when a child draws a horizontal line across the center of a marker board, blackboard, or paper, he has effectively divided that space into two parts. He is then able to learn the concepts of above/below and over/under. If the paper or board is relatively square, he has learned what a square is. If it is oblong, he will understand the shape of a rectangle. When a line is drawn vertically, he has divided the space into halves again, this time side by side. He learns right and left. By drawing a line from the upper left corner to the lower right corner, he has created two triangles. Such concepts, which we take for granted, will intrigue the intelligent minds of autistic children.

These exercises may seem absurdly simple to you, yet they are very complex and connect and stimulate both hemispheres of the brain. Each exercise has a goal beyond the mere physical act of creating a drawing. The exercises ultimately help children with psycho-neuro disorders understand, and interact with, the world beyond themselves. For all of these exercises, children should do all lines and circles freehand without the help of rulers or stencils.

Turn to page 267 of Part Two for specific exercises in spatial relationships.

Duplication

The entire world is composed of straight and curved lines in various formations. Children who are very fixed in their concepts—for example, those who keep holding on to a mental image or event—find it difficult to draw curved lines, and their pictures usually consist mainly of angles. Having a child duplicate your drawings of angles, straight lines, circles, and arcs enhances his fine motor skills and opens him up to various shapes beyond those that are his (perceived) limitations.

Duplication Exercises

Particularly useful activities involve instructing your child to duplicate what you have just drawn. This is important to help a child both to understand and follow directions and also to distinguish between, and create, straight and curvy lines. By drawing a straight line and then a curved one, children learn the two polaric principles of form. By alternating the use of these two lines, a sense of symmetry, instead of one-sidedness, will result.

Turn to page 269 of Part Two for exercises involving duplication.

Amazing Benefits of Energetic Art

A child with hyperactivity, epilepsy, schizophrenia, or autism frequently feels at the mercy of his condition. He feels that it is controlling him and often feels quite helpless. As a child begins to paint and draw, he releases many inhibitions and tensions that can increase the severity or frequency of his attacks or condition. He can infuse his art with feelings that cannot—or will not—be expressed in any other way. As one autistic girl said with surprise, "I didn't know I could do that!"

In addition to improving spatial perception, eye/hand coordination, and fine motor skills, this type of drawing arouses the thinking process as the child begins to learn fundamental geometry and the forms of sculpture. Conventional wisdom would hold that autistic children are impervious to the lessons we try to impart, but the truth is that these teachings are not lost on autistic children, who understand the concepts to the best of their ability. That ability continues to evolve as they do.

Moving Forward

As you continue with similar exercises, your child gains a sense of form that carries into his mind and physical body. Part of him wants to improve and will work very hard to accomplish this. It is as if he wants to perfect something within himself (that which is imperfect), just as he closes the gap of a circle's two halves to make a whole.

The "games" should be done for a few minutes of each session for several weeks and then intermittently during the remainder of the course of therapy.

The act of drawing a line, even as simple as one drawn vertically from the top of the board to the bottom or horizontally across the board, calls upon the child's strength of will, as was previously mentioned. Completing the downward or upward stroke is a victory for a child on several levels: physically, mentally, and spiritually.

There is more to duplicating a line, circle, or any geometric form than is readily apparent. It first calls upon the sense of hearing as the child is given directions; then it calls upon the senses of sight, touch, and action. Perception and observation are followed by the gross and fine motor involvement of picking up the crayon, chalk, or marker. And within that time, the child actively attempts to obey our instructions, which may have to be repeated several times.

Never "talk down" to or patronize any child, especially one with autism, Asperger's, or ADD. He is intelligent enough to know that you are being condescending and will show his displeasure in many ways—from being silent to doing something to annoy you deliberately. When you work with a non-verbal child, show your respect by speaking articulately and sincerity and warmth. Talk *to* him as if you were talking *with* him—which you are, even though his communication is non-verbal. He will respond and trust you as someone who is sincerely interested in his welfare.

Using Rectangular Crayons

A child who persists in attempting to draw, despite his awkwardness or difficulty in holding a crayon, is trying to control his inner chaos. It is a persistent struggle, and he needs all the encouragement you can give him with frequent and sincere praise. Rectangular, four-sided crayons are easier to grasp than the popular round ones we are all familiar with. Help your child learn how best to use them, since they are very different from the round crayons.

The broad side of the crayon can be used to make circles; this produces a different artistic effect. Demonstrate to him how this works. Then show him that by using any of the flat surfaces of a rectangular crayon, he can produce varied shades. This concept is more complex, and you will probably find that it takes some time for the child to understand it. The edges of these crayons are perfect for drawing horizontal and vertical lines as well as other designs.

Circles

The fact that most autistic children can—and want to—participate in Energetic Drawing is ample reason to believe an innate intelligence is at work within the child. They know the difference between a true and completed circle and one that is not. A circle is supposed to be perfectly round, and as our eyes follow the outline of a circle, our limbs are stimulated. We make minuscule, imperceptible motions with our fingers, hands, and arms as if we are physically duplicating the outline. Every slight movement strengthens the muscles.

If the circle is imperfect, it upsets our sense of balance. Geometric forms flow everywhere, from the round tires on our car to the straight lines of billboards along the road. We look around us and are confronted at every turn with variations of circles and straight lines.

We live in a physical, material world, but the world of art is quite different. Art frees us from the constraints of day-to-day existence and it gives us the freedom to create. Our creation can be one round circle on top of another, like so many scoops of ice cream in a cone. Or it can be a straight line depicting a low, flat building with squares and triangles for doors and windows. Imagination knows no bounds.

However, if a child draws only straight lines over and over, it is an instinctual process with no spiritual connection. A child who draws only a line is rigid and is not allowing his creativity to express itself. If a child draws only circles, he is expressing his feeling of being confined in a body that seems foreign to him. If he draws a circle with a "ruffled" or "jagged" outline, he is attempting to move beyond the confines of his reality and will need your help.

Children on the Spectrum, particularly around the age of eight or ten years, often feel unable to cope with events or their environment. The seemingly senseless act of drawing a circle with a dot in the center, or a dot with a circle around it, seems to benefit these children, who identify with living within a perimeter. The circle represents their conception of the outside world, and the dot represents them. Energetic Art allows a child to see and feel the difference when drawing both circles and lines.

Circle Exercises

By drawing two halves of a circle that are then joined, a child sees that a circle is composed of two sides, and that the arc also consists of two sides, one concave and the other convex. Although he may not grasp or remember the terms, he will see how this joining brings a completion in the form of a circle. He begins—on some level—to gain a sense of reality that will flow into his own shape and physical form.

Turn to page 271 of Part Two for exercises involving the creation of circles.

Completing What Is Incomplete

Children with autism and Asperger's have a sense that they are different from their peers. They may say that they feel something is missing in them because they do not think or act like other kids. Children on the Autism Spectrum enjoy exercises in which they recognize and replace a missing

---

Improved Kids: Threatened Parents

When a child begins to feel better about himself, is encouraged in his work, and is loved unconditionally, he is able to make decisions that change his behavior. It is an unfortunate fact that some mothers (in my experience it has always been the mother) are threatened by this newly discovered ability.

As the child develops a sense of independence, the mother is no longer the pivotal point in her child's life. Some mothers feel a loss of control that threatens their current position as caregiver. By constantly anticipating and attending to their child's every need, they undercut the absolute necessity that he use his own ability to think and act independently. They begin to feel unneeded by their child and antagonistic towards the therapist, sometimes finally removing him from the very source of nourishment that was enhancing his self-esteem as well as his motor, verbal, social, and academic skills.

It is important that parents be aware of the potential for this unpleasant reaction. If they are conscious of this possibility before the appearance of any such response, they may be able to monitor and control their sense of loss as their child becomes more independent.

element because they relate to having something missing in themselves and can take an active role in completing what is incomplete.

Completion Exercises

Completion exercises are fun and especially effective after a child has drawn circles, triangles, squares, and rectangles and can recognize the different shapes.

Turn to page 272 in Part Two for activities based upon completing what is missing or incomplete.

SUMMARY

Art takes many forms and all can be remedial, as well as fun, for your child. The creative process is beneficial to everyone, and you may be surprised at your child's progress and capabilities as a result of the exercises mentioned in this chapter. Painting allows your child's true spirit to emerge. There is a gentleness about painting; the colors are often ethereal and comforting. Their flow can be relaxing and intriguing to your child. Fingerpainting can be enjoyed even by children who are tactilely defensive. Painting is especially effective for a child whose breathing is affected by, for example, asthma.

Energetic Drawing helps your child expand his horizons when he removes the frames from his pictures and rigidity from his thoughts. He learns the difference between circles and lines, and the ability to observe and perceive his surroundings is heightened by completing drawings with a missing piece. Spatial perception is difficult for many children on the Spectrum, but Energetic Drawing techniques easily teach the concepts of up and down, right and left.

Every child is different and every day is different, and you have to be flexible about each of them. If you sense that what you are doing is not working because of the "space" your child is in, switch immediately to something else. Don't be afraid to let your "gut feeling" work for you. The most creative and fulfilled people in the world are perceptive and follow their intuition.

Parents, therapists, and teachers will find it helpful to have a working knowledge of the four temperaments. This interesting method of identifying a child's disposition describes the difference between his personality and his inborn, innate temperament. Continue reading to learn about the temperaments and why your child might be so different from his siblings and from other children.

CHAPTER 8

Taking the Mystery Out of Temperaments

The fictional Jones family has four children:

LuAnne is scattered, sweet, and hyper;

Scott is often sad and hard to cheer up;

Shawn has a temper and is always hitting his siblings;

Michelle is reserved and indifferent.

Mr. and Mrs. Jones often ask each other: "Why are our children all so different? They were all brought up the same way. What did we do wrong?"

The Jones family is very much like families all over the world whose children are not alike except for a slight facial resemblance to their parents or other relatives. There are many reasons why children are unique, including heredity, but this chapter will focus on the main influence: their temperaments. When we try to understand our children, ourselves, and other people, it helps to know that people are born with a particular temperament, or disposition, that remains with them throughout their lives.

THE HISTORICAL BASIS

Since the time of Aristotle, physicians and psychologists have attempted to distinguish the personalities of people by identifiable labels. This presented problems when it was discovered that human beings are a combination of characteristics. Eventually, it was found that although there are infinite traits among people, there are basically only four categories, known as the temperaments. Artistic extroverts (traditionally known as sanguines) love people and are often called flighty. Fiery managers (traditionally known as cholerics) are visionaries who are often called bossy. Quiet worriers (traditionally known as melancholics) are deep thinkers who are often called moody. Predictable introverts (traditionally known as phlegmatics) are the most balanced of all and are often called unflappable.

Human beings are a
puzzle, a complicated
entity of temperament,
personality, idiosyncrasies,
virtues, and vices.

Artistic extroverts are the most extroverted, and quiet worriers the most introverted, while fiery managers and predictable introverts appear to be a combination. An ideal temperament is formed by the best qualities of each of the four dispositions.

Everything in life is coordinated and impinges on something seemingly unrelated. Just as body, mind, and spirit are interconnected, so are we to our environment and the universe as a whole.

People are very complex riddles who show only the tip of the iceberg through their personalities. Beneath the surface is the large, hidden temperament that is joined to the "tip"—the personality seen by others. With all of our scientific and medical achievements, the source of one's temperament has remained puzzling and controversial.

Human beings are a puzzle, a complicated entity of personality, temperament, idiosyncrasies, virtues, and vices. Trying to analyze people on the basis of what we see and what they want us to see is fruitless, but an understanding of temperaments provides a revelation of the interconnected streams of influence.

THE ORIGIN OF TEMPERAMENTS

How are temperaments formed? According to Rudolf Steiner (1861–1925), who wrote and lectured extensively on children's sensitive natures, a child is the product of a physical stream of heredity and a spiritual stream of individuality. The resulting composite is the temperament, much as blue and yellow combine to make green. It is the basic and fundamental coloring of one's existence, and although it comes from within, it is shown to everyone as a visible part of one's body, mind, and spirit. Our inner, spiritual life provides feelings, sensitivities, and inspirations, while our heredity is responsible for our genetic makeup.

We will never understand a child simply by exploring her ancestry. There are certain traits and characteristics that may be evident, but that is only half of her makeup—the physical half. The other half is her individual, particular spiritual nature that still falls within the grouping of temperaments. Heredity provides physical qualities, and children in the same family may show similar characteristics. We need to look further and recognize the individuality of each child, which encompasses her heredity yet is unique. It is this uniqueness that is enhanced by her predisposition of the spirit, or "temperament."

Temperaments are seldom considered in the life of a child with autism, ADD, or Asperger's Syndrome, yet these dispositions do not distinguish between a gifted child and one who has a psycho-neuro disorder. All children fall into one of the four categories of temperaments. However, because of the variation created by Spectrum Disorders and one's personality, the temperament of a child with autism may be difficult to distinguish.

Temperaments are a subject of study for psychologists and therapists who look to the mind for an explanation, but unless the core of our existence, our spirit, is factored into the equation *body + mind + spirit = humanity*, the temperament will never be adequately explained. It is this aspect of the three-fold nature of every human being that eludes dissection and analysis by scientists, who may grant that the spirit is an integral part of religious teachings but, since it cannot be seen or touched, believe it probably does not exist. Only when natural or spiritual science and physical science coexist will the three-fold human being be understood.

Many people share an ancestry and inherited characteristics but it is one's spiritual nature that provides the endless variations that are presented to others. It is important that when we meet people, we engage our feelings and senses rather than analytical intelligence, since neither our spiritual nature nor the temperaments can be understood intellectually. Unless we are very observant and perceptive, our judgments will be based on only one aspect of a person: physical appearance. In all of our social and professional interactions, it is to everyone's benefit to sense what lies beyond one's obvious personality. This is of extreme importance for people who work in any capacity with children who have a disability of any kind.

The Masks We Wear

Persona is the Greek word for "mask," a description of our personality that changes with time or with situations. Most people have one personality in public and another, quite different, in the privacy of their homes. The mask changes from time to time, but temperaments are inborn qualities that remain constant. We probably all know people who are charming and tactful to people they meet in social or business situations but abrupt and tactless at home—or the other way around.

Impressions based on physical appearance can be misleading, since we are faced with what a person wants to project. Our clothes, hairstyle, and possible cosmetic surgery combine with thoughts and actions to create a persona that is presented to others. Movie stars are a prime example of mask wearers. We may never know the real person inside the façade that has been created in an effort to make a good impression. For this reason, it is necessary to be familiar with the temperaments, which are the true barometers of our inner selves.

Habitual, or even occasional, comparison of children by parents, teachers, physicians, or therapists is damaging to every child. There is an old saying that we cannot compare apples and oranges. We should be pleased to see that, as children mature, they all exhibit different traits and interests instead of lamenting, as did our fictional Mr. and Mrs. Jones, "I brought them all up the same. How can they all be so different?" In reality, it is impossible to bring all children up "the same."

When children express their individuality and independent thinking, adults should observe this growth with respect and awe because developing and evolving are major accomplishments at any age. We really would not want everyone to think and act alike, as if we had mass-produced plastic dolls on the assembly line instead of given birth to a unique individual with ancestral and spiritual influences.

Minimizing one's individuality is the first step towards manipulation by others, since balanced and secure individuals have a sense of identity, security, and confidence that people with a "mob mentality" lack. We know that some people are strong-willed and others are passive. These are basically leaders and followers. To learn more about yourself and your children, it is necessary to know the traits of each of the four temperaments.

CHARACTERISTICS OF THE TEMPERAMENTS

In each temperament there is the tendency to one-sidedness, or lack of balance, that, if not recognized in children, can lead to degeneration in adulthood. We need to allow our observation, perception, and intuition to discern how to work with each child and which programs are best suited to her spirit.

There are general characteristics of each temperament that are distinctive, but there are always exceptions. For example, a fiery manager can be short or tall, stocky or slim. Although physical appearance may differ slightly from the traditional characteristics of a child's temperament, her interests and behavior are reliable indicators. Some children are feisty and others are quiet. Another may be a loner while her sister is gregarious. With these perceptions, you can accurately determine how to approach your child most effectively.

All temperaments have negative qualities as well as virtues, and our objective as parents, therapists, and teachers is to encourage a child's virtues through methods that excite what is lacking. This is contrary to traditional thought, whereby vices and lacks are harmful and detrimental. You will at times be perplexed by a child, particularly one on the Spectrum, who seems to be an enigma. Awareness of the temperaments determines what kind of music to play, what art form may be of the greatest benefit, and how to engage her verbally and physically. An understanding of temperaments provides insight into what is needed to stimulate children in each of the four groups.

The type of music chosen to play while working with a child is based on your observation of her. We wouldn't ordinarily choose a rousing piece with emphasis on drums for fiery managers, or a morose piece for quiet worriers. Children who are artistically extroverted or predictably introverted seem to favor lighthearted pieces but there are times when both of these temperaments have to be roused by stimulating music or calmed by a waltz. Obviously, these are not hard and fast rules but instead are based on common sense. However, any well-scheduled plan for working with your child is often totally changed by her mood at the time, so flexibility is the key.

Simply because we can determine the temperament of a child does not mean that all children who share a temperament are the same. This false belief may be a snare that prevents us from seeing the whole child, in which case we fail to meet many of her needs. By working only with what is obvious, we do a disservice to children by failing to engage their disposition. This may lead a child to a life of one-sidedness by failing to encourage the strengths that will overcome her weaknesses. In each temperament there is the tendency to one-sidedness, or lack of balance, that, if not recognized in children, can lead to degeneration in adulthood. We need to allow our observation, perception, and intuition to discern how to work with each child and which programs are best suited to her spirit. Then her weakness becomes her strength.

Children must be purposefully stimulated in order to bring out the portion of their temperament that is lacking and in need of remedial therapy. In reading about dispositions, we must keep in mind that we are a blend of temperaments with one predominating. The predominant characteristics determine the temperament of a child. There are no "good" or "bad" characteristics; they are part of every person in every culture.

The Artistic Extrovert

The temperament of the artistic extrovert is the liveliest—sometimes lively to the point of hyperactivity. The artistic extrovert reacts emotionally instead of intellectually and often gets into trouble because of her spontaneity. She is imaginative, social, and the envy of shy children. All of the characteristics of an artistic extrovert's disposition are most readily apparent in children.

With all children, including those on the Spectrum, an informed parent or therapist works to build on what is lacking in a temperament. She doesn't attempt to change a child; instead, she works with what the child already possesses. It will do no good to try to force an artistic extrovert to learn something if she finds the subject totally uninteresting. Teachers need to make it interesting by bringing out seemingly insignificant facts that may capture her attention and proceed from there.

Artistic extroverts are delightful children, and their faces light up as their glance moves from one object to another, captivated by all things for a short time. Artistic extroverts are distracted by everything; they have sensitive nervous systems with rising and falling sensations. They are given over to a tide of images and impressions, as their interests are quickly aroused and just as quickly dismissed. Their short memory needs to be taken into consideration by teachers, therapists, and parents, who often want an immediate response and follow-through.

Children who are artistic extroverts cannot fix their attention on one subject if it does not captivate them, and they are often labeled as having ADHD. They may be prescribed a psychotropic drug, such as Ritalin, that may effectively destroy their ingenuity and individuality. Like children of all temperaments, they need to have their weaknesses stimulated and thus transformed into strengths. An understanding of temperaments is necessary to excite her spiritual nature properly.

Like people of all temperaments, artistic extroverts have very positive qualities that endear them to others. These include tenderness, compassion, agility, happiness, and versatility and flexibility among other people. Artistic extroverts are very rarely bored because they move easily from one activity or thought to another. They are loyal friends who forget past unpleasantness and love people.

The child who is an artistic extrovert needs to admire someone. It is only by indirect means that we can stimulate her. She must show an interest in her own way and own time, but we can encourage her interest by showing her a number of pictures of famous people and "newsmakers" from different walks of life. When she learns about their heroics or amazing inventions that have changed civilizations, she will want to know more.

A child who is an artistic extrovert has many interests, but they quickly disappear as new images or sensations appear to her. She enjoys the rush of stimulation and misses it when it fades.

Physically, artistic extroverts have a slim build with small muscles and move with apparent joy. Their body is well balanced and their step is so light that they seem to glide as they walk. Although it may seem odd, professional research and personal experience reveal that artistic extroverts very often have blue eyes, which appear to be lit from within, while fiery managers' eyes are intense and quiet worriers' eyes are dull and apparently colorless.

What Can I Do?

The artistically extroverted child has to be kept busy, her mind active. It is vital that you invest time in working with your child to help her improve her ability to observe, articulate, and focus.

One effective technique is to show her pictures that don't necessarily interest her. If she loves cartoon characters, you would not show her cartoon characters. If she is a star soccer player, you wouldn't show her soccer uniforms. Instead, you might show pictures of great people who were inventors, musicians, statesmen, or artists. Perhaps show her a picture of an architect and a picture of the Eiffel Tower, a picture of an artist and a picture of a famous painting, or a picture of a well-known ballerina and a picture of *Swan Lake* being performed by ballet dancers.

Artistic extroverts often have a very poetic nature that surfaces only as they mature. Show her, for another example, a picture of a well-known poet—Robert Browning perhaps—and a poem of his. Read a few lines and put them both away.

Let her scan the pictures for a few seconds, and then remove them from her sight. When this is done, the child will continue to think about those who especially attracted her. The next day or next session, the process is repeated. Each time, her thought process is lengthened until her ability to focus is greatly improved and she wants to explore further the history of the person she admires. She will want to emulate the positive traits and strengths of people she respects and holds in high esteem. In this way, her weakness becomes her strength.

With artistically extroverted children, as with children of all temperaments, we need to work with what is there, not with what is lacking. We want to bring out what is within but still latent. Again, as Socrates said, "Education is the kindling of a flame, not the filling of a vessel." This is exactly what this exercise does for a child. It stimulates an interest in something that had not occurred to her until that point. For example, if she has within her the capability to be an architect, pictures of Frank Lloyd Wright and his beautiful artistic buildings can trigger something that will urge her to learn more. Again, her weakness becomes her strength.

It will help an artistically extroverted child to realize her innate temperament and acknowledge her predisposition to inquisitiveness, activity, and difficulty in concentrating. By recognizing this part of her makeup, she can willfully take steps to control her wandering mind. In this way, her weakness becomes her strength as she settles down in school and absorbs her lessons.

In addition, she will be able to complete her homework and classwork without reminders from her parent or teacher. A key to helping her monitor herself is your encouragement and sincere praise of her accomplishments.

If you think your child is an artistic extrovert, you may have already discovered that by eliminating sugar and artificial coloring, her tendency towards inattention and flightiness is greatly improved.

If you have a child who is a quiet worrier, you may have noticed that it is easy for her to listen to a lengthy musical composition, while artistic extroverts can't sit still long enough to listen to a complete song. For example, four-year-old Lillian had an attention span of mere seconds unless there was something she really wanted to hear or do. I used various art forms during each of our sessions and had classical music playing in the background; as a result, her ability to focus increased each week.

If we were looking at a picture book and she showed clear signs of being ready to get up and wander about the room, I might point to the page and exclaim, "Look! Isn't this bird beautiful? Can you find another bird in the picture?" Then, "What color is the bird?" and finally, "What does a bird sound like?" If she didn't know, I would say, "Cheep, cheep." She loved the sound effects and the game. Then I would stop, put the book away, and move to another project. It is important that you stop when *you* want to, not when your child wants to.

This exercise translated into sitting still long enough in preschool to hear the complete reading of a story or listening to the full record the teacher was playing. She began to enjoy participating with the rest of her group in the amusing songs by repeating the words when asked and following instructions about moving her arms and legs to the music. You can easily do the same thing at home when your child is relaxed and cooperative. As with any child of any age and any temperament, whatever you do must be interesting and fun or the results will be negligible.

Artistically extroverted adults often show an interest in medicine, theater, education, and public speaking. Generally very sensitive to others' feelings, their compassion leads them frequently into the field of medicine, where their "bedside manner" encourages confidence and communication.

The Fiery Manager

The child who is a fiery manager is easy to identify, and there seem to be more and more children today with this temperament. They are noted for their interactions with other children. They are aggressive, bossy, and very confident, with a strong need to have activities regulated and well planned. A child who is a fiery manager cannot resist punching another child as they pass each other in the hall. Because of that urge, she is often in fights with her peers.

Fiery managers demand attention by asserting themselves, and because their ego is so strong, it often prevents lightness, tact, and social courtesy. They are frequently antisocial but can be friendly with peers and siblings as long as they have their own way. If they don't, their short fuse is ignited and their temper explodes. Afterwards they often regret the outburst, a common trait of Asperger's Syndrome. Parents usually have no idea how to deal with a child who is a fiery manager.

What Can I Do?

Fiery managers need to be faced with small challenges and obstacles—not to dampen their fiery nature, but rather to encourage them to think and reason instead of becoming angry and impatient. When presented with many small challenges, a child who is a fiery manager learns that life has numerous obstacles that can be overcome without the use of force.

If your child seems to fit into this category of temperament, you need to stimulate her by issuing a challenge that she is happy to accept. There are many small challenges that can be offered. For example, put all of the Scrabble pieces on the table right side up. Using a small hourglass, ask her to see how many three-letter words she can find before the sand runs out. That will be easy for her. Then ask her to look for four-letter words. That's a little harder, but she will enjoy this challenge. Use this method every few weeks so it's always fresh.

Challenge her to say something nice to someone she dislikes, and give her heartfelt praise when she tells you what she said and to whom.

If she's a math genius, tell her about your friend's son who doesn't understand math and could use some tutoring. Ask if she would like to help him for a week or so. That's a small challenge that will end at a definite time. You might further ask if she would like to attend advanced math classes at the local college or community center. That's a real challenge that she may eagerly accept.

When you go on a short trip, give your child a map and ask her to plan the shortest distance between your house and the destination and to estimate the time you will arrive. If you have a navigation system in your car, she will be interested to see if her directions are similar to those shown on the screen.

A child who is a fiery manager needs a strong authority figure in the home and school who will enforce rules and challenge her to excel. She has an admiration for authority. For this reason, parents, teachers, and therapists have to be knowledgeable about the subjects they are discussing.

Temper Tantrums and Temperaments

Temper tantrums happen to toddlers, children, and even adults of every temperament at some point. We all have outbursts of anger and temper at times, but it is how a person behaves afterwards that gives a clue to her temperament.

A child who is a fiery manager may feel regret or guilt, but it doesn't change her natural temperament, as a result of which other outbursts are bound to occur. An artistically extroverted child will think little of her tantrum and quickly return to her joyful, lighthearted manner. A quiet worrier will feel great regret and continue to brood about it. A predictable introvert will be surprised by her outburst of anger, but her reaction doesn't last as she finds something else to do.

Pay attention to a person's behavior after she has an explosion of frustration or emotion in order to gain some insight into her true temperament.

A child—regardless
of temperament—
responds to gentleness
and a soothing, soft
voice, since a gentle voice
penetrates her veneer
of indifference.

Respect and truth are key words for working with all children, but especially with fiery managers, who will think less of you if these qualities are missing. A child will know if an adult is untruthful or doesn't know the answer to a question and tries to bluff. It won't work. It's much better to say something like, "I'm not absolutely sure about that but I'll do some research and we can talk more about it next time. Is that all right with you?"

A child—regardless of temperament—responds to gentleness and a soothing, soft voice, since a gentle voice penetrates her veneer of indifference. Parents often react quickly and loudly when their child is disruptive or angry, but that does not solve the problem.

If both you and your child are stubborn, strong-willed, and absolutely sure of being right in an argument, chances are both of you are fiery managers. It is a paradox that because you are so alike you often "butt heads," but more often you have a very strong bond. Adult fiery managers are often in politics or medicine, but no matter what vocation they choose, they will do well because they are goal-oriented and determined to succeed.

Since fiery managers typically like spicy foods that seem to fuel their fiery temper, such foods should be reduced or eliminated from their diet.

The Quiet Worrier

The average person who is faced with obstacles in her daily life finds a way of dealing with them. But when quiet worriers feel inner obstacles cannot be conquered, they sink into a morass of sadness, pain, and listlessness. Children who are quiet worriers have little flexibility in their thoughts or actions. They may face a challenge and feel unable to meet it, much less surmount it. When obstacles cannot be overcome, the quiet worrier is absorbed in despair and unable to see the light at the end of the tunnel.

Quiet worriers are usually shy loners who may excel in the arts but have difficulty articulating thoughts and feelings. They do not have a need to surround themselves with people, although they may have a few friends to whom they are intensely loyal and considerate. They prefer to be alone and can be a wet blanket with a group of peers because they like to tell stories in great detail about their trials and tribulations.

Physically, children with this disposition are usually tall and slim with sloping shoulders and a gliding walk. They are often anemic. These generalities, however, do not always apply. One may have the build and walk of a fiery manager but the disposition of a quiet worrier.

As the artistically extroverted child is stimulated through interest and admiration, and the fiery manager needs to respect authority, the child who is a quiet worrier must be shown that there is suffering in the world and that other people also have problems. This helps the child turn her attention from deep within to outside of herself. It does no good to tell a child who is a quiet worrier to "snap out of it," because she isn't able to take control of her melancholy and simply become something or someone she is not.

Whatever a child who is a quiet worrier experiences makes a deep and lasting impression, and she replays it constantly, often with feelings of guilt and remorse for what she did or did not do.

What Can I Do?

Quiet worriers need more sugar in their diet because they are always brooding about something and need to be stirred into action. Natural fruit sugar gives them the boost they need. Your child's melancholy needs to be diverted because if you try to "talk her out of it" or try to do something you think will entertain her, she may retreat further within, thinking that no one understands her.

Quiet worriers like to dwell on past events or things of a spiritual nature that cannot be discussed with anyone. All in all, they are deep thinkers, and instead of enjoying the immediate beauty of the world around them, they often go within and find beauty in somber thoughts. This quality can be nourished in your child by understanding her need to be alone sometimes.

A child who is a quiet worrier cannot be forced into anything. If she doesn't want to participate in a group activity, quietly explain how disappointed other children will be if she doesn't do her part in the social interaction. She will forget about herself and join in. We need to appeal to her sense of fairness and compassion. Even though group activities are often difficult, she may agree to attend a group therapy session where art is used to elicit non-verbal emotions. In this way, she will soon discover that other boys and girls have difficulties that surface in their art, and her own problems may begin to seem very minor. She will empathize with them and want to help if she can.

When she knows that others experience pain, too, she will feel sympathy for them. Talk to her about your own experiences. If you have lost a beloved pet, relative, or friend, share this with her because she will relate to it. She will gradually lose her one-sidedness and show compassion for others. Naturally, things of a highly personal nature or particularly gruesome subject are inappropriate, but if a child who is a quiet worrier learns that an adult she respects has had seemingly insurmountable or painful experiences and not only survived, but was actually better for the experience, she will commiserate with her. When this occurs, a strong bond is created that is nourishing and stimulating to the child, and she begins to experience empathy for others. And since quiet worriers seem to feel most comfortable being listless and morose, it is pointless to try to cheer them up.

With the exception of severe cases, autistic children are intelligent and often brilliant and shouldn't have limits placed on them by the very people entrusted with the responsibility to help them grow into a healthy life.

Most quiet worriers are gifted in music, art, and poetry, but because they are antisocial they would rather do all of these activities solo than in a group. Most geniuses are quiet worriers who, with a rich inner life, are able to work through their emotions to reach a point of inspiration. Younger children are too shy to express this same rich inner life, but with the right environment, encouragement, support, and maturity, their innate talents will surface.

Your child who is a quiet worrier has to think carefully about something before she responds to a question or a statement. For example, if you ask how she feels, she will carefully consider whether she is hungry, hot, cold, angry, or happy, and then answer you. If you are a fiery manager, this will test your patience.

Now that you know your child is a perfectionist, be patient with her while she figures out the best way to clean her room or take out the trash. A fiery manager might throw everything in the closet or under the bed and consider the room clean, or scatter trash on the way to the dumpster. A quiet worrier will likely take a longer time and do a better job. She will carefully consider all possibilities and throw herself into the task with dedication. As an adult, the quiet worrier will discover that this trait is highly prized in most areas of business, although she will take more time than a fiery manager to finish a project.

As adults, quiet worriers are interested in details and may gravitate to the following vocations: mathematics, theoretical science, architecture, philosophy, writing, and diagnostic medicine. They have high standards of excellence that are difficult to live up to since they are perfectionists and take everything very seriously.

You may think that such careers are impossible aspirations for children on the Autism Spectrum, but remember: With the exception of severe cases, autistic children are intelligent and often brilliant and shouldn't have limits placed on them by the very people entrusted with the responsibility to help them grow into a healthy life.

The Predictable Introvert

Children who are predictable introverts have the most balanced of all temperaments. They have a delightful, dry sense of humor that shines through their façade of indifference at the least expected times, and teachers are never sure what to expect from day to day. They are friendly but reserved and pleasant to be with because they are easygoing and dependable. Very little affects them emotionally, and they seem to accept others' faults as easily as they accept their strengths.

Predictably introverted children experience feelings of inner comfort and show little interest in activities outside their minds. They are generally unaware of their environment and nothing much interests them without outside stimulation, such as that provided by other children. A solid relationship with peers is paramount to the predictable introvert's arousal of interest. Her apathy can be reduced by such interaction.

The predictably introverted child often appears uninterested in the activities of others around her, but she is actually stimulated by the play of her peers. Objects are of no interest to a predictable introvert; other children are. Through interaction with classmates of her age, she will be stirred by their interests, which will be reflected in relationships and behavior.

Like people of all temperaments, the predictable introvert has many fine qualities. These include being cheerful, objective, dependable, good-natured, faithful, practical, efficient, and neat.

Physically, predictable introverts are usually easy to spot, since many are overweight and indifferent although neat in appearance. They are often rather lazy and seem to drag themselves around instead of stepping. They sometimes seem to be moving in slow motion. Their glandular system is likely out of balance and provides an almost constant feeling of well-being. They are comfortable remaining in this state and are interested in what is happening in their environment, but have no desire to become involved in it.

What Can I Do?

If you believe your child is a predictable introvert, you must be direct in your conversation with her or she will lose interest. To stimulate a predictably introverted child, you must shock her into awareness by a sudden action, such as dropping a book on the floor or sharply clapping your hands once.

Another effective technique is to tell a story with great enthusiasm and then suddenly stop talking. Predictable introverts will be roused from their lethargy and want to know what happens next. You then continue the story with great enthusiasm, and if she has sunken back into herself, again stop abruptly and remain silent until she realizes something has changed. If she asks, "Why did you stop?" calmly tell her, "I wasn't sure you were listening. Would you like me to continue?" Of course, she will say "Yes" and the process is repeated. Soon the lapses into herself will become less frequent, and the time she spends listening will increase. This ability to focus will carry over into all of her activities and schoolwork.

Valuable teaching can be accomplished in this way. If you want a predictable introvert to do something, ask her to do you a favor. She will always want to help. We tend to use too many words when giving an instruction. When you ask your child to feed the dog, it isn't necessary to remind her that she didn't do it yesterday, or to detail how hungry Fido will be if he isn't fed at the same time every day. You probably already did that when you brought the dog home and discussed who does what in your pet's care and feeding. A simple "Laura, please feed the dog" is more effective than a long explanation of why this is important. Asking her to feed the dog should be one instruction. Asking her to empty the dishwasher should be another. Put the two together and one probably won't get done.

Most young girls—and many boys—like to help in the kitchen. This is a good time to enlist their assistance by asking them to bring you an ingredient or a spatula. Predictable introverts enjoy being helpful, and it's a great time for parent-child bonding. Many young children also like to help their mom with a new baby by fetching a diaper or talcum powder.

Predictable introverts—children and adults alike—think a great deal and conserve their physical energy. There is no use trying to drill something into them, but when they apply themselves they will work very hard to complete a project they are interested in. As adults, predictable introverts are good counselors, since one of their outstanding traits is the ability to listen to others. This positive trait is also clearly seen in predictably introverted children, who will listen without talking much. This clearly identifies a predictable introvert versus an artistic extrovert, who is more talkative and animated.

None of us, though, is on an even keel 100 percent of the time. We have our ups and downs, moods, and times when we are affected by outer circumstances that are beyond our control. All of these affect our personality and tend to be short-lived. They should not be mistaken for our true dispositions.

Pseudo-Temperaments

Therapists and teachers may find that there are times when children appear to show a change in temperament. This can usually be traced to a problem in the home. A normally calm child may suddenly become argumentative and aggressive although she shows no signs of being a true fiery manager. There may have been a disruption in her life, an ongoing problem between parents, or a change in familiar environment. A child who is carefree may become a pseudo–quiet worrier due to a great loss, perhaps the death of a friend, relative, or pet.

Parents, teachers, and therapists would do well to identify their own temperaments and learn what may be necessary to avoid one-sidedness in their lives. As is the case with children, particularly with those on the Autism Spectrum, we cannot hope to understand our own temperament intellectually. We have to know the characteristics of each temperament and, furthermore, how to work with what is missing. However, to comprehend how to stimulate the artistic extrovert, fiery manager, predictable introvert, or quiet worrier (including ourselves), we must call upon our perception or intuition.

It is logical to assume that to "fix" the problem of a specific temperament all we have to do is provide the child with the elements that are the opposite of her disposition. Actually, we have to appeal to the qualities that are present in the child. We have to kindle the flame that Socrates spoke of. To do this we have to reach her core of individuality and ask, "What is it that makes her different? What is it that arouses her interest?" This can be done only when a spiritual bond is established between the child and her parents, between the child and her therapist, and between the child and her teacher. Only then will what is necessary for the child be given to her.

Pseudo-temperaments due to outside influences are very common when a child is in a stressful situation, and they are easily identified once we know the characteristics of each disposition. Adults generally think that childhood is a carefree, stress-free time because kids don't have to pay the bills or deal with annoying coworkers. The truth is that children have a lot of stress in their lives. But it is not always verbalized; we therefore tend to think it does not exist. School is stressful; if they have a teacher they do not like or who appears not to like them, the stress factor is enormous. Part of the difficulty may be the temperament of the teacher.

TEACHERS AND TEMPERAMENTS

The most definitive works on this subject are *Teaching as a Lively Art* by Marjorie Spock and two of Rudolf Steiner's books, *A Modern Art of Education* and *The Essentials of Education*. This chapter will try to remove many of the mysteries of the temperaments. It is important for parents to recognize that adults also have temperaments with all of the characteristics of those listed for children. The temperaments of our children's teachers are rarely discussed or taken into consideration.

Teachers have a great responsibility to the children they have chosen to help along their individual paths. Their role is to educate in the truest sense of the word—to bring out of a child what is already within her and to help her grow by nurturing her innate abilities. We have to acknowledge the positive characteristics of teachers' temperaments and personalities that so greatly benefit children throughout their young lives while recognizing that, by virtue of their existence, teachers also have negative characteristics. The temperament of a teacher is impressed indelibly on the psyche of a child, and as adults we can often describe a particularly kind or cruel teacher we had years earlier.

Teachers have a great responsibility to the children they have chosen to help along their individual paths.

The connection between the temperaments of teachers and students helps explain why a few boys or girls are considered troublemakers by some teachers and hard workers by others. It may explain why Rachel feels Mrs. Johnson is mean while Brandon thinks she is the best teacher in school. This clashing of temperaments—and personalities—is often shown by not wanting to go to school or therapy or by becoming physically ill before school is about to start.

Teachers can be artistic extroverts, fiery managers, predictable introverts, or quiet worriers, with their own strengths, weaknesses, virtues, and vices. We need to ask, "What effect do teachers have on children?" Teachers who are unable to control their temperaments can do untold harm to sensitive children in the primary grades. Similarly, a therapist with a particular temperament can do irreparable damage to a child on the Autism Spectrum. However, I'm not suggesting that parents attempt to choose their children's teachers based on temperaments, because although it would be ideal, it's just not practical.

Teachers who are fiery managers may be loud and frightening to artistically extroverted children, who appear to forget the incident but bury it within their subconscious mind. A child is one large sense organ. She absorbs everything in her environment, and artistic extroverts are especially vulnerable to people, places, and things. Teachers who are fiery managers and who unconsciously instill fear in children may eventually cause permanent psychological damage to an artistically extroverted child.

Predictably introverted teachers are subtler in their influence; their suppressed spontaneity affects children and makes them restless. This is a form of smothering the creative impulse of young minds. Some say these teachers are "heavy" and that they make children nervous. This can have the effect of influencing the child even into adulthood. We know that the brain is an amazing storehouse of memories that are forgotten at the level of consciousness. As an adult, we may smell a familiar fragrance and remember suddenly that a predictably introverted teacher wore that fragrance as a perfume. This memory can produce a stifling, suffocating, or nervous reaction that is puzzling and frightening.

A teacher who is a quiet worrier may be so concerned about her own problems that she has difficulty relating to her students. She may be so self-centered that she deprives her students of warmth and interest. If she gives vent to her emotions in the classroom, the effect is to dampen the spiritual impulses of her students.

An artistically extroverted teacher confuses students by flitting from one subject or activity to another and, as a result, boys and girls may not have the will to follow through on a task or project that they have started or show enthusiasm for their work.

The important thing to remember is that although a person may be a very good teacher and able to educate students, her temperament is at all times influencing her and, through her, the children. It is of greatest importance that teachers primarily be a role model children want to emulate; the imparting of information is secondary. If this understanding is lacking, the educational process of centuries past will be repeated by ignoring the spiritual and emphasizing the mental, or by emphasizing the head and ignoring the heart. Establishing a relationship with a child means more than developing her potential and strengthening her spiritual nature; it means preparing her for her entire future.

The qualities of truth, beauty, and goodness that are conveyed to the child in her formative years will find expression in her adult life. For this reason, therapists, teachers, parents, and caregivers must be exemplary role models who live with ethics, morals, integrity, and an understanding of the relationship of body, mind, and spirit.

> It is of greatest importance that teachers primarily be a role model children want to emulate; the imparting of information is secondary. Establishing a relationship with a child means more than developing her potential and strengthening her spiritual nature; it means preparing her for her entire future.

Classroom Seating

Strange as it sounds because it breaks with tradition, it makes sense to seat children according to temperaments. For example, since fiery managers feel the need to hit, group them together in the back of the room where they can experience the discomfort they so generously bestow on others. They will soon realize that their actions are causing reactions and decide that they don't want to be punched; therefore, they won't punch anyone else. These disturbances are less disruptive to other students when fiery managers are seated in the rear of the room.

Artistic extroverts should be seated by the inside wall so they are not distracted by outside sounds and activity. When they see other children of a similar temperament darting about, they begin to identify it as a part of themselves, which has a subduing effect. As they see other boys and girls frequently sharpening their pencils or wanting to see the garbage truck as it passes the school, they begin to realize that roaming the room isn't the way a class is conducted. They see other students sitting at their desks and being attentive and soon begin to do the same. This has the effect of reducing or calming their need to be overly active.

Quiet worriers need to be attracted by outside activities, so they should be seated by the windows, where they are less apt to concentrate on themselves. When they are grouped together, children who are quiet worriers find they cannot compete with one another in terms of their sorrows, so their melancholy is less pronounced.

For example, we all know people who revel in their difficulties and want to dominate the conversation by describing the intimate details of their misfortune. A newcomer to the group may want to tell her story, but after listening to the tales of others, she realizes that her problem isn't all that serious. As she listens, she begins to commiserate with the person who is speaking. Children are no different. They will see that others have problems that cause distress and begin to think less about their own misery.

Predictable introverts are also less concerned with themselves if they are surrounded with like temperaments. They will be stirred out of their sluggishness if seated by windows, since they are sometimes overcome by inertia and need stimulation. If they see trucks, animals, or balloons, their interest perks up and they begin to listen to what the teacher is saying. They should also be close to the teacher, who can occasionally drop a book to jolt them back to awareness of their surroundings.

When we consider this unusual seating arrangement, we have to remember that we are grouping by temperaments, not by any other designation such as age or alphabetical last names. It's also important to understand that the children are responding through their spiritual nature, not through their personality. For example, it you tell a fiery manager to stop hitting, she won't because she can't, but if her innate sense of decency and compassion is stimulated, she will want to stop hitting because she senses that other children are in pain because of her actions.

Storytelling

Telling a story is one of the best ways to send a message without lecturing. If a character in a story is a soldier, there is usually a situation that requires bravery and courage. At this point, the teacher (or therapist) may look at the fiery managers, who are immediately caught up in the story and captivated by such daring. By including many changes of scene, the teacher appeals to an artistically extroverted child, whose mind quickly visualizes and grasps the story.

Telling a story is one of the best ways to send a message without lecturing.

Since children who are quiet worriers love detail, stories should include precise descriptions of many objects and people, including color and size. This approach helps a child with this temperament to forget her miseries as the storyteller weaves a tale of challenges, misfortunes, and victories that envelop the characters.

Predictable introverts listlessly listen to stories. To gain the attention of a predictably introverted child, the storyteller should stop suddenly in the telling of the high point of the suspense, to the surprise of everyone. The predictable introvert is more affected than the artistic extrovert, fiery manager, and quiet worrier because this snaps her out of her somnambulant state, and she looks at the teacher in wonder and surprise. After the storyteller has her attention, the story continues and the predictable introvert listens—until the next time.

A skilled teacher finds or writes stories that contain all these scenarios and looks at each group of temperaments as she tells the tale in several different voices and accents. She needs to add a lot of animation and exaggerated physical movements and then ask questions, focusing on each temperament to bring every child into the group dynamic.

Teachers are remembered for decades. We either think of them fondly for their happy, smiling face, obvious affection for all children, and love of teaching, or we recall their harsh voice, penchant for punishment, and unpleasant personality. Teachers can make or break a child. If you feel there is a conflict between your child and her teacher, it might help to have a conference. Now that you know about your child's temperament, you may discover that the teacher needs a little education as well.

SUMMARY

An understanding of the four temperaments is one more key to unlocking the hidden world of children's behavior, those both with and without a neurological disorder. You may ask why this subject is included in a book about autism, Attention Deficit Disorder, and Asperger's, and the answer is simple: All children, including those with autism, are influenced by the temperament with which they were born. People are independent entities who are part of a universal group. All of humankind can be separated into the four dispositions: the artistic extrovert (sanguine), the fiery manager (choleric), the quiet worrier (melancholic), and the predictable introvert (phlegmatic). Each of us is a combination of temperaments, with one being predominant.

Comparing one unique child to another unique child is a gross injustice to each. Classroom seating according to temperaments appears to be a revolutionary approach, but when you think about it, it is logical. A child who is easily distracted should obviously not be seated next to the windows where she sees students, birds, trees, and planes. She is stimulated. School is forgotten. Why would it not be? Rather than recommend Ritalin, move her to another part of the room with the other artistic extroverts.

Although all children are different, they share one thing: the love of fairy tales. In the next chapter, we will explore why these timeless stories are of such importance in the life of a child.

CHAPTER 9

*F*airy Tales

The Hidden Truths

*F*airy tales probably provoke thoughts of fantasy or fiction, yet these stories of values, virtues, and goodness are meant to help children develop meaningful images of spiritual qualities. Thousands of years before the printed word appeared, legends, morals, and skills were taught through the art of storytelling, the power of speech. In all cultures, fairy stories were passed down from elders to children to assure that truths were kept alive in their minds and hearts. Aesop (619–564 BC) wrote his fables in which animals are the main characters of stories that teach virtues and integrity. Aesop's Fables are known and cherished throughout the world.

The brothers Jakob and Wilhelm Grimm are the most well-known and prolific writers and collectors of these stories, although they never used the word "fairy" in their writings, since very few of the stories mentioned fairies. Through their search for ancient beliefs and tales from other cultures, they found that spiritual beings were described in a veiled manner and that these stories were more than mere entertainment.

Common sense would have us ask: "Why have fairy tales that are so filled with fear, violence, fighting, and puzzling events lasted for so many centuries? Is there more than meets the eye, or are they simply scary or silly stories to occupy a child's mind? There must be something more to them than a make-believe story."

There is. Children accept the messages of fairy tales without question, as if they know intuitively that these stories are guiding them to become better people through kindness, generosity, compassion, and goodness. They may not be familiar with these words, but they do know the difference between right and wrong—the basis of all fairy tales and fables. Virtues and vices never change, and the battle of good versus evil will always be part of the growth and learning process of humanity. Fairy tales contain them all.

Fairy tales tell about reality, although it may not be obvious. That's the best part about fairy tales—morals and messages are hidden in a fascinating story with many turns of plot. The stories describe spiritual truths in visual concepts that children clearly understand.

Children on the Autism Spectrum love fairy tales. Although they are aware of being different in reality, they often live in an inner world of fantasy where they are no different from their peers. Children enjoy using their imagination, and so fairy tales are the perfect vehicle for introducing them to morals, virtues, and the possibility of overcoming obstacles and hardship—all of which are extremely valuable in their challenging young lives.

THE POLARITIES OF FAIRY TALES

Fairy tales clearly tell us about the polarity of good and bad in human beings and the struggle between the material and the spiritual elements of life. These lessons should always be part of a young child's learning process, because it is only by knowing evil that we can know its opposite.

The polarity of good and evil is shown in fairy tales through themes such as darkness and light, the wicked stepmother and the guardian angel, and the dragon and the knight. Light dispels darkness, and children learn that goodness overpowers evil. This lesson is absorbed and children will remember that those who perpetrate bad deeds can be punished. Once we understand the hidden meanings of fairy tales, they become clear to our intellect, which always tries to dissect, analyze, and judge. Intellect keeps us bound to the material world, while fairy tales introduce us, metaphorically, to the world of spirit.

Often in fairy tales, a person feels totally alone and in despair, yet comfort and encouragement appear in the form of a guardian angel, a nature spirit, or a voice offering hope. Most children on the Autism Spectrum can easily relate to the isolation of main characters in fairy tales and rejoice in their triumph over impossible odds. These stories invariably contain the elements of life. Children also learn that they are never truly alone and that if they lead a virtuous life they will find their way home. This is a common theme in fairy stories, one that is comforting to a child. In actuality, "home" may mean something far more than simply returning to a house, because these stories tell the tale of strife, redemption, and return to one's source.

OBJECTIONS TO FAIRY TALES

Because the average person did not—or could not—read until the nineteenth century, young people were educated through allegories, sagas, legends, folk tales, and fairy stories. All of these verbal recitations created pictures and images that were assimilated by children and that strengthened their spiritual forces. As humanity became more intellectually oriented, the storyteller was regarded as ignorant and uneducated. The truths of life were ridiculed by academics who were now too well educated to believe such nonsense. They scoffed at fairy-tale wisdom and Aesop's fables. They proclaimed, "Animals don't talk. How absurd!" Supposedly, we were enlightened.

As a result, humanity gradually became hardened to the beauty and genius of fairy-tale wisdom. Spirituality was stifled in its attempt to guide life, and people began reacting to situations instead of responding to them. People became indifferent to the sufferings of others and gained riches by thoughtlessly ruining others financially. They spoke harshly, as the soft-spoken words of sensitivity were muffled. Objective and analytical thinking dissected fairy tales and pronounced them worthless. After all, they were now "educated," and talk of one's spirit had no place in life.

Today, some "enlightened" people want to remove fairy tales from schools and libraries, complaining they are too intense. Meanwhile, many children play harsh, chaotic video games that are meant to imitate life. In our high-tech society, fairy tales are often scoffed at, along with the arts. They are considered old-fashioned and useless by some people; however, they are exactly the opposite. We need them more than ever in our hectic, materialistic lives. Disregarding fairy tales would eliminate a rich source of moral literature, where children relate to the struggles between good and evil. Children learn that the anger, greed, stubbornness, or arrogance in the stories is a part of them, and that saying or doing things related to those qualities has consequences.

The stories teach that we have two sides to our personality and are capable of the greatest compassion as well as the greatest harm. The "violence" of these teaching tools is simply a way of depicting universal challenges and the dichotomy within each of us. Children learn that there is good and bad in the world and that there will always be a struggle between the two. They absorb the message that if they are honest, sincere, and strive to help others, good will always triumph.

There are esoteric truths hidden in fairy tales, and by saying that children shouldn't be exposed to the stories because they are "violent," we are denying young people practical knowledge of all the ups and downs of life, which will prepare them for every eventuality up to and beyond death. We do a disservice if we try to "protect" them from the idea that they will come into contact with people who may not be as pure as they are and whose motives may not be in their best interests. Children need to know these facts of life, which teach such valuable lessons in a way that touches their inner self and sensitive nature.

> We do a disservice if we try to "protect" them from the idea that they will come into contact with people who may not be as pure as they are and whose motives may not be in their best interests.

There is a remnant in each of us that recognizes the truth of these stories. It may be ignored, but it is deep in the imagination of all people who want to better themselves by seeking truth. Storytelling has never died out. In fact, it is making a comeback as people realize the depth and wisdom of tales that convey messages of hope, liberation, and success.

It's always nice to read and tell stories of a beautiful princess who met a handsome prince and lived happily ever after in wedded bliss. Apparently, these royals never experienced any hardships or confrontations—no darker side of life. Some people prefer only sweet and tender stories that leave out the symbolic witches, goblins, wicked stepmothers, and magicians. If children hear only stories that have no conflict, no need for decisions, and no challenges, a false sense of protection will cause them to lack the resolve they should have learned through fairy tales.

Nothing is one-sided. To tell stories of only good, happy, and perfect times is the most far-fetched fairy tale of all. The messages in these stories are seeds of wisdom that sink into the subconscious mind, strengthening the essence of a child in ways that will be called upon as he experiences life's twists, turns, and temptations. Fairy tales invariably contain the elements of life.

SIGNIFICANCE OF SYMBOLS

Fairy tales tell us in numerous ways of our search for personal improvement, an adventure fraught with obstacles, the overcoming of danger, tasks, and circuitous routes to conquering all odds and victoriously finding our way home at last. In graphic images, children learn how morals, ethics, and virtues triumph over vices that we all will encounter. Stories may begin in a house where an adult subjects children to emotional, verbal, or physical abuse. The house is symbolically the world. Children live in a world filled with unpleasantness, yet they manage to retain their wonderful innocence and naiveté that guides them as they search for something meaningful.

As they start their journey, children in the stories may decide to rest and eventually fall into a sleep that lasts for years. We all do the same thing as we begin any journey of development that starts with the thought, "There must be something more to life than this." This recurring thought has been described as Divine Discontent, or our spiritual nature striving to make itself known.

In other words, we begin our individual search for "something more." We make progress. We falter. We fall into a symbolic sleep that may last for a few days, weeks, months, years, or a lifetime. We wake and begin the process again, each time further along the path.

This search is no different from that of children on the Autism Spectrum who are constantly, unconsciously searching for a balance in their lives. They make gains, they slip, and make more gains. It is an ongoing process of growth, as a child begins to take control of his life and his thoughts. His will to think, speak, and act is strengthened each time he slips and moves forward once again. This persistent struggle is a common theme in fairy tales, and children of all ages relate to it in their own way.

We begin to see this clearly as we become familiar with fairy tales and the identification with our lower selves, or animal instincts. Many tales have beasts that have to be conquered, and the animal is often transformed through the kindness of a human being. The "beast" represents the animal part of our nature that must be tamed in order for us to become moral, honest, and kind. Our inner beast must be conquered if we are to become the best person we can be. Often a wise person enters the story in various guises that may include old men, angels, fairies, gnomes, and dwarves. This wise person serves as a guide who shows the way. Children understand the message that people who are selfish, cruel, immoral, and arrogant will not prevail.

Children love fairy tales because they identify with the characters, who are trying to find their way in this world. Our world is confusing, chaotic, and unintelligible to children up to about the age of seven. After that, they are more familiar with their surroundings and the physical world. Around the age of ten, they feel—and become—more independent. Around fourteen, their thinking powers begin to develop as they prepare for adulthood. Because of this natural evolution, fairy tales were designed for different age groups according to the children's ability to comprehend and absorb the meanings.

> Children love fairy tales because they identify with the characters, who are trying to find their way in this world.

TALES RECOMMENDED BY AGE

The ages of children in fairy stories are important, as they correspond to the stages of spiritual development through which each child progresses. These tales are written for children according to their ability to imagine, understand, and take the morals into their hearts and minds. Children with autism, Asperger's Syndrome, and ADHD go through periods of mental, emotional, and physical development, although they may be different from children who have no disabilities. Because of their innate intelligence and sensitive spiritual nature, they understand the lessons of fairy tales, perhaps more readily than do "typical" children.

Fairy tales are written for various age groups, according to the child's ability to understand the message. Young three-year olds like simple stories with a straightforward moral, while older children are able to visualize the characters, action, and ultimate outcome. All fairy tales tell a story of good and bad, hardship and triumph. These states of mind and activity change with age. Adversity for a preschooler is different from what it is for a teenager or an adult, so it is handled differently. As we mature, we go through many experiences of trials and hardships as well as joy.

The following list contains suggested fairy tales based on a child's age, and was compiled by Joan Almon, past Chair of the Waldorf Early Childhood Association of North America:

Suggested Stories for Three-Year Olds

- "Goldilocks and the Three Bears"
- "Little Louse and Little Flea"
- "Little Madam"
- "Sweet Porridge"
- "The Gingerbread Man"
- "The Johnny Cake"
- "The Mitten"
- "The Turnip"

Suggested Stories for Four- and Five-Year Olds

- "The Pancake Mill"
- "The Three Billy Goats Gruff"
- "The Three Little Pigs"
- "The Shoemaker and the Elves"
- "The Wolf and the Seven Goats"

Suggested Stories for Five- and Six-Year Olds

- "Breman Town Musicians"
- "Frog Prince"
- "Golden Goose"
- "Hansel and Gretel"
- "Hut in the Forest"
- "Little Red Cap"
- "Little Briar Rose"
- "Mother Hulda"
- "Princess and the Flaming Castle"
- "The Queen Bee"
- "Rumpelstiltskin"
- "Snow Maiden"
- "Snow White and the Seven Dwarves"
- "Snow White and Rose Red"
- "Spindle, Shuttle and Needle"
- "Star Money"
- "The Donkey"
- "The Seven Ravens"

Stories Suggested for Preparation for First Grade

- "Beauty and the Beast"
- "Cinderella"
- "Featherlight"
- "Jorinde and Joringel"
- "Little Brother and Little Sister"
- "The Handless Maiden"

- "The Land of the Blue Flower"
- "The Seven-Year-Old Wonder Book"
- "The Six Swans"
- "The Wonderful Adventures of Nils"
- "Rapunzel: A Fairy Tale"
- "Sam Luckless: The Unlucky Lad"

This listing based on age groups may seem unfamiliar, but when we read the stories and relate them to our own children of different ages, it makes perfect sense. As a child matures, his feelings, emotions, and thoughts need to be stimulated in ways different from when he was younger. He becomes aware of polarities and the negative and positive in all things and all people.

VIRTUES AND VICES

As early as the fourth century, the Seven Virtues and Seven Vices were identified and described as the battle between good and evil, where virtue overcomes vice. The Seven Vices include pride; greed, or avarice; lust; anger; gluttony; envy; and sloth. The Seven Virtues are humility; mercy; chastity, or continence; patience, or meekness; temperance; love of God, neighbor, and enemy; and fortitude, or courage. Virtues and vices are present throughout many fairy tales.

In some tales, a princess is locked away in a dark tower until rescued by a prince. This is the path of the human being who has to go through darkness before he can see the light. In other words, one has to experience the dark side of life before one can emerge as a truly enlightened human being. One cannot truly appreciate the light until one has survived the darkness.

Lessons for living a virtuous life have been handed down by word of mouth from generation to generation. All fairy tales have a spiritual component that tells of the need to be kind to others. This can be done only by abandoning a life based on selfishness, greed, envy, hate, and other brutish, negative thoughts. As this is an ongoing process throughout life, one gradually replaces heartless, unfeeling, and inhumane behavior with that behavior is kind, helpful, caring, and positive. This transformation ultimately brings one happiness, which is the message of fairy tales.

Fairy tales awaken slumbering virtues in children. Imagination is piqued as their fantasies create images of battles, ogres, dragons, heroes, victory, and defeat. These images and fantasies teach morals and virtues as nothing else can, because fairy stories were written for children to absorb the messages deep into their spirit, which identifies with truth, beauty, and goodness. Boys and girls learn how to face problems that confront every person.

The polarities of virtues and vices, or of good and bad, are clearly represented in the story of the three brothers and the queen bee. It also shows the inherent innocence and goodness of young children versus the "worldliness" of older people. Please see the inset "The Queen Bee" for a description of this fairy tale.

IMPORTANT ROLES OF FAIRY TALES

Fairy tales are for boys and girls, all social classes, and all cultures. Every person can relate to the stories of hardship and adversity, of good and wicked people. Every child is satisfied when a fairy tale reaches a conclusion they can relate to at some level.

Obviously, these stories are entertaining. When told in a group, a closeness develops within that group, and when told by a parent, there is a closeness and bonding between parent and child. The parent is a protector, and the group serves the same purpose.

A constant message in fairy tales is that we are never abandoned. If we persist in our struggle through life's challenges, we will succeed. This is supportive and encouraging to children on the Spectrum, who are frequently frustrated by their limitations and feel no one understands them.

Children with autism or Asperger's Syndrome often cannot relate to— or recognize—facial expressions such as surprise and fear. These are two emotions that can be greatly exaggerated by the storyteller for effect while describing action that is taking place in a fairy tale. This may help children identify and better understand facial expressions and body language in their everyday lives.

As the child becomes involved in the story, his heart beats faster and his blood flows more quickly. Stories with twists and turns of plot have the effect of creating tension and release within the child as he, for example, imagines the unarmed hero confronted with a fire-eating dragon. His muscles are affected and strengthened as they alternately tense and relax. Motor skills are also affected as the muscles are invigorated, even to a slight degree. This complicated process takes place in a split second and is repeated throughout the exciting parts of the story.

As the story progresses, a great deal depends upon the storyteller's ability to arouse children as they are taken on an emotional rollercoaster: frightened one moment, relieved the next, as the hero or heroine faces, and

The Queen Bee

Fairy tales teach a reverence for animals and insects. When we look at nature with respect, we see the amazing intelligence of the plant and animal kingdoms as well as that of humankind. Children or adults who have a tyrannical nature enjoy destroying such creativity instead of experiencing the awe of creation. From fairy tales, children learn compassion and appreciation for all living things. The sadistic pleasure some children feel at pulling wings off of flies or uprooting plants will intensify in proportion to their age unless checked. This impulse can lead to rage and destruction in people who have little or no control over their emotions and no respect for themselves.

Tales such as "The Queen Bee" appeal to a child's sensitivity and address this lack of respect. This classic tells of three brothers who are sons of an elderly king. They are wandering through the woods when they come upon an anthill. The two older brothers want to tear apart the anthill but are stopped by the third, youngest brother, named Simpleton. Then, the two decide to kill and roast ducks swimming in a pond, but again are prevented from this carnage by their brother. Finally, they decide to destroy a beehive, but once again are stopped from their cruelty by Simpleton.

They continue their journey and approach a castle. Next to it is a stable with horses made of stone. They go into the castle and enter a small room where an old man sits at a table. He tells them that the castle was bewitched by a spell that is turning everything into stone, a metaphor for being enclosed in the animal or mineral kingdoms where the creative spirit is held captive. The only thing that can save him and the brothers is if each completes a task. If they don't complete even the smallest part of the task, they would be turned to stone.

He picks one of the brothers who wanted to kill the ants and tells him his task is to find 1,000 of the princess's pearls that had been buried. He can find only 999, so he is turned to stone. Simpleton says he will try, and the ants that he had saved from destruction lead him to the pearls, and he recovers all 1,000 of them.

The task of the second cruel brother is to dive into the lake and find the key to the door of the princess's bedroom. He is unable to find it and he, too, is turned to stone. But when Simpleton dives into the lake, the ducks that he had saved from a fiery death lead him to the key, and his life is spared.

Now Simpleton is told he has to identify which of the king's three daughters had eaten honey before going to sleep. The other two girls had eaten sugar or syrup. Simpleton does not know how he could solve this problem, but just then, the queen bee of the hive he had protected flies into the room and directly to the princess who had eaten honey. It hovers over her lips, and Simpleton kisses the beautiful princess, who then awakens, and the entire castle, including his brothers, is released from its enchantment.

Soon after, the brothers' father dies of old age. Simpleton becomes king and marries the princess he had wakened from the spell. His two brothers marry the other two sisters, and they all live happily ever after.

Children with ADD and Asperger's easily grasp the message that compassion and kindness reap rewards, and haughtiness, cruelty, and arrogance will be our eventual downfall. They learn that actions have consequences.

is saved from, one crisis after another. As we tell fairy tales, our delivery—our inflection and animation—makes children come alive and draws them into the plot.

All fairy tales convey a moral and may include harshness or even cruelty as a means of teaching a lesson, which is far different from the gratuitous violence shown in movies or on television. Most important, fairy tales stimulate the imagination, which is slowly fading in children of today as they play with toys that require them to follow instructions instead of making up a game themselves. Similarly, talking dolls that say phrases when a string is pulled or a button is pushed may discourage a little girl from being creative in her play. Too many young people spend their free time watching television and playing computer games. All of these energize the mind, body, and emotions, but none of them stimulates a child's spiritual nature as fairy stories do.

Imagination is the connecting link between the hemispheres of the brain, between the left/logical/linear side and the right/creative/artistic side. It is the bridge between intellect and intuition. The intellect of children is being stimulated in our high-tech society out of proportion to the creative aspect. Computers, electronic gadgetry, and many toys are designed for left-brain activity, and to balance this, we need imagination and imagery. Fairy tales provide an imaginative release from structure while conveying valuable teachings. Books and stories in general allow each child to create his own mental image of the characters and their surroundings.

Fairy tales have traditionally been part of growing up. They are stories that describe real spiritual events that are part of humankind. Children identify with the hero of the story; they absorb the message of fighting evil and being a prince who wins the fair maiden after slaying the dragon or overcoming some other adversity. These lessons—but not necessarily a particular story—will stay with them into their adult years and form the basis for making decisions. Fairy tales strengthen the inner lives of children, which would be weakened if boys and girls were prevented from hearing them. They would be unable to make firm and wise decisions based on courage and perception as they reach adulthood.

Fairy tales are the same around the world for one simple reason: Humanity's search for betterment is within each of us, with the struggles, challenges, and successes that confront us all. Beauty, truth, and goodness exist side by side with body, mind, and spirit. These tales always encompass the two basic elements of life—good and bad. Someone is always saved from the clutches of a witch or some other personification of evil.

These stories should be told (not read) to children without explanation or analysis because the personality of the storyteller might otherwise taint

> Humanity's search for betterment is within each of us, with the struggles, challenges, and successes that confront us all. Beauty, truth, and goodness exist side by side with body, mind, and spirit.

the message and lessons being conveyed. Explanations aren't necessary because children create visual images that are individual and highly personal. These images are archetypes of the characters that face all of the challenges, obstacles, and rewards of a spirit-directed life. Although the goal is the same for every human being, the method of attaining that goal varies from person to person. The storyteller's explanation will be different from the one visualized by the child.

It is important that children have activities to build their inner lives of thinking, feeling, and willing. Their spiritual nature needs nourishment as much as their physical body does. If the spirit of a child is not filled with positive, healthy, and virtuous images, his mind will be filled with crass, unimaginative bits of information that flood into, and throughout, his mind, eliminating the truth, beauty, and goodness that build strong character.

The story of the wolf and the seven kids tells how young children can be easily deceived by someone determined to do harm and how important it is to obey one's parents. Please see the inset, "The Wolf and the Seven Goats."

What Can I Do?

All children should be read to and told stories, especially fairy tales. Telling stories is the best way of reaching children and capturing their attention, but if your young child is very hyperactive, you may have to be flexible in your expectations, at least for a while. Reading with great animation and inflection is effective for a child who needs to focus on something—in this case, on the images. Children sit wide-eyed with anticipation when a story is told with feeling and inflection, regardless of how many times they have heard it before.

Sitting side by side in a comfortable chair with a child gives him a sense of security; he can feel solidity on both sides and is not as apt to wriggle or want to wander about the room. If your child is older, sit next to each other on the couch. If he is tactilely defensive, this provides an opportunity for you to move slightly closer during the reading. Emphasize a point by quickly and lightly touching his leg or arm. If you do this, he does not have time to register an objection and gradually learns that there is nothing to be afraid of. This is an excellent strategy for a child with Asperger's and is a good first step towards massage, since it helps to reduce his aversion to touch.

When your child asks if a fairy tale is true, a lengthy, complex answer is not necessary. At some level he already knows about right and wrong, so it is enough to say that the story is telling us about how we have to make choices; making good choices may not be easy, but it is the best thing to do.

The Wolf and the Seven Goats

The story about the wolf and the seven kids describes the conflicting emotions of seven young goats whose mother had to fetch wood in the forest, leaving them alone and vulnerable. She gave strict instructions to be on guard against the wolf, who was very good at disguising himself to deceive children. However, she said, they will recognize him by his rough voice and black paws.

When their mother left, like all children do, the kids felt a sense of freedom from parental control. They felt they couldn't possibly be fooled and that their mother was exaggerating the danger. They were sure they were capable of handling the wolf, should he appear.

Soon, there was a knock at the door and a low, gravelly voice said, "Open the door. It's your mother." The wolf did not fool the kids at all, and they refused to open the door. But the wolf didn't give up. He thought of a devious way to disguise his voice, so he ate chalk, which made his voice soft. Then he went back to the goats' house and tried again.

"Open the door," he said. "It is your mother with treats for you." The voice sounded like their mother's and they almost opened the door, but the wolf had laid his black paws on the window, and the kids said they were not fooled because their mother didn't have black feet.

Still determined to get in the house and devour the baby goats for lunch, he put flour on his paws, and when the children saw his white feet and heard his soft voice, they opened the door. Suddenly, the wolf charged into the room, taking them by surprise. His deceitful and evil plan to seduce the children had worked. The young goats scattered and tried to hide, but the wolf found six of them

and swallowed them whole. He then walked into the forest and fell into a deep sleep. The youngest kid, who had hidden in a large clock case, ran into the forest to tell his mother the terrible news.

Their mother had such love for her children and anger towards the evil wolf that she decided to take desperate measures. She took scissors, a needle and thread, and gathered six rocks. She found the wolf in a deep sleep and cut open his belly. She removed her babies and replaced them with the rocks and then sewed up the wolf.

When he woke, he stumbled to the well for a drink, and, laden with such weight, fell into the water and drowned. At home, the mother and her seven healthy baby goats sang and danced because they were all safe and sound. All the kids had learned a valuable lesson that they would never forget, and, as in most fairy tales, they lived happily ever after.

What Is the Meaning of This Story?

Fairy tales often tell about deceit and greed. The message is that we need to be discerning and able to sense when people are lying or interested only in themselves. A common theme is that children disobey their parents (usually the mother) and become involved in uncomfortable or potentially dangerous situations. The moral is that it is wiser to listen to our parents than to indulge our whims—an issue applicable to all children, but especially to those on the Autism Spectrum.

The first part of the story contains elements recognizable even to three- or four-year-old children, all of whom have been told by their father or mother not to do something, but may have been encouraged and talked into it and ended up in trouble—or in this case, in the wolf.

Every character in a fairy tale is an aspect of each of us. We have good aspects that we allow to be perceived by others and other aspects that may be kept hidden, either because we aren't aware they are part of our psyche or because we are aware but don't want to accept our negative side.

In this story, the kids listen to their mother (their innate wisdom) and are strong in their obedience until the wolf (temptation, vices, evil) uses devious means (greed, avarice) to seduce them into opening the door. At that point, the kids try to escape and hide from their poor decisions, to little avail. Six of the seven are swallowed whole and find themselves in a dark, confined place.

The seventh is the youngest and not yet tainted by worldly things and temptations. He senses evil and eludes the fate of his siblings by seeking protection in the clock case and is able to tell his mother what happened. When the mother goat finds the wolf sleeping, she cuts open his belly and retrieves her kids, unharmed. She then replaces them with stones that eventually cause his demise.

The moral is that although we may believe we are safe from deceit, treachery, and harm, we must never become complacent, for this leads to carelessness and opening the door to evil. If we are strong enough to resist temptation and seek a place or state of grace, in time (as represented by the clock) we will be reunited with our mother (wisdom) and be able to help others through the lessons of our experiences. The wolf has been outwitted (justice), and he drowns as a result of his gluttony (vice).

Children can relate to such stories involving disobedience, discipline, and a mother who cares about them and trusts them to do the right thing. They know there are times when they won't do the right thing. In the end, mother in all her wisdom and experience is still there as a loving and nurturing figure.

When telling a fairy tale you should start by saying that you're going to tell a story that will show that everyone at some time feels lost and frightened, but that we can overcome and deal with anything that we might meet. Tell him a fairy tale and ask him to let you know when someone is faced with a choice. Ask him if the characters in the story made a good decision and why he feels that way.

Exercises After Listening to Fairy Tales

Children think in images as you tell them a fairy tale. Pictures flood into their minds as they "see" what they are hearing. There are several creative ways to stimulate a child's imagination and strengthen the message of the story after you've finished telling him the tale.

After telling a fairy tale, ask your child to draw a picture of or write about what he just experienced. This is much more effective than simply asking what he felt or if he liked the story. When using an art form, children are more in touch with their creative nature and the ability to express themselves. While listening to the stories, they are flooded with images, which can then be represented through painting, writing, role playing, and more.

Turn to page 275 of Part Two for activities that will strengthen your child's memory and artistic expression after he has finished listening to a fairy tale.

SUMMARY

Fairy tales are an antidote to the harshness of everyday life with which all of us are involved in one way or another. Simply by being alive and living on this planet, we cannot possibly escape materiality; however, it doesn't have to govern our lives or those of our children. With an understanding of the meaning of fairy tales, we can help children "find their way" through stories and creative arts.

As you can see, fairy tales serve a vital purpose in the development of children's spiritual nature; they're not just silly stories. They teach valuable lessons that children will remember throughout life and will help them face difficult situations with awareness. We need to keep fairy tales alive in the hearts, minds, and spirits of all children so their resolve and discernment will be strengthened.

Fairy tales are noted for their wisdom and ability to teach right from wrong, often by a test that will determine the outcome of an adventure. Many stories feature the unpleasant results of encounters with unsavory characters. Eventually, goodness triumphs and children learn lessons. People who object to the "violence" in fairy tales ignore the value of these life lessons, which have been handed down from generation to generation for thousands of years.

When we remove the elements of temptation, vices, evil, seduction, and ultimate rescue from these time-honored stories, we fail to teach our young children about morals and virtues in ways that sink into their spirit and remain with them forever. Truths that are learned are never forgotten when they become part of a child's sensitive nature.

The recurring themes of a guardian angel or a wise king, seemingly impossible odds, and the surmounting of obstacles are comforting to children with ADD, ADHD, autism, and Asperger's, who are often wracked with stress, frustration, and fears. Fairy tales provide an imaginative, creative way of teaching morals and encouraging children who may be absorbed in their own sensitive, isolated world.

In the following chapter, you will learn of another way to reach the inner nature of children on the Autism Spectrum: through music.

CHAPTER 10

The Latent Power of Music

Music is different from other art forms, many of which have models in the physical world. An artist may create in an attempt to replicate an earthly object or image, but we have to *experience* music. It is often a spiritual experience that has to be sensed; we cannot touch, see, or smell it—we have to *feel* it.

Arthur Schopenhaurer (1788–1860), a German philosopher and psychologist, wrote extensively on a variety of topics including the aesthetics, or appreciation of the beauty, of art, including music. He stated that the role of music is to portray the essence of the cosmos.

Our body is musical; consider the heartbeat, respiration, and other physical cycles. We are primed to respond to rhythm, and children with psycho-neuro disorders are "ready" for a therapist to bring this experience to the surface and into their consciousness. If we are to believe Socrates' statement that "Education is the kindling of a flame, not the filling of a vessel," we must also believe that there is something latent within a child that will blossom and emerge with the proper "kindling" or encouragement.

Through everyday activities, neurotypical children will experience rhythm in a way that others may not. They are frequently exposed to music in some form, perhaps the car radio, a stereo in their room, or an iPod. They move instinctively to this rhythm, where most children with psycho-neuro disorders, particularly autism, may like music but have little or no sense of rhythm. They are usually unable to "feel" the beat unless someone demonstrates it by patting their back or leg in time to the music.

This chapter will help you in selecting the most effective musical compositions to use with your child. You will learn about the amazing potential for development and progress when music is incorporated into a therapeutic program for your child. To understand why music is so powerful and respected, we should first look at its long and varied history.

HISTORY OF MUSIC AND SPIRITUALITY

Throughout recorded history, music has played an important part in all cultures. Egyptian drawings on monuments show seated men holding instruments, and a man, apparently the conductor, with his arms raised, standing in front of them. Historically, music has been used to appease angry gods and to ward off evil spirits, and it has been used in religious ceremonies to create a mood of reverence and unity. Even today, music is a vital part of the worship services of virtually all religions. For the Aztecs, the chief function of music was to obtain mystical communication with a particular god. We are close to the same ritual when we go to a place of worship to sing and pray. Music has a fundamental spiritual quality that brings people together.

The first divine messages were given in musical form—the Psalms of David, the Song of Solomon, the Bathas of Zoroaster, and the Gita of Krishna, who was always shown playing the flute. Pythagoras compared the seven-stringed lyre of Apollo to the human body, and taught that each note generated a specific tone, or vibration, to which the body and mind responded. Hippocrates, the Father of Medicine, is said to have taken his patients to the Temple of Aesculapius, the Greco-Roman god of healing, where music was accepted as a valid form of healing.

For thousands of years, people lived with the knowledge that the arts were a gift from God and a privilege to experience. Socrates, Martin Luther, Darwin, Plato, and Kepler were a few of the respected men who have spoken of the importance of music in our lives. Until relatively recent times, people felt music was sacred and placed musicians in a loft, with the audience below, to honor their standing. Today the audience soars above the orchestra, which is in a pit. At one time, when people lived in a state of awe and closeness to their spiritual source, instruments were created in an attempt to capture the voices of angels.

In the twelfth century, physicians prescribed music as a healing agent for their patients, and musicians were asked to play in orphanages to calm unruly children and to help develop their talents. This led to the creation of children's choirs during the medieval days, when troubadours were honored guests of monasteries. The Church obviously retained its knowledge of the healing power of music when, in the fourteenth century, it stationed choirs around the dome of St. Peter's Basilica to sing in an attempt to end the plague.

Music in The Middle Ages and Beyond

During the medieval period, when many famous cathedrals of Europe were built, the well-known French Cathedral of Chartres was begun in 1194 and dedicated in 1260. As the church was being built, orchestras played for the workers because it was felt that an atmosphere of fellow-

The Stages of Life

Rhythm exists in the developmental stages of human life, each of which is seven years. We have all heard about the various stages of childhood, especially "The Terrible Twos." I like to call the stage of these toddlers "The Terrific Twos" since these little people are in the process of constant learning and testing your patience. Knowledge of these developmental stages can help you to understand why children react and respond the way they do and gives invaluable insight into the most loving way to bring up a child.

0–6

From birth through age six, a child is a sponge, absorbing everything she hears, sees, or smells. During these formative years, she learns by imitating the people in her environment. She learns morals and virtues. She is developing her senses and begins to externalize her spiritual qualities, showing her love for painting, dancing, and music.

7–13

Around the age of six or seven, her second teeth appear, and a major shift in consciousness takes place. Her mind begins to develop, as she begins to understand the important differences between right and wrong. She starts putting into practice everything she has learned up to this time. She is beginning to apprehend the differences between memory training and thinking, and between objective events and their subjective causes. She is learning the law of cause and effect.

14–20

At the age of fourteen, at puberty, a child really begins to understand science. Until then, it's a gray area with basic ideas and thoughts that have formed, but the mechanics of science still elude her. At the age of twenty-one, she is considered an adult.

ship and cooperation was created with the music, and the walls of the cathedral absorbed sound. If an argument did occur, all work stopped until it was resolved. Families traveled great distances to watch, listen, and enjoy a picnic lunch while observing the cathedral being built, in the belief that the combination of a spiritual endeavor and music created a healing environment, similar to that of Lourdes today.

As the great universities were built in the fourteenth, fifteenth, and sixteenth centuries, humanity became more materialistic, and respect for music faded as people became increasingly logical and intellectual. Because music cannot be analyzed or seen in the usual ways, the intellect can have difficulty understanding it; it was therefore deemed unimportant.

Fortunately for the world, many great musicians were born in the seventeenth, eighteenth, and nineteenth centuries. They wrote brilliant and moving compositions that will never die. As if to counter the effects of this shift to intellectualism, musical masters appeared and left a legacy of their work at a time when it was needed most. Their great classics created a natural balance of the literal/creative, material/spiritual, and left/right hemispheres of the brain.

Fine classical music touches our spirit; it stimulates imagination and inspiration. These qualities are the polar opposite of the analytical, intellectual thought that flourished in universities at the time. Whenever our interests are one-sided, we are out of balance. (This single, consuming interest is notable in people with obsessions.) When the universities were established, people were eager to learn, often ignoring their feeling nature. Many became hardened and "lopsided" until their spirit was stimulated by the classics that became so popular and highly praised. Instead of only thinking and analyzing, they began to listen and sense. This process encompassed many generations as they began to balance their heads and their hearts.

We need to rekindle the reverence our ancestors had for music, art, nature, and the human spirit.

RHYTHM IS EVERYWHERE

Rhythm is found in nature, in the universe, and in every man, woman, and child. An approximate average rhythm of the heart and respiration is seventy-two beats and eighteen breaths; in other words, for every seventy-two heartbeats, the average person takes eighteen breaths. If the ratio of the heart to respiration differs greatly, there is a disruption in other functions of the body, since everything works in a coordinated effort—just as gears have to mesh for machinery to work properly.

Rhythm is found in nature, in the universe, and in every man, woman, and child.

Music has the ability to disrupt the four-to-one ratio, and since we live in a world of sound, we are frequently affected without knowing it. When this disruption is long-lasting or continuous, we have a disturbance of the rhythmic patterns of the body, creating arrhythmia, or a disrupted rhythm, that can usually be restored with remedial therapies.

Adolescents may turn to rock music not because they like it but because it makes them feel part of a group and offers an outlet for blossoming sexual energy. Little or no thought is given to the effect of music on our bodies, yet we know certain rock beats disturb the rhythm of the heart, and riots sometimes result at rock concerts, as the audience is swept up in a frenzy of emotion.

Although we still do not know exactly how it works, we have learned a great deal about the effects of sound. According to an article in the March 27, 1981 issue of *Science News*, monkeys were used in an experiment to determine their reaction to the noises that are around us every day. They heard alarm clocks, running water, toilets flushing, electric razors, radio and television shows, construction equipment, and televised football games. They experienced an average rise in blood pressure of 27 percent over that of the control animals, which were exposed to no unusual noise. Not only did their blood pressure rise; it stayed elevated for over a month. Even though there was no physical damage to their hearing, the study indicated that noise could have long-lasting effects of which we are probably unaware. The results of this study are still valid and give us something to think about.

Fortunately, children are not subjected to a laboratory of noise, but even so, everyday sounds can be stressful. Children on the Autism Spectrum are even more affected by loud sounds than other kids are. To counteract stress, eliminate as much as possible any unnecessary noise in your home, and encourage your child to listen to the sounds of nature, which are much more soothing.

Music in Nature

When you take your child to the park, listen for the sounds that are not immediately obvious and point them out to her. She may not hear what you do at first, but soon she will be able to discern individual sounds. You might hear:

- The buzz of a bee
- The chirp of a cricket
- The burble of water flowing over rocks in a stream
- The song of the birds
- The breeze through the trees
- The call of tree frogs in a pond
- The distinctive call of snow geese

Children are fascinated when they hear the sound of water flowing over different-sized rocks or falling from various heights. Each has a different tone, and when put together, they create a symphony of nature—if we take the time to listen.

When children absorb these basic sounds of nature, they become aware of other sounds in their environment. To enlarge their perception and understanding of the natural world, the next step might be to introduce them to the cycles and rhythm of nature—for instance, the ebb and flow of tides, the blooming and fading of flowers, the rhythm of the seasons, and the waxing and waning of the moon.

These examples are graphic illustrations of the rhythm of nature, which can be emphasized by photographs in science books or videos for children. Knowledge of nature is essential for boys and girls in order for them to understand that there is a time and season for everything—even for people.

Music Within Us

We are surrounded by sounds, but few consider that we have music within us, as an article in the March 2004 issue of *Smithsonian Magazine* reveals.

We are rhythmic human beings—even down to the smallest cell, which is affected by external influences.

Jim Gimzewski, a chemist at UCLA, was intrigued when a colleague told him that when living heart cells were placed in a petri dish with nutrients, the cells continued to pulsate. He wondered if there might be a sound produced by the beating cells, and, hoping to detect cellular noise, he built a delicate instrument called an atomic force microscope.

Yeast cells were placed in a dish, and it was discovered that the cells vibrated an average of 1,000 beats per second. The frequency of the yeast cells was in the range of C-sharp to D. When alcohol was placed on live cells to kill them, it raised the pitch before they died, and the remaining dead cells gave off a low, rumbling sound. This is yet more proof that we are rhythmic human beings—even down to the smallest cell, which is affected by external influences.

The Effects of Sound and Rhythm

Many references to music are found in the Bible, the Bhagavad Gita (the Sanskrit text held sacred by many Hindus), medicine, and philosophy. One Bible story states that Joshua was leading the Israelites to the Promised Land when they approached the walled city of Jericho. He asked God what to do and was told to march the group around the walls for six days, and on the seventh day, to sound a trumpet blast. Even if we are not familiar with the Bible, we may know the result, "And the walls came tumbling down." This parable tells of the power of rhythm and sound.

Another example of the power of rhythm is illustrated by the United States military, which knows the wisdom of marching out of step when crossing a bridge so the steady pounding of many boots in rhythm will not compromise the integrity of the structure. A tragic failure to account for the power of rhythmic energy, on the other hand, occured on July 18, 1981, a day of disaster for the 1,500 to 2,000 people who were attending a popular function at the Hyatt Regency Hotel in Kansas City, Missouri. The tea dance had become a pleasant way of spending a few hours listening to music and dancing. On a walkway, four floors above the main floor, 100 people were dancing. Suddenly there were cracking sounds, and the walkway plunged into the crowd below, killing 114 people and injuring hundreds of others. The cause was declared to be extreme stress on the structure of the walkway by so many people dancing in unison to the rhythm of the band.

If recurrent rhythm and stress can destroy a building, it is logical to assume that it could have harmful effects on the human body. Continued exposure to repetitive beats and loud music, particularly at rock concerts, has caused people to complain of "rubbery legs," pain in the chest, and temporary or permanent loss of hearing.

Although we do not know for sure, this might be what normal noise and voices sound and feel like to children with autism. The hearing of autistic children is so acute, they often cover their ears to block common environmental sounds and voices. We need not only to understand mentally the effect of music on children; we need to sense it in ourselves.

HOW DOES MUSIC AFFECT US?

Just as we have a three-fold nature of body, mind, and spirit, there are three parts of music: rhythm, melody, and harmony, which affect different parts of our body. Rhythm is almost always generated by a drum beat, while a melody is the repeating refrain of a song that we can remember and sing or hum. Harmony is the playing or singing of notes that are joined with the melody to create a pleasing blend of notes and chords.

Rhythm can stimulate a sluggish pulse and give us more energy. Who can resist tapping her foot when she hears a song with a strong rhythm? When rhythm is used therapeutically, it can activate brain rhythms, regulate heartbeat, and encourage movement of the limbs.

Melodies help us to step aside from pain and stress. We can put ourselves in a state of meditation by listening to a melody, which cannot be done with rhythm, since rhythm is stimulating to our body and mind. This is the opposite of the state we strive for in order to relax, meditate, or sleep. Melody is pleasant to listen to, but without harmony and rhythm, it is incomplete.

While a favorite melody is easily remembered, when combined with harmony it produces feelings of joy or sorrow, pleasure or regret. Harmony is more pleasing to the ear and moves the spirit. Melody and rhythm without harmony produce the urge to jump up and down. It creates sensual motions easily seen in the popular music of today, the majority of which contains more rhythm than melody or harmony. All three components, usually heard in a beautiful piece of classical music, stir our spiritual essence, often bringing us close to tears.

Musical Triplets

The three-fold nature of willing, thinking, and feeling governs different organs or body parts. For example, rhythm has a beat, which the body, especially the limbs, responds to by moving. We move only when our will is involved. We may think about dancing but until we will ourselves to do it, it is still a thought. Our mind creates the melodies of songs; therefore, our ability to think is called into play. Feelings originate in our spiritual nature, which brings harmony to a musical composition—and to our lives. There are many references to triplicities in our bodies, all of which have a correlation to music. There are interesting correlations among humanity, music, and instruments.

When we look at the columns in Table 10.1 on page 188, we see that under the heading of "Body" are willing, rhythm, limbs, and percussion—

all of which are forceful and energetic. Under the second heading, "Mind," the correlations are more passive and involve our thinking capability. Wind instruments traditionally carry the melody of a song, which is thought about before being written by the composer. Under the third heading, "Spirit," the words themselves have a kinder, gentler feel, coming from the heart and harmony. The string section of an orchestra brings a light, often ethereal effect or it may be deep and soulful. Either way, it might affect our sensitive nature to the point of tears.

TABLE 10.1. MUSICAL TRIPLICITIES

	Body	Mind	Spirit
The three aspects of our conscious activities are:	Willing	Thinking	Feeling
When we add the three components of music, we have:	Rhythm	Melody	Harmony
Each of these stimulates activity in the involuntary functions of:	Limbs	Head	Heart
An additional triplicity in music is found in an orchestra that contains three major groups:	Percussion	Wind	Strings

Communication Through Music

Non-verbal children often respond musically. For example, Harley was nine years old and seldom spoke. He liked to sit at the piano while I played a simple song and sang the words. I played four notes and sang, "Hello, Harley." He was surprised and pleased. I said, "Now, it's your turn Harley. It's your turn to say, 'Hello, Janet.'"

I played the four notes and sang to him, then four notes and waited. This was repeated several times until, in a soft voice, he said, "Janet." It wasn't in tune with the notes but it didn't matter. He soon added, "Hello," and tried to sing the words.

Our next session began in the same way, but this time I changed it slightly by singing and playing, "How are you today?" Then I said, "Now it's your turn to answer. Are you fine today?" He nodded and mumbled, "Today."

Then I asked if I could touch his hand, and when he agreed, I encouraged him to press the keys, with my finger over his, as he responded.

This continued for several weeks until he decided to hit the keys without urging. Harley would ask and answer simple questions by pressing the keys. This was an ideal way to communicate with each other, and it was fun for both of us. He began to talk a little more freely without the "crutch" of the piano.

Children who are antisocial may benefit from private music lessons, where there is no competition with other children. Music helps them to compensate, and if they can play an instrument, their self-esteem will increase as they grow more proficient. As they become more secure, they may move on to small groups, and later to a school band.

Tony: Classical Calm

Tony was a nine-year-old boy with autism. He was hyperactive but calmed down during his therapy sessions as soon as classical music started playing. His mother was pleased with his progress, but had one complaint: He wouldn't go to sleep at night, or would wake in the middle of the night and wander throughout the house. She was exhausted from lack of sleep and becoming very angry with her son.

I made a tape of his favorite classical album and told him it would help him sleep. The following week, his mother was ecstatic. For the past week at bedtime, she had told me, Tony had put the tape in the player, turned it on, and went right to sleep. If he woke during the night, instead of walking around the house he would rewind the tape and play it again as he fell back to sleep.

This was a simple solution to an ongoing, frustrating problem. The beautiful combination of rhythm, melody, and harmony in his preferred classical music soothed his hyperactive nature and eventually allowed sleep and relaxation to come naturally without the tape. Consequently, the entire family was sleeping normally once again.

We begin to recognize a pattern in music and in life, as all of these aspects must work in unison to create a work of art, whether it's an orchestra or a healthy body. If one aspect of music is missing, there is discord, and if there is one aspect of the physical body missing, there is disease. If left untreated, it will probably become worse or at least will not greatly improve without some intervention. In therapy, the same comparison can be used.

All children show four major reactions to music: physical, sensuous, intellectual, and emotional. Most react to the impact of rhythm because it provokes a primitive, physical reaction. Many obtain sensuous reactions similar to stroking a piece of fabric.

Children with developmental disorders, particularly autism, are very sensitive to touch. They are repelled by some fabrics and attracted to others, which they may stroke repeatedly or rub on their arms. This is often the case when they are seated or standing quietly, listening to music for a few minutes. If the child shows an attraction to a certain piece of fabric, let her hold it if she is upset or hyperactive, since it may have a calming effect.

Other children are intellectually stimulated and want to remember the words and notes. Still others are emotionally aroused and may feel happy, sad, angry, and/or fearful in response to the music heard. Sometimes, non-verbal children will communicate through music. The inset on page 188 details an example of this triumph.

For exercises that will help your child recognize her feelings and reactions to music, and express them creatively, turn to page 279 of Part Two.

We can clearly see how all three aspects of music work in coordination to provide an integrated piece of art. Remedial therapies utilize all three to create carefully selected music to stimulate or calm the body, mind, and spirit, thereby initiating the healing process. That is, music with an emphasis on rhythm, melody, or harmony is chosen for specific children with specific needs. It is played as a child is involved in drawing, sculpture, or other artistic activities. If you play a piece with strong rhythm one day, she may not need or want it during the next session and instead may respond to something with more harmony or melody.

See the inset on page 189 to learn how classical music can calm a hyperactive child.

WHY IS MUSIC SO IMPORTANT?

Since music is heard and not seen, we are not influenced by a visual form, and our responses are based on feelings the music elicits.

Music is different from other art forms because our feelings in response to it come solely from within and are not based on what we see. It is not the brain or the mind that responds to the arts and to music in particular; our spiritual essence does. One does not need a perfect brain to respond to music. In fact, intelligence often stifles feelings, and we need the ability to feel in order to appreciate and be affected by music.

When we look at a piece of art or sculpture, we are influenced by the artist's ability or lack of technique. We may analyze and criticize it based on our personal preferences for color or style. Since music is heard and not seen, we are not influenced by a visual form, and our responses are based on feelings the music elicits.

As children learn to enjoy classical music, they become less hyperactive and their attention span increases. Muscular coordination is improved if they play an instrument, and they are able to release tensions and anxieties. The spasms of cerebral palsy and seizures of epilepsy are often greatly reduced by music.

Children Need Music

Even the youngest of children seem to need music and movement. Their sounds are vocalizations of the beginning of speech and tone. They love being rocked and sung to. As toddlers, they love to bang pot covers together for their cymbals. They tell us in many ways that they like sounds. What they can't tell us is that, at their deepest level, they love music. More than that, they *need* music. Toddlers love senseless but rhythmical nursery rhymes such as "Tom, Tom the Piper's Son" and "Pat-a-Cake." Waving bye-bye and clapping their hands are as rhythmical and intrinsic to toddlers as rocking in their crib or playpen.

Playing music and dancing provide an emotional release. At the same time, these actions enhance a child's self-image. Often it is only through music that children with Spectrum Disorders can express themselves. Children on the Spectrum may be withdrawn, aggressive, dependent, antisocial, and/or depressed. Selected music is helpful in changing their behavior and responses.

When in a group, singing and playing an instrument often has several beneficial effects. Sociability in a group is very supportive and positive, since children learn to become less self-centered. Children are being directly creative by making sounds (as opposed to listening), which is re-creative and requires interpretation of what they are hearing. In addition, children often listen to—and respond to—instructions, directions, or comments when the words are sung instead of spoken. Although we don't know why, it could be the cadence and tone of a singing voice that captures their attention. Also, perhaps the pitch of the spoken word is difficult for some children to hear and process.

Although children with psycho-neuro disorders will not respond to music in exactly the same way as "typical" children do, they may show reactions by tensing or relaxing muscles or with a slight smile or an inquiring look. They may not, and need not, be able to read music, keep time, play an instrument properly, or possess a pleasant singing voice, but if they are able to express themselves in any way and derive pleasure from it, they will have been helped enormously and may more readily respond to other therapies.

Like most autistic children, Brent, a beautiful three-year old with a fondness for the piano, had no sense of rhythm. While I played, he would walk around the room, sometimes turning in circles, dancing. He would stand by the piano and either move his feet or move his body up and down. He liked sitting next to me and playing with one finger. To help him feel the rhythm of playing music, I would pat his back in time to the beat as I sang a simple song and played with one hand. He began keeping time by patting his thigh in an attempt to imitate me.

Musical instruments were brought out for him to play with. He was intrigued with the small cymbals but didn't know what to do with them. His gross motor and fine motor skills were underdeveloped, and he had difficulty picking up any of the instruments. I showed him how to hold the cymbals by holding his hands over the cymbals, then how to clap them together to make a sound. This noise frightened him at first, but he soon realized that it was a sound that he had made himself. Although he never could keep time to the music, he tried by hitting the cymbals together while music was playing. His mother later stated that he was starting to play with his instruments at home.

When Brent started the program, he had an attention span of about twenty seconds. He liked the books in my office but would never sit still long enough to look at one. After a month of weekly sessions, Brent would sit comfortably next to me in a chair and listen to an entire story while I pointed out animals and drawings in the book, all the while gently touching his arm or leg to the beat of the music. Instead of for twenty seconds, he was now able to focus for twenty minutes while classical music played in the background. His father watched through the window in disbelief, since his son was usually in constant motion.

Just as we should never underestimate the humor and intelligence of children on the Autism Spectrum, we should never forget that music is one of the most powerful and effective means of reaching and teaching children with autism, Asperger's Syndrome, and ADHD.

MUSIC AS THERAPY

Music can evoke deep-seated emotions and liberate tensions in order to help a person express what cannot otherwise be articulated. No one disputes the effect of music on people with various disorders. Aristotle stated that music affects the body and emotions. When we hear certain music, we associate with past events, pleasant or not, and music stirs memories that may be helpful in unlocking repressed thoughts such as anger, fear, and hostility, which can then be dealt with by working with a therapist. We can see that music is more than just something to listen to while shopping or as background sound—it is very therapeutic.

> Music can evoke deep-seated emotions and liberate tensions in order to help a person express what cannot otherwise be articulated.

In the twentieth century, we "discovered" that music does indeed have charms that soothe the savage beast. During World War II, volunteers played music in veterans' hospitals to boost morale, and the successful experiment led to the formation of the first school of Music Therapy at Michigan State University in 1944. The program and field were still in their rudimentary academic stages at that point.

Music Therapy has become one of the most popular therapy courses for children with disabilities. It's now offered in universities throughout the United States as academicians have learned what people have known instinctively for thousands of years: Music has intangible, but very real, healing qualities.

Although the term "Music Therapy" is only a few decades old, the concept has been recognized and implemented for thousands of years. Mental disabilities were recorded as long ago as 1500 BC, when they were called "the shadow accompanying man." Pythagoras felt that each note of the musical scale affected a different part of the body and a different organ. This sounds remarkably like Music Therapy today, through which certain music is chosen for specific conditions.

SELECTING MUSIC FOR YOUR CHILD

Choosing music to play for a child can be done in several ways. We can, and should, do it intuitively, in which case it will vary from day to day and we won't know which selection to play until the child arrives for her session. We may have an idea of a piece to play, but her demeanor may require something quite different.

Another method is to play music by different composers and observe the child's reaction of like, dislike, or indifference. If she likes it, play it often. If she doesn't, it may be hurting her ears, it may have discordant notes, or perhaps she simply doesn't like the style. If she is indifferent, alternate it with other pieces she likes. A third method is to listen to a complete album and select tracks that you feel would be ideal for playing during a session.

If the child shows a fondness for one composer or piece of music, she will probably do her best work while it is playing. Unless a child has a specific problem, such as with breathing or lethargy, any piece of fine classical music will have a nice balance of rhythm, melody, and harmony.

What is lacking can be drawn out of the child's sensitive, spiritual nature by various techniques. There are musical strategies for working with children on the Autism Spectrum, and if something is lacking in the body, we may supplement it with music. Before playing therapeutic music for your children, it is important to listen to it in order to determine which pieces are stimulating and which are calming.

For example, children who are lethargic and those who have weak limbs need to be stimulated with rhythm. They can be invigorated with music that contains pronounced rhythmic percussion; Ravel's "Boléro" is a good example. Hyperactive children respond to soft, flowing orchestral selections such as Debussy's "Afternoon of a Fawn." For emotionally disturbed children, we need to emphasize harmony, which may be insufficient in the composition of their brain. It makes sense that for literal, left-brained children, we need to emphasize harmony, which will balance their one-pointed intellect.

Aristotle (384–322 BC) said, "Emotions of any kind are produced by melody and rhythm; therefore by music a man becomes accustomed to feeling the right emotions; music has the power to form character." These words were true then, and they are true today, which tells us that music therapy was known as a powerful force a long time ago. The following are a few suggestions for applying music to specific conditions in order to "form character":

• For weak muscles and limbs and to energize the body, play stimulating music with volume slightly louder than usual.

Select: "Boléro" by Ravel, "Mephisto Waltz" by Liszt

- To calm a child who is hyperactive, play music that has more melody and harmony than rhythm and percussion. Instead of being physically and mentally active, she will be relaxed and soothed.
  Select: "Romeo and Juliet" by Tchaikovsky

- Children who are anxious need music with a pronounced rhythm and melody.
  Select: Waltzes by Strauss

- Chronically ill children benefit from soft music.
  Select: "La Mer" by Debussy

- Hyperactive behavior is often reduced when soft songs are played.
  Select: "Carmen Suite" nos. 1–2 by Bizet

- Children who live in their feelings benefit from songs with a lot of harmony.
  Select: "Jupiter Symphony" by Mozart

- Lethargic children are energized when music with rhythm and horns are played.
  Select: "Stars and Stripes Forever" by Sousa

The temperament of a child could also be considered. For example, Ravel's "Boléro" would not be played for a hyperactive child, as it would be too stimulating, but might be a good choice for one who is lethargic. In his book *Discussions With Teachers,* Rudolf Steiner describes therapy for the temperaments:

- Predictable introverts should play the piano and sing in chorus. They benefit from harmony.

- Artistic extroverts benefit most from wind instruments and playing in a group rather than solo. They benefit from melody.

- Fiery managers should play the drums or other percussion instruments, preferably solo. They benefit from rhythm.

- Quiet worriers benefit most from stringed instruments and solo singing. They also benefit from counterpoint, which occurs when a second melody is played above or below the main one.

There is another method of selecting the music of the masters that is little known but greatly effective. It is based on the time of year and the great musical composers. It is a child's three-fold state that is being addressed, rather than her temperament. She is born with a specific disposition, but the body, mind, and spirit are subject to outside influences.

Time of Year and Time of Birth

How can you determine the best music to be played during one-on-one or group sessions? A simple, effective formula is based upon the time of year of the session and the birth date of the composers. If that sounds strange, remember that the concept of Music Therapy itself is impossible to describe without speaking in rather esoteric terms, as it deals with the nebulous psyche of an individual.

All of the great composers had a distinct temperament and talent, which are reflected in their music. Virtually all musical geniuses have written about spiritual experiences that have influenced and inspired them. They feel they were privileged to hear the "harmony of the spheres" or "celestial music" and reproduce it for humankind to enjoy.

Coincidentally, some pieces by composers who share an approximate birth date are similar in sound, content, or in the responses they evoke. For this reason, the following list (see Table 10.2) was compiled from various sources and provides a guideline for selecting compositions to be played during the year, as you choose the pieces according to the month indicated.

For example, when selecting music to play on the dates from May 22 to June 21, you would choose from the pieces by Wagner, Gounod, Grieg, Schumann, or Strauss. There are no doubt others born during the same timeframe, and you will improve your knowledge and appreciation of music by searching for them. Naturally, some compositions are vibrant and loud, while others are soft and soothing. This requires you to listen first to determine which pieces are appropriate for a child. With this suggested list, as with most classical music in general, orchestral versions are better than those with lyrics, since many people, young and old, will listen to the music, but become restless with words—especially opera.

It has been my experience over the past twenty-five years that selecting music according to the birth time of the year—not the precise birth date—of great composers and correlating it to the current calendar month is a very effective, although unorthodox, method of reaching and teaching children. The following list will simplify your search for appropriate music and encourage you to find other pieces in your collection of albums.

> All of the great composers had a distinct temperament and talent, which are reflected in their music.

TABLE 10.2. SELECTING MUSIC BASED ON DATE

Date	Composer	Work
March 22–April 21	Johann Sebastian Bach	"St. Matthew Passion" "St. John Passion" Midsummer Eve (St. John the Baptist) Michaelmas (St. Michael) Fugues, Chorals, Cantatas
April 22–May 21	Peter Ilich Tchaikovsky	"None But the Lonely Heart" "Swan Lake" Fourth Symphony "Romeo and Juliet"
May 22–June 21	Richard Wagner	"The Flying Dutchman" "Tannhäuser" "Lohengrin" "Tristan and Isolde" The "Ring" Cycle "Parsifal"
	Charles Gounod	"Faust"
	Edvard Grieg	"Peer Gynt Suite" "In the Hall of the Mountain King" "Solveig's Song"
	Robert Schumann	"Traumerei" "Carnival" "Kinderszenen" "Papillons"
	Richard Strauss	"Salome" "Rosenkavalier" "Electra"
June 22–July 21	Gustav Mahler	"Resurrection" Symphony Eighth Symphony
July 22–August 21	Achille-Claude Debussy	"The Afternoon of a Faun" "Pelléas and Mélisande" "Jardins Sous la Pluie" "Nuages" "La Mer" "Reflets Dans l'Eau"
August 22–September 21	Giacomo Meyerbeer	"Les Huguenots" "Robert le Diable" "The Prophet" "L'Africaine"

Date	Composer	Work
September 22–October 21	Giuseppe Verdi	"Nabucco" "Aïda" "Rigoletto" "Don Carlos" "Il Trovatore" "Macbeth" "Falstaff"
October 22–November 21	Domenico Scarlatti Franz Liszt	Sonatas "Mephisto Waltz"
November 22–December 21	Ludwig van Beethoven	Symphony No. 3—"Eroica" Symphony No. 6—"Pastoral" Other symphonies "Appassionata" Concertos
	César Franck	"The Beatitudes" "Violin Sonata" "Pianoforte Quintet"
December 21–January 22	Giacomo Puccini	"Madam Butterfly" "Tosca" "La Bohème"
	Alexander Scriabin	"Mysterium" "Prometheus"
January 22–February 21	Franz Schubert	"Ave Maria" Unfinished Symphony in B Minor
	Wolfgang Mozart	"Requiem Mass" "The Magic Flute" "Jupiter Symphony"
	Felix Mendelssohn	"A Midsummer Night's Dream" "Songs Without Words" "Scherzo"
February 22–March 21	Georg Frideric Handel	"Passion" "Israel in Egypt" "The Messiah"
	Maurice Ravel	"Boléro" "Jeux d'Eau" "Ondine"
	Modest Mussorgsky	"Khovanshchina" "Boris Godunov" "Pictures At An Exhibition"

As with most recommended lists, this one is given as a guideline. By adding your favorites or eliminating those you or your child don't care for, you will have a library of classics that will suit the various moods and needs of your child.

How to Help Kids With Epilepsy, Asthma, and Hearing Loss

The skin is our largest sense organ, and through it deaf children can feel the pulsation of rhythm from stereo speakers, by touching a piano, or by simply feeling the vibrations of the floor through their feet. Hearing-impaired children can often play the drums, cymbals, or other instruments if they can "feel" the beat and watch the conductor who cues them.

Playing a wind instrument helps children with asthma and other breathing difficulties. Children with epilepsy and asthma respond to creative therapies. If both of these disorders are made worse by stress and inhibition, it makes sense to approach treatment with the goal of releasing the tensions through a creative outlet.

Children with pent-up emotions and no effective method of release may explode in any number of ways from a mild case of the "blahs" to more severe withdrawal, physical illness, or violence. Some suppressed anxieties affect the physical body; some, the physical brain; and some, the emotions, producing more anxiety. Symptoms are often masked by medication, which in itself frequently can produce bizarre and puzzling reactions such as tics, grunts, confusion, and depression, in addition to other known side effects.

It is not uncommon for autistic children to have hundreds of petit mal (mild) seizures every day. These may or may not be noticeable to the casual observer, but a parent is aware of a difference in the child's actions and appearance. It may be for a split second, where consciousness is lost and she has a "far-away" look. She may stumble or fall, regaining her composure so quickly that one wonders if a seizure has actually taken place.

Rudolf Steiner (1861–1925) established elementary schools, known as Waldorf Schools, for children throughout Europe, and also residential schools where children with disabilities would go to sleep and wake to classical music. This practice can reduce epileptic seizures, since episodes frequently occur just before or after falling asleep and soon after awakening.

Classical music has a calming effect that helps children fall asleep. In the morning as we begin to wake, we are between sleep and waking, and it is in this stage that classical music has a beneficial effect. It calms children as they begin to awaken for the day. At bedtime, children are soothed as they prepare for sleep. This form of therapy can easily be done in the home.

Seizures can be brought on by the flickering of a television or video game, or by looking at the blades of a rotating fan or the glittering surface of a lake. They can be induced by being a passenger in a car while driving down a road with the sunlight flickering through the trees. Some children deliberately induce a seizure by moving the fingers in front of the eyes while looking towards the sun. Many adults report a feeling of pleasure just before having a seizure.

Frequently the time before the seizure is compared to a thunderstorm that is building up, and the attack is a release, or an attempt to release the pent-up power. If seizures are caused by stress, as many doctors believe, it is important to reduce tension in the child's life, and one of the best ways is through music.

Music Is Individual

Autistic children are almost universally responsive to music. While the love of music is a commonly mentioned characteristic of autism, it is rarely noted in children with schizophrenia. Developmentally delayed children usually do not mind if there is dissonance in a musical piece, but psychotic, schizophrenic, or otherwise disturbed individuals are upset by it. Some very intelligent adults do not like dissonance because it is irritating and it does not conform to a pattern. On the other hand, some enjoy it because they feel dissonance adds to the totality of the musical composition.

Obviously, music affects everyone differently. We cannot say that because a child has autism, she should be exposed to only one kind of music, and Aspies to another, and children with ADD to still other classical pieces. Young children have their favorite types, just as we do, and may respond to them more readily than to some we might select for them.

It helps to think of a child with a neurological disorder as an artist who is playing with a faulty instrument.

Our Body Is Our Instrument

No matter how good a pianist is, if she is playing a piano that is out of tune, it will be irritating to the listeners. They may walk out, laugh, or boo her performance, which makes it only worse. The pianist may get flustered, make mistakes, and finally quit in tears. But if the audience knows the pianist and knows the piano is out of tune, they are much more understanding. In fact, they admire her persistence and ability to play despite the obstacles of a piano that badly needs tuning.

Now think of the pianist as a child with autism, and the piano as her body and mind. We now thoroughly support her in her efforts to overcome challenges. We applaud her attempts to play on a faulty instrument, and because of our attitude, she is given the strength she needs to continue in her learning and improvement. Even an out-of-tune piano hits a few good notes, as do these children. They have some things that they are good or gifted at, so no one is "totally broken."

As parents, you'll find many ways to bring music into your child's life. You have a greater opportunity to affect them than do therapists who may see them one hour a week. Since you aren't a Music Therapist, you may ask how you can help your child. Don't worry.

WHAT CAN I DO?

To instill the love of music in a child, homes should be filled with the beauty of the classics. Like appreciation of good food and art, appreciation of music begins early in life. A young child may not be able to grasp the mechanics of a classical composition intellectually, but she will feel and sense tones and vibrations as they course through her body. Just as a harsh voice causes a toddler to cringe in fright, so does music that is not pleasing to the ear create a desire to escape the noise. Autistic children often cover their ears and cry for no apparent reason, yet a child who is verbal may tell you the noise hurts her ears.

To understand how to best select music for your child, it helps to remember the correlation of rhythm, melody, and harmony to her limbs, head, and heart—to the process of willing, thinking, and feeling. (See page 188.) This will soon be second nature to you as you learn more about your child, her needs, and how to fulfill them.

To instill the love of music in a child, homes should be filled with the beauty of the classics. Like appreciation of good food and art, appreciation of music begins early in life.

There are many things you can do for and with your child that involve music. The easiest first step is simply to listen. You will be surprised by how many sounds you will be able to identify in your environment. Take a moment right now and close your eyes—and listen. Both the hum of the refrigerator that is always in the background and the ticking clock in the next room may seem unusually loud, yet when we go about our daily routine they aren't noticeable. Children on the Autism Spectrum have incredibly acute hearing. The refrigerator and clock may be unbearable to them. One can only imagine how unpleasant very loud sounds like sirens and raised voices must be to sensitive ears.

Just being aware of noise in your home is a huge first step in working with your child. Then you can begin to create an environment of good music by learning about the great masters such as Debussy, Mozart, and Liszt. If you don't have a collection of albums from which to choose, your local library probably has CDs that can be checked out. This is a good way to explore various composers and types of music to play without having to purchase a lot of new music. If your child doesn't respond to a particular selection, don't give up; try another piece. Choosing music is 99 percent intuition, so let that work for you.

Simply dancing and playing games with your child is important in building a relationship. When a relationship is developed, many paths of communication are opened. If she expresses an interest in playing an instrument, allow her to have the experience, if possible. Many children with autism are musical savants who play beautifully. You will never know if your child has a musical talent unless she has access to the proper tools, whatever they may be.

Buy small instruments that are of good quality. Inexpensive toy cymbals, for example, usually have a harsh, metallic sound that is not very pleasing to the ear. Buy a good recorder; if you can find one made of pear wood, so much the better. Maracas are a great way for your autistic child to learn how to keep time to the rhythm of the beat. They are easy to hold and usually made of wood. A xylophone is a wonderful instrument for all children. Don't expect your young child to play a song; it may be enough that she can hold the sticks and hammer at the keys with obvious enjoyment.

It helps to remember that our voices are our instruments and conversations become symphonies, complete with lilting flutes, soft strings, staccato drums, and clashing cymbals. Too many drums and cymbals produce discomfort, and most people get tired of nothing but strings. Using this analogy, a family needs to work together to create a harmonious atmosphere. When working with your child, enjoy it. Make it fun, not a chore, because she will know the difference.

Musical Games You Can Play

There are various musical exercises you can do with your child. Her participation naturally depends on her disorder and the severity of her condition. Never give up. Siblings, grandparents, aunts, uncles, and even babysitters—all of whom will feel a sense of gratification just by taking part in the activities—can do all of the exercises with your child.

Try playing a lively march and exaggerating stepping in time to the beat of the drums. Stomp while counting aloud to four, with emphasis on the "one" as you march around the room—"ONE two three four, ONE two three four." All children love to stomp because it may not be normally allowed. This exercise helps them to stomp as hard as they want to on the beat of one, and they begin to feel a rhythmic pattern. This sense of rhythm is related to proper breathing.

Turn to page 279 of Part Two for more fun exercises involving music, memory, and awareness.

SUMMARY

Music has a long and revered history in cultures throughout the world. The last half of the twentieth century brought great insights into the effective remedial use of music, as Music Therapy was taught in universities as a viable form of treatment.

We have learned a great deal about the different parts of music and how each affects our body, mind, and spirit. Because music can be only felt—not seen or touched—it has a deep-rooted effect on a child's inner nature. Her spirit responds to the beauty of music, especially to the moving compositions of some of the great masters of classical music.

Music affects us in different ways. Physically, it increases body motion. Mentally, it satisfies the intellect. Artistically, it has beauty and grace, touching the heart and promoting a spiritual experience.

Children don't just love music and rhythm. They *need* it. They show this by their musical sounds and rhythmic movements. Toddlers pull pots and pans from the kitchen cupboard and discover how to make music by banging pot covers together.

Just as we have the three components of body, mind, and spirit, music has the three components of rhythm, melody, and harmony. All three have to be synchronized to have a whole person or a full symphony. If one part is missing, there is an imbalance that can be overcome with the right choice of music and other creative remedial therapies.

Music is different from other art forms such as painting or physical creation because it can't be seen; it has to be *experienced*. Although color can be seen, it also has to be experienced for its fullest impression. We will learn more about color in the next chapter.

CHAPTER 11

*T*he Inner Nature
of Color

Colors stir our spirit just as music does, and just as there must be a balance of music, activities, and food for a healthy body, there must be a balance of color. We take color for granted, yet without it our lives would be uninteresting and uninspired. For a therapist, understanding color is as important as understanding music or any other art form. Since it subtly affects the way we think, feel, and act during the time we are awake, it is logical that learning about it would be to our benefit. As we learn, we are consciously able to help children on the Spectrum, who are extraordinarily sensitive to color.

If someone were to ask, "What is color?" we might say that the grass is green or that the sky is blue, but the definitive answer to this question remains elusive. We can create colors with a prism, but that doesn't answer the question either. Science may tell us that light and color are two ends of the vibratory spectrum, but again, this does not explain what color truly is.

While Sir Isaac Newton (1642–1727) felt that color was caused by light striking objects and entering our eyes, Johann Wolfgang Goethe (1749–1821) maintained that color is formed by our perception. He said that everything we see is composed of light, shade, and color, and it is through these that we construct our visible, physical world. He was the first person to understand the psychological effect of each color and created the color wheel that defines the complementary colors.

The famous artist Claude Monet (1840–1926) forever changed the way we look at objects by his series of paintings of haystacks. For one day, he painted a single haystack at half-hour intervals, and at the end of the day, each painting was different, showing that the haystack had absorbed colors. At the start of the day, the haystack appeared yellowish brown, but it clearly had changed to shades of orange and red as the day progressed. Obviously, there was more to consider than the theory that everything had its own color.

There is energy in color that is transferred to a solid surface. Research has proven that we can feel color by placing our hands over a piece of fabric or paper; shades of blue and green feel cooler to us than do red, yellow, or orange. (This is a fun game for children, who are very good at identifying colors, much to their surprise.) This ability was first discovered in Russia over thirty years ago and has been proven throughout the years with people who are blind.

There are many more colors in our environment than we are aware of, simply because we have never seen them. It is difficult to believe that there are vivid colors inside of a crystal that are invisible to the naked eye, yet a gifted photographer and artist, Donald W. Gill, has developed a technique to photograph the interior of thousands of crystals. When printed, with no computer enhancement, the result is a spectacular, colorful wall hanging that is easily mistaken for a fine piece of art.

It would be unthinkable to decorate our homes in shades of gray or to buy a gray painting that will hang on a gray wall. We need color in our lives just as we do in our homes and businesses. Because we too often believe that what we see is all there is, we place limitations on our ability to learn and be educated. Intellect is valuable, but in creative activities such as photographing crystals or painting a picture, it may have drawbacks. The experience of color is closely linked to our spiritual essence.

"Uncivilized" Man

Until humanity became "civilized," color always had a spiritual meaning. For example:

- Early people tied colored string or cloth around their wrist or neck, not to be attractive but to communicate with the spirits of the universe.

- They felt that color, like music, was a gift from the gods, and that by concentrating on a particular shade they could commune with a specific deity.

- In Ancient Greece, the rainbow was called Iris, the name that has remained with us as the color of our eyes.

- God is frequently shown upon a rainbow throne.

- Ezekiel mentioned the "bow in the cloud."

- Rainbows as a spiritual reflection are seen in the art of both the East and the West. They were always revered and held a spiritual significance for early humans.

Clothing was carefully chosen to bring to earth the colors of the spiritual world. The clothes people wore and the buildings they designed and built were reflections of their feelings for the living and the dead. Some modern cultures celebrate festivals by dressing in native costumes, but today this practice reflects tradition more than an understanding of the significance of color.

This chapter will explore color psychology as well as the importance of, and need for, color in our lives. You will learn how to use color both to calm a hyperactive child and to stimulate a lethargic one. Most important, you will learn how color can help children, especially those on the Autism Spectrum, to express themselves and attune themselves to their spiritual nature.

WHY IS COLOR IMPORTANT?

Color has fascinated people for hundreds of years, but only recently has it been taken seriously by researchers hoping to discover why some colors make us feel happy and positive and others have the opposite effect. Color psychology is a science in itself, and studies have shown that certain colors are relaxing, some are invigorating, and others are irritating. Knowing that, we can learn to use colors to our advantage by creating a pleasant environment in our homes, schools, offices, and clinics. We need to be flexible, though, because our like and dislike of colors are subjective feelings that may change over the years as we undergo changes in the way we think and feel.

Color draping or consulting had its beginning in the 1980s when someone stated what is now obvious, common knowledge—that we are attracted to some colors and repelled by others. Color draping is the demonstration of how colors influence our appearance and emotions, since some are more flattering and give us a feeling of well-being while others may make us uncomfortable.

In color draping, pieces of fabric are placed around your body as you look at yourself in a full-length mirror. Most people immediately react to colors they feel are unflattering or flattering, or to colors that they are repelled by or attracted to. However, if we are in tune with our feelings, we already know this intuitively. We feel better in some colors than in others and choose our clothing accordingly.

Colors affect us more than we may realize, and since we don't live in a colorless world, we are constantly influenced by the colors of our surroundings. All businesses are aware of the immediate impact of color in the advertising and marketing of their products. Millions of dollars are spent annually to determine the best way to package their products in order to attract buyers, and some products that don't sell are simply repackaged in another color and swept off the shelves by shoppers. Although everyone is affected by color, each of us reacts differently. This is clearly shown by the child who rebels when a blue shirt is selected by his mother and he insists he wants to wear the red one.

Colors affect us more than we may realize, and since we don't live in a colorless world, we are constantly influenced by the colors of our surroundings. Although everyone is affected by color, each of us reacts differently.

COMPLEMENTARY COLORS

Although it may seem unlikely, color's effect on children is different from its effect on adults. Many adults instinctively wear red when they are tired since it is a stimulating color and boosts their energy levels. While red may invigorate an adult, it is calming to hyperactive children, who actually experience it's complementary color, blue.

Children do not make the conscious association of red (or blue) with its effects; therefore, they are unable to articulate their experiences or sensations with relation to a particular color. They know only that they feel "better," and their behavior will be obvious to their parent or therapist. Along the same lines, amphetamines, also known as "speed," and specifically Ritalin, are prescribed for children with ADHD since their effect on children is opposite their effect on adults: Children are calmed instead of stimulated.

If we stare at a red square of paper and then quickly look at a white surface, we will see a green square. If we look at a blue paper and then at a white surface, we will see the complementary color of orange-yellow. This is an interesting parlor trick, but a child automatically creates it within himself. This is why red calms a child and blue invigorates him, which is the exact opposite of how adults are affected. He inwardly creates the complementary color and experiences the consequent effects. This creation of the complementary color is one of the mysteries of color and its effect on children.

Although it may seem unlikely, color's effect on children is different from its effect on adults.

Contrary to the common logic that shades of red are stimulating to everyone, a restless child should be surrounded with orange and rose-red walls, sheets, and curtains in his bedroom to help calm him. You may experiment even further by trying different shades of red to see which is the most effective. When sheets, pajamas, drapes, rugs, and/or walls are of these colors, a hyperactive or restless child will soon be more cheerful, calm, and rested.

Conversely, a lethargic and inactive child should be surrounded with blue and blue/green, which will energize him and produce within the child the complementary stimulating color of orange/yellow.

Investigate his closet to see what colors are predominant. Changing a wardrobe or the colors of a bedroom are easy methods for determining which colors are beneficial to your child. The image of Goethe's color wheel may be very helpful in your selections. Once we recognize how colors affect us all, we become more aware of the décor in our homes and businesses.

FIRST IMPRESSIONS

For most of us, introductions to places, things, or people are accompanied by lasting visual impressions that often have to do with color. Most bars and cocktail lounges use a lot of red and orange because it encourages eating and drinking. These colors are associated with increased energy and very strong emotions and passions, ranging from a desire for food and drink to sex and/or violence, depending on the person. (Mars has always been known as "The God of War" and is known as "the red planet.") On the other hand, fast food restaurants are almost devoid of color, and, whether we are conscious of it or not, this lack of color is uncomfortable to us. As a result, people don't generally linger after eating; this creates a greater flow of customers and business.

We are drawn to the colors we like and sometimes irritated by those we don't. (See "What Color Are You?" below for examples of how color has permeated our language of emotions and feelings.) Similarly, we may be attracted to people who share our love of blue and repelled by those who wear only black, which we may associate with gloom, doom, and sadness. We experience this attraction/repulsion or sympathy/antipathy constantly in our lives, since we live in a world of individuals and their preferences. We also have to realize that children are surrounded by a variety of colors during their waking hours and affected by them all.

Goethe stated that he was meant to "uncover color's secrets" and to understand how people reacted to color. His groundbreaking work is the basis of color psychology as we know it today. (Goethe's color wheel,

---

What Color Are You?

There are many familiar references to color in figures of speech used in everyday language. For example:

- green with envy
- got the blues
- seeing red
- in the pink

- under a black cloud
- white with fear
- green-eyed monster
- yellow coward

- blushing scarlet
- rose-colored glasses
- good as gold
- silver lining

If color weren't such an important part of our lives, there wouldn't be so many references to it in connection with our emotions.

often taught to children in elementary school, is an important tool for identifying colors and their complements.) Indeed, people react to color instantly and strongly. We are naturaly affected by it because color is a light wave that penetrates our body.

LIGHT WAVES

In 1666 Sir Isaac Newton admitted sunlight through a prism and established the familiar seven basic colors of the spectrum—red, orange, yellow, green, blue, indigo, and violet.

Light is radiant energy and travels through space in the form of waves, some of which we can see and hear within a certain range of wavelengths. Traveling through space at 186,000 miles per second, wavelengths vary in size, energy, and vibration. Color, light, and heat are related to wavelengths. We tend to isolate music and color into distinct categories although they are, in fact, just variations of energy on a spectrum.

Electromagnetic energies from space can be detected by sophisticated scientific instruments. We are surrounded by a continuum of these waves, including radio waves, microwaves, infrared waves, visible light waves, ultraviolet waves, X-ray waves, and gamma waves. Although most of these are familiar names to us, visible light waves are the only ones we can see. When we see a complete rainbow, we are looking at what is known as an optical spectrum, or range, of all the colors that are visible to us, ranging from the deepest red to the lightest violet. The length of the light wave determines its density and our ability to see or hear it. As it speeds through space, it loses heat and dissipates until the most easily seen color is red. The denser the energy, the more visible it is. Like sound, light has "pitch." The red end of the spectrum has a lower pitch, or frequency, than the blue end. In musical terms, red would sound like low notes and blue would sound like high notes.

Ancient teachings have always held that music and color are just two ends of the spectrum, colors being the denser element. This is similar to the Autism Spectrum—ADD is considered a very mild disorder that is easily overlooked, and classic autism is much more obvious to the observer.

Full-Spectrum Lighting

Full-spectrum lighting is meant to recreate sunlight. The most well-known researcher in this field is pioneer Dr. John Ott, the inventor of full-spectrum lighting. A photobiologist, Dr. Ott has worked for over forty years with color and its effects on plant growth and development. He found that plants grown under different-colored glass and lights had different rates of growth and strength. Color affects human beings just as it influences the development of plants, since both are living things responsive to their environment.

The idea that plants are affected by color is not new. In 1876, an article was published by Augustus Pleasanton about the work he did with plants in greenhouses. He stated that the size of his grapes and yield were much larger when he used green and red panes of glass. This was undoubtedly startling news at the time.

Sunlight is the healthiest of all light since it contains all the colors of the spectrum and affects our endocrine system. It stimulates hormones that affect us on all levels: physical, mental, emotional, and spiritual. Obviously, what we see enters our eyes and travels to the brain, but everything we don't see does as well.

In addition to being affected by what we see each day, we are, at the same time, impressed by things we hear, smell, taste, and touch. Even though we may not see the source of these sensations, they are registered by the brain. We may be unaware of them, but it is impossible to escape sensory input from our environment. The sun contains all the colors of the spectrum, and these colors enter our eyes and subsequently our brain's hypothalamus, which regulates various functions of the body.

There is still a lot to learn about color and its effects. We do know that it is a form of radiation, like microwaves, ultraviolet rays, and X-rays. Like each of those, it enters the body with a profound effect. Learning how we respond to various shades is an experience we can use to observe our children. For a healthy body, we need sunlight, full-spectrum lighting, or color in some other form in our environment.

Sunlight Deprivation

We know that plants become spindly and sick without sunlight, but we often fail to understand that people react the same way. Pliny the Elder (AD 23–79) wrote that Rome was such a powerful nation for 600 years because Roman structures had solariums on roofs for sunbathing. Sunlight starvation, or sunlight deprivation, is common in northern areas during the long winter months, when days are gloomy. People are generally more irritable and experience fatigue, depression, and illness from November through May.

If natural sunlight is not available to you—for example, during dreary days or when in an enclosed space—use full-spectrum lighting, which contains all of the colors of sunlight and is widely used in clinics and homes. It has been found that the flickering of common fluorescent tubes increases hyperactive behavior and irritability, but that full-spectrum lights calm children.

Sunlight is the healthiest of all light since it contains all the colors of the spectrum and affects our endocrine system. It stimulates hormones that affect us on all levels: physical, mental, emotional, and spiritual.

Feng Shui

Feng Shui—the Chinese art of placement and color—has long been used in East Asia to ensure good luck, health, and prosperity through knowledge of form, shape, locale, and color. It is becoming very popular in the United States as people learn about this ancient method of transformation. Parents and therapists who work in their homes with children on the Autism Spectrum should be especially cognizant of the colors that are used throughout the house.

The following is a good example of the use of Feng Shui. One time, decorating my house in which I worked with children on the Autism Spectrum, I selected colors specifically for the effects they would have on them. All rooms were visible from a certain point in my living room, where I worked with the children.

All windows and sliding glass doors had vertical blinds. The interior doors to the rooms were painted the same color as the room itself. This provided for a nicer flow of color into the room itself than the standard white door. The trim throughout was very pale lilac, which, although it sounds odd, pulled all of the rooms together in a beautiful rainbow of color. Table 11.1 lists the colors I carefully selected in my former home.

TABLE 11.1. FENG SHUI IN ACTION

Room	Walls	Blinds
Living Room/Dining Area	Apricot	Sage Green
Bedroom	Dusty Rose	Lemon Yellow
Office	Deep Yellow	Midnight Blue
Bathroom	Lighter Rose	(no window)
Kitchen	Dark Rose (also ceiling)	Deep Pink

The effect was mesmerizing to young children who, seeing the colors for the first time, simply stood for several minutes, absorbing them. Parents soon commented that their children were sleeping better and seemed happier and less hyperactive. First-time visitors were taken aback by the array of colors, but, like the children, they soon grew to like the various blends of colors.

Off-white walls and ceilings are the most popular interior colors in houses today, especially in the Southwestern United States. This can lead to boredom if more vibrant colors are not used elsewhere throughout the house in accessories, paintings, and rugs. Because there is a lack of understanding in our culture of the importance of color and how it affects us physically, mentally, emotionally, and spiritually, it may be the responsibility of a child's therapist to educate parents—and other therapists—about how colors affect their children and clients.

Cathedrals, especially in Europe, are known for their spectacular stained-glass windows. As the sun is reflected through the glass, it bathes the room in colors and adds a serene, healing quality to the prayers of the worshippers. In this setting, colors, combined with fervent prayers, create a powerful force for balancing one's body, mind, and spirit. The largest stained-glass window in the world is in St. Mary's Cathedral Basilica of the Assumption in Covington, Kentucky. This immense window is sixty-seven feet tall by twenty-four feet wide and the focal point of the cathedral, which was modeled after the Notre Dame Cathedral in Paris. In addition, there are two enormous round rose windows, so the overall effect is one of walking through a rainbow.

People in East Asia have always taken for granted that art has spiritual roots, while the Western world has generally lost its reverence for the arts. Science, art, and religion were always inextricably intertwined until the rise of materialism in the Middle Ages. In the high-tech age of the twenty-first century, we now have scientists, artists, and religionists, few of whom can relate to the others in terms of each being one-third of a homogenous spiritual entity. To bring wholeness to future generations, science, art, and personal beliefs have to be recognized as the three spiritual qualities of a coordinated civilization. Color is an important part of the equation.

> To bring wholeness to future generations, science, art, and personal beliefs have to be recognized as the three spiritual qualities of a coordinated civilization. Color Is an Important part of the equation.

Spiritual Expression Through Color

A person can express his spiritual nature in color as well as in words, tones, and forms. Many traditional tribes still first decorate and then clothe themselves in colors that represent how their spirits feel about their place in the world. (See the inset on page 204 about the traditional spiritual significance of color.) The way we combine colors is indicative of our appreciation of the spiritual nature of color, or lack thereof. We need to represent our inner selves by consciously choosing our clothing, since this symbolizes our true selves to people we meet on a business or social level.

When color itself creates the boundaries, shapes and forms will naturally flow through the colors. This appears to be a radical concept, but it can best be explained by the example of first using coloring books for children who are hyperactive and unable to focus. Using crayons and observing how they are coloring in their book, they learn that they should be coloring within the lines. This gives them a concept of boundaries and order.

From there it's a short step to working with watercolors on plain white paper, where there are no guidelines, nothing to say, "This is a tree. It has green leaves," or, "This is the sky and I know the sky is blue so this has to be blue." When painting on a plain white sheet of paper, a child must use his imagination even to begin the first brush stroke. His first tentative step with the color red may look like an irregular circle or oval, but suddenly his creativity kicks in and he adds four little legs. Then he adds dots of color to the pool of red and suddenly he has painted a ladybug—all without boundaries. The paint, shape, and color have inspired him to create what is for him something quite extraordinary. It was copied not from a real ladybug sitting before him but from his own mind. His excitement is contagious—he wants to paint more and more.

THE MANY USES OF COLOR

Artistic therapy, including the use of color, may be used to strengthen the will and memory of a child with special needs—or rather, a child in need of special care of his spiritual needs. Intellect is often a hindrance in artistic endeavors such as painting or drawing, since we usually want to recreate what we see with our physical eye. But, if we allow ourselves to paint what we see with spiritual vision we will use colors that evoke feelings that come from our inner life experience, not from intellectual analysis. This is the exact opposite of mathematics, science, mechanics, and physics, where emotions must be overshadowed by one's intellect.

When a child is attuned to his spiritual nature, he is able to paint more than a copy of something tangible, such as flowers or trees. His imagination flows through the colors as he transcends the purely physical. Art lessons teach spatial relationships by guiding children to draw lines that indicate background, foreground, and objects. The purpose is to create a picture that is spatially correct. The spiritual artist, on the other hand, simply paints with color. He may have no preconceived idea of what the outcome will be or how he will accomplish it. This is not to suggest that a child shouldn't know about spatial perspective—only that he may understand it while instead consciously using his knowledge of color to express his spiritual nature.

Color can give the impression of objects being in the background or foreground. The object's size does not have to be changed, as is usually the case in creating perspective, because color can give the impression of size. It also gives the impression of weight, since objects appear to be heavier or lighter depending on what colors are used. Color can be used to indicate something or someone seemingly moving forward by the use of red-yellow. If the artist intends to show an object in the background, or retreating, he will use blue-violet.

This color perspective is found in the art of many Renaissance masters. Once a child begins to sense how the use of color can make a picture come alive, he will produce inspired art that will be helpful to a therapist's interpretation. He may not intellectually grasp the theory, but he will feel it is a natural way to paint. Whether he creates a painting or simply enjoys looking at one, he senses the spiritual meaning of color, which is both an inner and an outer experience.

A child who is left alone with paints will use colors and shapes that speak to and through him. As soon as he is told to paint an object, he is no longer creating art but instead a copy of something material. It becomes an original piece of art when a child uses colors to depict action or movement that he feels or "sees" in his mind. Painting from an image in one's mind is different from painting something that already has physical form. One is true creative art and the other is duplication. There is nothing wrong with copying something we see; it is simply a different mental process. In fact, many children and adults are more comfortable reproducing something they can actually see, and we cannot say that their finished product is not art.

When one appreciates art, like the artist one "tastes" the color—not literally, of course, but through a subtle imaginative process that takes place at the back of the tongue, much like "eating" with our eyes before we actually eat and enjoy an attractive meal. Artists can smell the vague nuances of color—again not literally, but with something deep within that is moved as they immerse themselves in color.

SYNESTHESIA

Some people have an unusual ability to see colors as they hear sounds. This is an example of what is known as synesthesia, which means, "mingling of the senses." They literally feel colors. For example, the ringing of a telephone may cause a synesthete to see and feel jagged red lines, and the whole effect can be painful. This may be a reason why autistic children are so jolted by noise. Perhaps the sound is accompanied by disturbing visual and sensory images.

Synesthesia affects one in every 500,000 people, and those with this condition may say the taste of a lemon feels like points pressing against their face. This could also explain why some children on the Autism Spectrum refuse to eat certain foods. If they are tactilely defensive, the texture may be repugnant or physically painful.

For a synesthete, the spoken word and the vowels all have different colors. Some synesthetes can enjoy listening to classical music with the

> When one appreciates art, like the artist one "tastes" the color—not literally, of course, but through a subtle imaginative process that takes place at the back of the tongue, much like "eating" with our eyes before we actually eat and enjoy an attractive meal.

added pleasure of seeing colors that correspond to the various instruments. They are able to see and hear a symphony with all the flowing of hues and tones that the average person cannot. Research has shown that varying the pitch of cycles per second alters the colors seen by a synesthete.

If we think about light waves and their differences in frequency, it seems logical that, when the pitch of a note is increased, there is a corresponding change in wavelength and frequency. In other words, if a low bass note is sounded on a cello, the wave is lengthened and the synesthete will see deep colors such as dark red. The shorter the wavelength, the higher the pitch and the lighter the colors that are seen by people with this ability.

Synesthetes' lives can be complicated, since in extreme cases words spoken by people during the course of a day are accompanied by visual effects such as smoke, fog, blocks of wood, and streaks of color. Children with synesthesia love music and can carry a tune. But for some, when they have to sing words, they are confused by the colors and images produced by the words and the music. Some children who are gifted piano players are annoyed when they try to add words to their compositions and continually see colors and objects.

Although true synesthesia is relatively rare and perplexing, some "average" people can also "see" the colors of different instruments in a piece of classical music by relaxing and "looking" with closed eyes. Colors begin to move in the darkness and it soon becomes quite pleasurable. To these people, it is a game or diversion that is turned on and off at will. Not so with the true synesthete, who has no control over it since it is due to the structure of his brain.

COLOR VISION DEFICIENCY

Although most children will enjoy this game, some may be frustrated because they are unable to tell one color from another. It is estimated that one out of every ten females and one out of every twelve males are color-blind, or what is now known as "color vision deficient." This deficiency is an inherited inability to distinguish between certain colors, especially between red and green, more rarely between blue and yellow.

Many adults first realize they have a problem when they notice that traffic lights are confusing, since red and green look alike to them. They soon figure out that red is on top, green on the bottom, and yellow in the middle. However, a yellow caution light may be puzzling when they aren't sure what color it is. When traveling to other places, they may find that traffic lights are horizontal rather than the familiar vertical, which means they now have to learn left and right instead of up and down for the rules of driving.

Such adults may have had problems as children and not known it. For example, if a teacher asks children to use a red crayon, they will pick the right one only if they have learned how to spell "red," which is printed on the covering. As a result, some children are very careful about not ripping the paper off of their crayons. Others always ask their parents to buy the smallest possible box of crayons because the larger ones include more fancy names, like cinnamon, and too many choices.

A malfunction of the retina, color vision deficiency can be frustrating. Women may have a problem applying their cosmetics, and men may have

Color Vision Deficiency: A Personal Story

Kathy Koewler, a friend of mine, has a teenage son, Al, who is colorblind. I feel their personal experience might be helpful to other parents whose children may have a color vision deficiency. The following is an email she sent me.

When an adult asked (young) Al how he liked the red sweater, then whatever he saw he considered red. It was later on when he had to learn to plug in the correct colors that we found he had a problem. In his case, he has trouble telling red from orange if they are side by side.

As he has gotten older we have found that he does see the different colors in some form, but I don't think that he sees different shades as most people do. Al has always liked the extreme contrast of black and white. I am guessing that the black, white, and gray are easy for him to see clearly. He went through a time when he wanted sheets and his room in all black and white. He also wears a lot of black, white, or gray tee shirts. I think that if I pushed him, he would say it is because he KNOWS what color they are. It is safe.

I am not really sure just how he knows or if he knows colors. He must have some way to figure it out. He took a computer graphics class and the final was to recreate a picture that the teacher had drawn. I know that to match the color was really, really hard for him. He did well in the class but failed the final because it took him too long to match colors. But he never would tell the teacher why. Here is something else strange . . . he can see a rainbow, which I would think would be hard, as the color is so faint.

My dad was what I would call profoundly color blind. He saw almost no color. Most things were just on a gray or tan scale . . . sort of like looking at an old black and white photo or a sepia print. Odd as it sounds, Dad was a very good photographer. He would shoot in color, but only for us to see. He was not so distracted by the color but his lighting and shadows were always good. He looked more at the composition than the colors.

We did know that Dad could not see any pastels. We learned that when his new tan pants were really a pastel pink. He was really angry about that Mom didn't tell him and he wore pink pants to work, but oh well, it was the 70s!

a hard time grilling steaks to perfection because they can't tell if they are rare or well done.

Parents whose children may have a color vision deficiency may find the personal experiences in the inset on page 215 insightful. Although color vision deficiency is inherited, it obviously can skip a generation, since neither Kathy nor any of her siblings has a problem distinguishing colors. Al had the intelligence, even as a young child, to develop coping skills, and will continue to find ways to compensate for his inability to distinguish colors. If your child is colorblind, ask him how he knows what crayon or paint to use. His ingenuity may surprise and delight you.

COLOR THERAPY

Color therapy, also known as chromotherapy, was taught in medical schools for hundreds of years until the beginning of the twentieth century, when the American Medical Association outlawed it as dangerous. In the twenty-first century, this seems ludicrous, since we know about all of the potentially dangerous side effects of drugs and all of the benefits of artistic therapy.

Color therapy is based on the fact that certain colors affect various organs of the body, and if an organ is malfunctioning or isn't healthy, the proper application of color may bring improvement or total healing. Color therapists may use glass slides of different colors that are projected onto the body of an ill person, and some simply use colored cloths placed over the afflicted area. Both may sound absurd to the scientific, analytical mind, or to one who simply has never heard of chromotherapy.

Children with psycho-neuro disorders such as autism, ADHD, and Asperger's Syndrome can be helped with the thoughtful use of color. Ideally, schools and therapists' offices would have one area decorated in red pillows, rugs, and/or walls, and another in blue. Children who are anxious or lethargic could sit in red or blue beanbag chairs, cover themselves with the appropriate color throw, and read a book, work on a puzzle, do their homework, or take a nap.

Changing a "busy" or cluttered environment also has a beneficial effect on the emotions. Homes and therapists' offices should be places of serenity with soft colors, fine music, and tasteful accessories. If you've ever entered a home or office and experienced an uncomfortable feeling for no obvious reason, the effects of colors used in the décor may have been to blame. Pay attention to these reactions, whether they are positive or negative, and note the colors of walls, rugs, and furniture. We can create a colorful healing environment in our home or clinic more with awareness than with money.

Color therapy is based on the fact that certain colors affect various organs of the body, and if an organ is malfunctioning or isn't healthy, the proper application of color may bring improvement or total healing.

Color has healing qualities beyond color draping, although this practice has the right idea about the healing effects of color on the emotions. The remedial use of color recognizes its effects on the totality of our body, mind, and spirit, not on just one aspect of our nature. It is of particular importance to a child in the early stages of development, since color is as nourishing as good food and a healthy lifestyle.

Often, major changes in a child can occur when color is used extensively, as we can see by the following case:

Therapeutic Use of the Color Red

Kari was a bright, very hyperactive five-year-old girl with ADHD whose preschool teachers constantly complained about her inability to sit still for more than a few seconds. As she began a series of weekly one-on-one sessions involving the therapeutic use of color, art, and music, Kari experienced a series of dramatic improvements. The following are some notes I made of her sessions:

First session: I drew traffic lights with the appropriate colors, which Kari could not comprehend. Her attention span was just seconds. Suggestions were made to her mother about her diet and color in her environment. Red and red/orange were recommended colors for Kari's clothes and room.

Second session: Kari's ability to focus had increased to ten minutes. Her mother stated that she had made the suggested changes and noticed an improvement almost immediately in terms of her daughter's greater attention span and reduced hyperactivity.

Third session: Kari worked with clay for about twenty minutes. She danced around with flowing scarves and named all the colors. She lay on the floor, surrounded with yellow and red scarves. In addition to focusing on color, I introduced a variety of modalities, including massage. Kari enjoyed and responded to them all.

Fourth session: Kari easily assembled a jigsaw puzzle. In school, she was able to string macaroni, showing her fine motor skills had improved along with her attention span. Teachers were impressed with her newfound ability to perform this task.

Fifth session: Kari was wearing a T-shirt she was given in preschool for sitting still the longest during story time.

These improvements continued as Kari's mother conscientiously worked with her at home and monitored her diet. She stated that red was now Kari's favorite color. Interestingly, it was also the mother's. For years she had needed greater energy to keep up with Kari, but as her daughter gradually improved, blues and greens (calming colors for adults) were added to Kari's mother's wardrobe. Both mother and daughter were calmer and happier. The change in Kari would probably not have happened if her mother felt that colors have no effect on people. Because she was willing to try anything to help her daughter, everyone benefited. You can create changes in your child, too.

WHAT CAN I DO?

As a parent, you can do many more things with your child at home than any teacher or therapist can because you are with him for a much longer time and have a sustained and personal interest.

Now that you know how color affects us, you may want to think about changing the décor of your child's room. Curtains, paint, and bedding can be chosen according to his needs or temperament. Color affects us on many levels, and we unconsciously gravitate to clothing that provides a certain energy that is needed at that particular time. If left to their own resources, children intuitively pick clothing that will give them exactly what they need, whether it is for a soccer game, a test, or just to relax.

Encourage your child to express himself creatively through drawing, painting, or other artistic means. This is a good way of seeing the colors that he is subconsciously attracted to. Young, hyperactive children should be given mostly red, yellow, and orange crayons or paints; blue, green, and violet should be provided for quiet, withdrawn children.

To add more color to the paintings of your child, he can paint white wooden or plastic frames to match one of the colors in the picture. Since it is your child's artwork, ask him what color frame he thinks would look nice with the picture. It probably won't be the same shade you had in mind, but it is his work of art and he will have a greater sense of ownership and self-esteem by selecting the frame, the color, and actually painting it himself. He may decide he doesn't like the color he chose and wants another. It's easy either to wash off the existing color or to repaint it. This may happen several times, but it's something he can do and enjoy.

As a parent, you can do many more things with your child at home than any teacher or therapist can because you are with him for a much longer time and have a sustained and personal interest.

When children—with or without autism—listen to classical music and are surrounded with the colors they need, wonderful benefits are achieved. They become more aware that we live in a world of color and tone and easily visualize colors or images as they hear the music. They exercise their brains and create new synapses, through which nerve impulses pass from one neuron to another. They learn more easily since their mind is not bombarded with the sounds of television, stereo, or video games. Their IQ increases and speech improves as a result of the filling of their mind and body with inspiring music and colors appropriate to their needs.

Games of Memory and Color

Some of the exercises relating to color may be difficult for most children with autism, but they should be given the opportunity to participate to the best of their ability. Others on the Spectrum, such as those who have ADHD or Asperger's Syndrome, will thoroughly enjoy entering into the spirit of these challenging games without realizing how much they are learning. Naturally, it all depends on their age and level of comprehension.

Turn to page 283 of Part Two for exercises using color to encourage and enhance creativity, observation, and memory.

SUMMARY

Whether we are aware of it or not, we are constantly affected by colors, just as we are by music, noise, and people in our environment. Color has more of an effect on us than we may realize and can be used in a variety of ways to create a positive environment or effect for children and adults. We are energized or calmed by the colors we choose, and we often select the wrong colors for our children, who don't respond to color in the same way adults do. Red may invigorate us adults, but children find it relaxing.

Color therapy is an ancient art that is experiencing a revival as more people begin to understand the healing power of colors. Like music, color has its roots in the spiritual world. Neither can be intellectually analyzed; we need to feel music and feel color. As we learn the true nature of color, we can more effectively help children regain the sense of beauty and awe that once permeated painting, music, dance, poetry, and sculpture. The suggestions given in this chapter for changes in color schemes are part of basic color therapy, and have been proven to benefit children on the Autism Spectrum.

Color games and activities exercise a child's memory and imagination and can be easily done in the home as well as in therapy or the classroom. But before a child can fully enter into any activities or a whole, healthy, normal life, he has to have proper speech, breathing, and hearing capabilities, which are discussed in the next chapter.

CHAPTER 12

Speech and Hearing

Children on the Autism Spectrum often also suffer from frustrating challenges involving speaking, hearing, and breathing. These three processes, often taken for granted, are interconnected. Such disorders further disrupt the body's balance and three-fold nature. Each of us is affected by speech, breathing, and hearing, all of which should ideally flow easily throughout our lives.

We rarely, if ever, think about the process and powerful impact of speech. However, respect and attention should be carefully considered when choosing our words. The sounds of our words have an energy, rhythm, and tone, all of which have a direct impact upon the listener. This is especially true for children on the Autism Spectrum, who love the arts and respond to cadence and rhythm, both in music and in speech.

Music, art, and other alternative therapeutic methods can be very effective for children who have been diagnosed with a Spectrum Disorder. All of these are viable options that can be explored after a proper diagnosis is reached. That can be done only after a complete physical examination of your child, after which the doctor may feel your child also needs help with her speech and suggest a speech therapist.

These specialists work with people who have difficulty pronouncing certain words or sounds. They frequently work within the school system and are available for therapeutic sessions during school hours. Many also have their own business, within a group or as a sole practitioner. They also work with adults, many of whom have speech difficulties following a stroke.

If the doctor feels your child either is not responsive to her name being called or fails to react to loud sounds in her environment, she may also suggest a hearing test by an audiologist. These specialists have advanced training in either a master's or doctoral program. They diagnose and treat people who have problems with hearing or with their balance, the latter of which may be the result of an inner ear disturbance. They may work in

Speech is an art through which we can create. Every sound has its own energy and rhythm.

tandem with other therapists to provide an integrative approach for children on the Spectrum.

This chapter will explore how to nurture and guide your child through the powerful process of speech. Speech is an art through which we can create. Every sound has its own energy and rhythm. In addition to carefully selecting the words you say to your child, you can use other techniques to help her. Massage can be more than just relaxing; it can help children with speech disorders and those who are overwhelmed by external noise. The concept of Touch and Tone provides a sensory experience that combines voice, massage, tactile sensations, and imagination while crossing the mid-poles of the body through touching the back. The power of speech cannot be ignored.

THE POWER OF SPEECH

We know that our words can be either constructive or destructive. Both kinds can occur in the same thought, as this ten-year-old girl discovered: "Martha, that's a lovely blue dress." (Martha is pleased that Aunt Lillian noticed.) "It's too bad that color looks awful on you." (Martha is devastated. Aunt Lillian is oblivious.) Words can hurt.

There is power in speech that is often overlooked. Words have—in addition to sound—form and energy. If you have ever been on the receiving end of someone's anger, you know the physical and emotional reactions to their outburst and what it feels like to have an index finger jabbed at you to make a point. It is a threatening gesture, and you can almost see the sparks flying from the finger. Angry words actually attack our physical body and can cause trembling and nausea. Negative words hurt, and positive words have the opposite effect—it is that simple. Because we find it so easy and automatic, we often lash out verbally at our children without thinking of the damage that can be done, especially to those on the Spectrum, who can be very sensitive.

Some people find there is more to sounds than simply hearing; they can also "see" words. As discussed in the previous chapter, synesthesia is a rare condition that causes senses to blend together. A synesthete, for instance, might perceive sounds, words, and music as color and form, in which case each word and each note may have a distinctive color and shape as words and music flow in colorful waves. Synesthetes are either very grateful for or very irritated by these experiences, which cannot be turned on and off at will. If we could see the color and form of words as synesthetes do, we would realize that there is more to speech than we can imagine. We might learn to give our words form, texture, and color to make them more effective and pleasing.

Using Words Wisely

Speaking releases energy that strikes the nearest object, which is usually a person. If we can keep that in mind, we can see that we need to speak articulately and without anger, hate, or gossip, all of which are damaging to the sensitive natures of those involved. We need to learn how to use words wisely.

There is a saying, "A soft voice turns away wrath." A calm voice can diffuse just about any situation that might escalate and end up in an argument. I discovered this when I had four young children and, like all youngsters, they were often rambunctious and loud. Raising my voice accomplished nothing, but if I lowered it to almost a whisper they suddenly stopped yelling or running and listened to what I was saying. In a soft voice, I would ask them please to play more quietly, and they did. At that young age, they knew that when their mother lowered her voice, she was serious.

A soft voice encourages dialogue and communication with children who may have difficulty verbalizing their deepest thoughts. When words are sung instead of spoken, they will usually get the attention of an autistic child, who tends to ignore the spoken word. This is a great technique for asking questions, giving instructions, and opening lines of communication.

Talking with a child about a variety of topics while offering a lot of supportive, sincere praise and engaging with him in activities such as painting or working with clay is doubly therapeutic. This is especially important for a non-verbal child who may have little or no support from people who assume that, because she cannot talk, her hearing is impaired. Do not be misled by the lack of verbal response; if her hearing is intact, she is listening to and absorbing everything you say.

If you watch her face carefully, you will see a quick sideways glance, a flicker of an expression, or a very slight smile. Because she is so aware, it is important to choose your words wisely. While both of you paint or work with clay, talk about an interesting documentary you saw on television, a trip you took to the Grand Canyon, or anything that is intriguing and filled with images. Be graphic and descriptive; be humorous and enthusiastic. Above all, be respectful and talk to her as you would to a child two or three years older. In other words, talk up to her; do not talk down to her.

Children with autism, ADD/ADHD, or Asperger's Syndrome should always be talked to in words appropriate for kids who are years ahead of their age. If a child of three years can understand an older child of eight whose speech is developed, why do we always "dumb down" our language? Do not be afraid to use complete sentences, and remember that tone is just as important as the words themselves.

As a society, we have become lazy in many areas, not the least of which is our speech. It is filled with slang that is now in the dictionary, and teens think there is nothing wrong with four-letter words that are seeping into our everyday language. If a child is surrounded only by slovenly or poorly articulated speech, she will not be able to develop imaginary thought. Instead, she'll constantly be exposed to dead words that will stunt her mental, emotional, and spiritual growth. The ability to form images as we speak and hear stimulates our creativity and speech. Slang, vulgarity, and strident tones are paralyzing to the spiritual nature of a child who yearns for truth, beauty, and goodness.

Slovenly speech is symptomatic of an unorganized mind and careless personality. We don't want our body to starve, so we feed it, but if we don't feed our children with words that nourish them, they are deprived of what they need for emotional and spiritual growth. They can't tell us they are hungry for this nurturing, so it is up to us to provide it through our words and behavior, which can shape the personality of a child.

Painting With Words

Every time we speak, we influence people with the energy of our words. Even before we open our mouths, we are transmitting our thoughts to others.

Words from our mouths are every bit as creative as paint flowing from a brush on canvas because we paint a word picture as we speak with colorful language, humor, enthusiasm, and passion. This is important when we are talking with children on the Autism Spectrum—especially those with Asperger's Syndrome, who take everything literally. We have to articulate clearly so that they know we respect them as people and don't think of them as "just kids" who can barely understand the most basic linguistic expression.

For example, if you walk down a path in the park with your child and pick up your pace, she will run to keep up with you. She is interested in where you are going and what new things you might discover. She doesn't want to miss out on anything. In a similar vein, when speaking to your child, you must elevate the level of your words to encourage her to rise to a higher level of understanding and articulation. She will want to stretch herself to see what she can discover.

Every time we speak, we influence people with the energy of our words. Even before we open our mouths, we are transmitting our thoughts to others. Because thoughts are so powerful and children are so intuitive, they trust more what their therapists or parents think than what they say. If someone dislikes a painting by a child but tells her how wonderful it is, she hasn't been fooled. There is an energy that precedes and accompanies speech that is obvious to a sensitive person and impossible to disguise.

When we think of our words as art that we have created, we can become more articulate and less strident.

The Overlooked Art

Speech is an art. Our voice reveals our inner self or spiritual nature, our true personality, how we perceive ourselves, and/or the image we want to project. A soft voice has healing qualities just as a loud, raucous voice is destructive to the feeling nature of all people, regardless of age. We no longer consider speech an art, as did the Greeks who recited poetry. They recognized the impact of the number of syllables in a word and the relationship of rhythm and speed to breathing and blood circulation.

We often take words for granted and give little thought to the effect of our words on the people we are talking to. Words create in the same manner as art, music, or sculpture, with a major difference: They have the power to elevate or destroy, to build up or tear down. In the final analysis, it is not the words that cause their effect—it is the psyche of the speaker who gives her words power.

An inspired speaker can stir the positive sensitivity of her listeners and a fanatic can purposely ignite the emotions of her audience. The difference is clear—one speaks from her spiritual nature with no ulterior motive, and the other seeks to seduce and manipulate. People who try to influence the minds of other people with their aggressive monologues aren't interested in dialogue or communication.

Charismatic speakers manipulate through their speech as they raise and lower their voices to attract, and keep, the listeners' attention. We need to learn the positive aspects of doing the same thing when reaching and teaching children on the Spectrum. A monotone will not keep their attention, but animation, enthusiasm, and variations of tone will.

As we learn more about breathing, sound, and words, we become more aware of our voice as an instrument. A soft flute captures the attention of a child who listens closely, while a crashing cymbal causes her to shut down and turn off her hearing. We need to listen to our voice and ask, "What instrument am I?"

We can often forget that children are very sensitive young people. This sensibility is greatly magnified in children on the Spectrum who are vulnerable to sound. (See the inset on page 227 for information on filters that help control intolerable sounds.) Angry words from a parent must be especially hard for a child with autism, since she probably understands them but neither knows the cause nor can articulate her concerns. A child may also have a hearing problem that compounds her articulation disorder.

EXPRESSIVE/RECEPTIVE DISORDERS

When children have a chronic medical condition with hearing, vision, or other physical problems, their days are filled with discomfort that they are unable to verbalize.

Children may be diagnosed with an expressive disorder, a receptive disorder, or a mixed expressive/receptive disorder. These are variations of an inability of a child to express her thoughts or to understand the words of another person. In an expressive disorder, she may have trouble verbalizing or articulating her thoughts. In a receptive disorder, she may have difficulty understanding what is said to her and therefore be unable to process information as quickly as other children.

Mixed expressive/receptive language disorders include both of these disorders, and children may also have a combination of impairments in speech, hearing, and vision. They may stutter, have difficulty articulating their thoughts, and exhibit language delays. Because of these conditions, they may be inaccurately diagnosed and not receive appropriate treatment. All avenues should be explored when assessing the condition of children suspected of having expressive/receptive disorders.

Evaluation on a psychological/developmental level must be done. Testing by a qualified professional is very important in order to identify a disorder that can then be treated with various therapies, such as counseling and artistic exercises that improve verbal skills.

Any underlying physical conditions must be addressed. A complete physical examination can confirm or rule out the possiblity that any existing illness is the cause of the impairment in speech, hearing, or vision, or of any other potential medical problems. Vision impairment may be a factor. Testing by a Developmental Ophthalmologist will identify visual problems a child may have that might interfere with her ability to read or see clearly. A child's hearing must be evaluated. Testing by an audiologist will rule out deafness or loss of hearing, which may account for inattention in school or at home. A dental examination is in order. Teeth should be checked because any infection might result in speaking difficulties, discomfort, or pain.

When children have a chronic medical condition with hearing, vision, or other physical problems, their days are filled with discomfort that they are unable to verbalize. They also suffer from allergies as well as digestive problems resulting in frequent stomachaches, both of which are common among children on the Autism Spectrum.

Speech impediments have to be understood to lie deep within the body, and treatment cannot be undertaken as easily as massage to the limbs, torso, or head. Since you cannot touch the organs of speech, it is often frustrating for both the child and the therapist, who is trying to encourage sounds and verbalization. It is exasperating for the child when she obviously wants to communicate verbally but cannot. This is similar to the plight of stroke patients, who often express their frustration by crying. Is it any wonder autistic children cry a great deal? Their senses are overloaded with the noises, smells, and sights of their environment, and they can show their fear, pain, or anger only by putting their hands over their ears or crying.

When we speak to a child or ask her a question, we expect an immediate response. For most children on the Spectrum, information processing is different from or slower than for the average child. Adults—and other children—often fail to give a child time to respond and impatiently barge ahead with more words. This is defeating for a youngster who is still trying to assimilate the first bit of information and formulate a response. Be patient. Give her time to answer. If it is obvious that she is not going to respond, repeat what you said or asked, but do wait for a response.

If a child's hearing has been checked and found to be normal, it is important for parents to understand that although their child may be nonverbal, may not respond to questions or commands, and may seem to be off in her own world, she isn't deaf. Such children hear and understand every word that is said in their presence. They absorb from an environment that is often loud, angry, frustrated, unhappy, discouraging, and filled with resentment. They learn behavioral traits in the first three years that influence their own behavior and activities. Children can "read" body

Controlling Intolerable Sounds

We know that many children on the Autism Spectrum experience a painful, extreme sensitivity to certain sounds—noises that we may encounter every day but take for granted due to tolerance. Because of children's sensitivity to sound, an audiologist may recommend the use of a filter—especially for kids with Asperger's, who are more able to understand a filter's purpose than children with autism and therefore more willing to accept a foreign object in their ears.

These devices filter out the high or middle tones that bring pain to sensitive Aspies. As the child matures and her sensitivity relents, the filters can be changed according to her ability to tolerate certain noises. She can control the sounds she wants to hear by removing the filters and replacing them when noises are too loud or too high in frequency.

The audiologist may suggest a particular filter, but some older teens and adults like the soft foam earplugs found in drug stores. They are pliable and can be shaped into a form that is unobtrusive and comfortable. They filter out loud noises but not conversation or other sounds people find comforting. For example, they may filter out the screeching of a siren but allow one to hear one's cell phone ringing.

language and facial expressions that may be in direct opposition to the spoken words.

Parents have the capacity to affect their child's personality positively as their own morals, ethics, and integrity flow through the tone and modulation of their voice and penetrate to the deepest levels. We say that people who talk continuously about uninteresting things are babbling, yet when babies babble, we laugh with pleasure. So, the question is: What is babbling?

BABBLING

Infancy may be the only time people of the world are united, since babbling is universal. All babies, regardless of culture, vocalize the same sounds. As Karl König wrote in *The First Three Years of Life*, "Every baby is still a citizen of the world and not yet of his country of birth. He has the potential to speak any language and the babble of deaf babies is identical to the babies with normal hearing."

Infant babbling isn't speech; it is motor movement that is building the base for formation of words. Words aren't usually spoken until the tenth to twelfth month of life, but the beginning of speech starts with the baby's first cry, and then the infant goes through three stages. She begins babbling at about the third month in imitation of her parents and in reaction to certain words.

Vowels and Consonants: Warmth and Will

We learn at an early age that language comprises consonants and vowels, but we are not taught that vowel sounds engage the warmth in our feel-

Every Child Is Different

With hundreds of books and websites that delineate when children should begin to talk, parents eagerly anticipate the day their child reaches that milestone. When their child doesn't begin speaking at the age the books say she should, parents often are filled with worry and fear. It's so important to remember that every child is different. Little do parents know that this toddler likely has her own schedule, which doesn't coincide with the experts' timetable. When she doesn't perform on cue, she may be taken to a pediatrician, who may refer the family to a psychologist, who will schedule a series of tests to see why three-year-old Nicole isn't talking—and they may all turn out fine. Maybe Nicole has nothing to say. Maybe she's just a slow talker, and if so, she's not alone. Don't automatically assume your child must conform to the generalities you read about.

ing life and consonants stimulate the will. Vocalizing a repeated "T" or "D" has a totally different feel from "AH" or "O." This is true for all consonants and vowels. You can feel the throat opening with a vowel, and tone seems to come from deep within. There is warmth to the sound of an intoned vowel that is lacking in a consonant.

Think of an orchestra, where the strings and woodwinds are vowels, and the percussion and brass are consonants. Our response to music with a lot of melody or harmony is different from our response to music that emphasizes percussion. You can also think of the difference between a lullaby and a march. One stirs our feeling, sensitive nature—or inner warmth—and the other energizes our will to act and move. For this reason, having a child repeat consonants by themselves or in words will help those with autism, because they often seem to have little will to act.

Naturally, in speech, the vowels and consonants have to work together to form an intelligible word. The same happens within a child when she repeats vowels and consonants; she is activating both her feeling nature and her will. She does this without conscious thought, while a therapist who is familiar with the concept of Touch and Tone (see page 231) will knowingly plan an exercise according to what the child is lacking: sensitivity and feeling or will and force.

An infant's first sounds are vowels because her sense of feeling and spiritual nature are in the process of becoming. Later, she adds consonants, among the first of which are "ma-ma" and "da-da." Babbling starts as a single sound, and then progresses to a string of sounds, none of which can be described as an attempt to communicate with anyone other than the baby herself. It is sometimes called "gibberish" because we cannot understand what is being said, but in reality, babbling and gibberish are quite different.

Gibberish

Gibberish is language that sounds unintelligible, but that is only because we don't understand it. Some toddlers often speak in gibberish with body and facial gestures, great animation, and inflection that is fascinating to hear and watch. It's obvious that they know exactly what they are saying and trying to convey. Even though (most) others cannot understand their words, their body language, gestures, and sounds are often very clear.

I saw a great example of this when a mother, father, and their eighteen-month-old son entered a doctor's office. The boy went immediately to a basket of toys and took out the Lincoln Logs. He quickly began putting together a building but could not get the roof to stay on. He was frustrated, stood up, and began talking to his parents in gibberish. With one hand

Some toddlers often speak in gibberish with body and facial gestures, great animation, and inflection that is fascinating to hear and watch. It's obvious that they know exactly what they are saying and trying to convey.

on his hip, the other gesturing to them and the building he was obvious-ly telling them with amazing inflection and animation about his problem.

When his father said, "Jason, put the roof on," the boy responded with what appeared to be irritation and more unintelligible words, probably telling him, "I already tried, but it doesn't stay on!" Just then another family came into the office with a boy who was about five years old. Jason proceeded to tell him the same thing he told his father. The older boy looked at him, listened, and obviously understood because he went right to the building and put the roof on so that it stayed in place. Jason stood with both hands on his hips, satisfied that somebody finally understood what he was saying. Even more intriguing was that the older boy clearly understood what Jason's parents could not.

Gibberish is not unusual between twins, who have been known to have their own "secret" language, and is interesting to experience. It demonstrates that there is much more to speech than merely mimicking what we hear. There is imagination and originality that is beyond the average person's act of speaking.

THE PROCESS OF SPEECH

Actual speech is an intricate process that starts with thinking of what we want to say. Then the muscles and fine motor movements are called into play and words are formed. Both sensory and motor skills are involved because on the motor side we speak and on the sensory side we hear. They have to work together so we can hear what we say, and if that synergy is lacking, speech, sensory, and motor/muscle therapies can help.

In the cycle of speech, we have long and short syllables and tones that are stressed or de-emphasized in the rhythm of speech formation. When we speak, our words are carried on air in our lungs, throat, and mouth and by our tongue and lips, and are finally expelled as sounds. This is a beautifully complex process that is usually accomplished with no thought.

This communication system is used as a signal among animals, who communicate more clearly than human beings who create confusion with their words. An animal is not deeply affected by a loud, bellowing, angry voice, while a person absorbs it throughout her entire body. Although we have many similarities to animals, particularly to apes, only humans can speak, since speech is communication on a deeper level.

Articulated speech is possible only when a child hears the correctly spoken word. Speech and language are formed by imitation, and if a child's hearing is impaired, her speech will be as well. It is estimated that 5 percent of school-aged children have speech-language disorders. Children with such disorders used to be removed from their classes for individualized therapy. Today, the preferred method is to leave the child in the classroom and provide her the support services of a speech therapist, perhaps at home. This combined effort is beneficial to most children, who can thus be mainstreamed as long as possible.

Many creative, remedial therapists have a rudimentary knowledge of sign language and hand gestures for the most common words or acts, such as "more," "drink," "potty," "come," "sleep," "eat," "hurt," etc. Some parents do not want their hearing-impaired child to learn sign language, feeling it is better that she learn to verbalize her needs. Therapists and teachers should check with parents before using sign language, just as they should if they plan to implement massage.

TOUCH AND TONE (T&T)

Touch and Tone (T&T) is a form of massage in which a note is sounded by the therapist, perhaps by softly singing a vowel, while touching or stroking an area of the back. Words are also softly spoken or whispered while the back is massaged. By using different tones and words while massaging a child's back, the therapist is creating energy that permeates the child's sensory system. This, in turn, affects the organs, and then the brain and mind resonate in kind.

> We hear a sound not only through our ears. Our entire body hears it because we absorb it through the skin, which is our largest sense organ.

We hear a sound not only through our ears. Our entire body hears it because we absorb it through the skin, which is our largest sense organ. The epidermis is the uppermost layer of skin and the most sensitive to physical touch. Its minuscule sensory organs are embedded deep within the corium, which is the layer beneath the epidermis. The sympathetic and parasympathetic nerve endings are located in the epidermis, which is why Touch and Tone prompts an immediate response from the child.

Although a child may be seemingly uninterested in this exercise, she is acutely aware of the touch and words of the therapist. By tapping a child's back as you sing a song, you make the music and words more readily understood than you would by simply singing. Instructions and teachings that may not be clearly understood when spoken alone can be implemented during this process.

Autistic children cannot imitate their parents at the crucial stages of learning and are therefore unable to articulate their feelings and needs. Many seem to have the ability to turn off their hearing, a condition known as selective deafness. If this occurs during the stage of mimicking speech, they will lack the ability to communicate verbally. In this case, T&T is of greatest importance, since it intones notes and words, acknowledging that the entire body is a sense organ that hears and feels. Because we cannot see our back, we are protective of it and its vulnerability. It is because of this vulnerability that massage and toning are especially effective in returning balance to the body.

When a child cannot speak clearly on account of an inability to imitate words, Touch and Tone is especially effective, since sounds on the back cannot be turned off or ignored as aural sounds can be. If there is profound damage to the speech center of the brain, Touch and Tone will probably not work in helping a child to speak; however, even if the child cannot talk, she can hear, feel, and sense.

Parents can assume a proactive role in their child's learning and healing process by making a game of T&T. Although it may seem at first that a child is making no progress, she will usually begin to show some results in three months or a little longer. Also be sure to read the section on rhythmic massage, beginning on page 262. Rhythmic massage balances the body and brain through a specific method of crossing the mid-pole and stimulating the sensory system. Rhythmic massage and Touch and Tone have many similarities, but they are different forms of therapy.

Touch and Tone creates a vibration through the nerve endings and can create change as the sensory system is either invigorated or calmed depending on the types of stroking, massage, or tones used. Toning is more than singing a random song as we work with the back. Some sounds affect specific problem areas, which is the basis of Music Therapy. But Toning goes one step beyond that by combining touch and the use of certain vowels to achieve a desired effect. Again, the concept that vowel sounds encourage an inner warmth and our sensitive, feeling nature while consonant sounds stimulate our strength and will applies to Touch and Tone.

Energy of the Vowels

All religions and healing practitioners have used toning in one way or another. What most people do not realize is that toning, or vocalizing, creates a vibration within the entire body and actually has the healing effect of increasing the flow of oxygen in and strengthening the natural rhythm of the body.

Toning is not new, although its modern use may be. All religions and healing practitioners have used toning in one way or another. We have all heard of the sounds "Om" and "Aum" being used in meditation, chanted to reach a deep level of peace and serenity. What most people do not realize is that toning, or vocalizing, creates a vibration within the entire body and actually has the healing effect of increasing the flow of oxygen in and strengthening the natural rhythm of the body. Think of toning as an inner massage.

We do not have to be experts or even good singers to produce tones. Anyone can sing the notes of a scale, even if they are off-tune. To start, intone just the sounds of "oh" and "ah," and move on to other vowels as you feel comfortable. To be effective, your voice should be soft and low.

Just as words carry energy, so do the components of words; every uttered sound carries an energy of its own. It would be very difficult to outline the energy each sound produces. It is known, though, that children who stutter are helped by intoning the vowels I, A, and O, since these vowels have a beneficial effect on breathing problems.

There are two methods of toning that may be helpful. During a session in which the child and therapist are seated, the child repeats the tones of the therapist, not unlike traditional Speech Therapy. Or, the child may lie on her stomach as the therapist vocalizes, touches, and massages her back.

All vowels can be used with different notes of the scale. Much of this process is intuitive, and it soon becomes a "knowing" of what, where, when, and why sounding and touching are applied.

If this is a new process for you, it may take repeated attempts to notice your child's response or lack thereof. If you have a piano, you can play the scale while singing the vowels on each note. You will soon recognize which note she responds to; however, it may not be what is needed next time. It's at this point that you begin to rely on your own perception and sense of what her needs are.

This method can be used congruently with rhythmic massage. By massaging the torso from top to bottom and bottom to top, and then left to right and right to left (arms and legs are done separately), you are balancing and aligning the mid-poles of the body.

MASSAGE

Massage helps to restore proper breathing through relaxation, physical touch, and the vibration of sound. Anyone can do massage if they understand its purpose and have the desire to help children regain or retain their balance and well-being. There are many forms of massage, and some require specific training and membership in national or international organizations. Others who do massage have taken workshops, read about the process, or perhaps seen a documentary. Therapists who plan to use massage should read the inset below. However, you don't need special training if you apply the methods you will learn about in this chapter.

Always Ask Permission

If you are a therapist, check with the parents before using Touch and Tone or any form of massage. Tell them why you would like to use these methods, what you hope to accomplish, and exactly how it is done. Show them the techniques and encourage them to practice on their child. In a program that includes various remedial therapies, T&T and massage should be discussed with every parent so they know exactly what a session involves. Parents should also be made aware when the plan changes and some methods are eliminated and others added. Include all of this in an agreement, and have it signed and dated. It is for their information and your protection, since you will be touching their child's body.

Not all children on the Spectrum respond to massage in the same way:

- **ADD**—Children with ADD or ADHD usually have little or no hesitation when asked if they would like a massage, because many have had the experience and liked it. If a child says "No," accept it and go on to something else, but try again another day. She'll probably soon be curious and then look forward to it as part of her session.

- **Asperger's Syndrome**—Explain to children with Asperger's Syndrome that massage will help them to relax and let go of tension. Describe how you will gently rub their legs, arms, and back while they are on their stomach. Children with Asperger's are often a little leery of massage because they are reluctant to being touched, especially by someone they do not know well. This reaction isn't as dramatic as that of a tactilely defensive child with autism, but even so, Touch and Tone has to be introduced a little at a time so the therapist can gain the child's trust.

- **Autism**—There are so many different degrees of autism that it is difficult to say with certainty how a child will respond to massage. Touch and Tone can often be initiated as the child is involved in another activity, such as painting or working with clay. An arm, shoulder, or back can be gently touched, then stroked, if she will allow you to touch her. If she enjoys it, other sensory activities can be introduced, and eventually her tactile defensiveness will be greatly reduced.

Massage is easily performed when an autistic child is tired and lying down. However, it is also effective in calming a child who is hyperactive and/or crying. Obviously there are no rules for when to massage a child with autism, because she will change the rules.

Parents can do a form of T&T at home by singing softly and massaging their child's back. When done at bedtime, it relaxes and helps children sleep more restfully. This is a good time for a full massage of legs, arms, neck, and torso.

The body is a complex system of nerves. Autistic children, with their exquisite sensitivity, are constantly attacked from every direction by various energies, and they react by crying or screaming. They seem to be in pain, and they are. One of the most sensitive parts of the body is the back; we all know the feeling of sitting uncomfortably in a chair with a wooden back or enjoying the warmth of a heating pad on our back. Because the back has so many nerve endings, children who are able to relax and participate with a therapist enjoy the rhythmic harmony of massage. Children need harmony and rhythm to strengthen their three-fold nature of body, mind, and spirit. If there is disharmony in one of these elements, the child will not be in balance and may become ill.

If your purpose is to relax your child and prepare her for sleep, a gentle massage, soft voice, and classical music are an unbeatable combination. However, if your child has ADD, ADHD, or Asperger's and is compliant, massage can be fun for both of you as well as therapeutic for your child. (See page 236 for the story of Monica, a girl with ADHD who significantly improved while having fun.) Even as you stroke your child, keep her mind occupied by talking to her, asking questions, and telling stories.

When a child with autism is allowed to retreat into her shell during times of inactivity, she is not fully engaged with the world in which she lives. It is a mistake to think that because your child does not respond, she is incapable of hearing or communicating. She constantly needs to be talked with—not at—in a soft, soothing voice using graphic and colorful images.

THE IMPORTANCE OF PROPER BREATHING

Good speech and articulation are possible only through normal breathing. There is a difference between the voice of a healthy person and the voice of a sick person because the breath changes with illness. Most people breathe shallowly, which decreases the amount of oxygen in the body. As a result, carbon dioxide is not completely expelled and it builds up. When there is too much in the blood, it causes illness and discomfort, including rheumatism, constipation, liver disorders, diabetes, migraine headaches, kidney disease, and lethargy.

Years ago in hospitals, nurses made nightly rounds to remove plants and flowers from patients' rooms as a preventive measure, since it was widely believed that plants drew oxygen from people. They obviously meant well but were misinformed. People give off carbon dioxide, which is absorbed by plants, and plants give off oxygen, which is absorbed by people. It is a perfect symbiotic relationship, wherein each needs and supplies the other.

If you feel that you, your client, or your child needs more oxygen, one solution, in addition to simply making a conscious effort to take slower, deeper breaths, is to open the bedroom windows at night and during the day to let in the fresh air. Another is to have a variety of living plants throughout your office or house, especially in the bedroom.

By combining breath and speech we create a balance between the nerve-sense system and the metabolic system as one "morphs" into the other. In other words, they begin to work together for the greatest benefit to the child.

By combining breath and speech we create a balance between the nerve-sense system and the metabolic system as one "morphs" into the other. In other words, they begin to work together for the greatest benefit to the child.

The goal of remedial creative therapies is to provide children the means to bring their spiritual nature into everyday experience. Fear, doubt, and worry are the antithesis of creative therapy and our spiritual

Monica: A Dramatic Change

Monica was a six-year-old girl with ADHD who was constantly getting into trouble at school. She bit, punched, kicked, screamed, and refused to do her schoolwork. Her report cards consistently stated she needed improvement, and her parents were frantic because the school advised them that Monica would have to leave if she didn't improve her grades and control her behavior. People had a sense that she was jumping out of her skin as her heightened senses kept her in a state of constant physical and mental activity, which she seemed to struggle to control. Even while she was involved in drawing a picture with many objects, her eyes would dart from one item in the room to another.

I developed a program of the remedial therapies of music, art, and sensory integration, which she enjoyed. She especially liked massage and frequently asked me to "write" on her back. Since different geometric forms have different energy (the basis of Feng Shui, the art of color and placement), I would "draw" shapes with my index finger one at a time on Monica's back, and she would then identify them. Small and large circles, squares, and rectangles were alternated with ovals and lemniscates, both horizontal and vertical. (A lemniscate is the symbol of infinity, similar to a figure "8" on its side, and is ideal for crossing the mid-poles of the body.)

At other times, I would draw a number or letter while intoning the sounds of the vowels. A variation would be to draw the letter and have Monica identify it and use it in a word, which she then spelled. Another variation was to draw part of a letter—for example an "N" without the final upward stroke or half of an "O." This was a little more difficult, but Monica correctly identified the letter most of the time. Obviously, she was a very bright six-year old.

She soon asked me to "do a story" on her back. The stories involved drawing a scene such as a square block with stores and houses of different sizes and shapes. There was always a cast of characters, some with names, who walked about, in and out of stores and restaurants, or stopped to chat with someone as I traced their motions in straight or zigzag lines, in circles or spirals, weaving the movements into the story. Monica visualized all of these stories and would later draw them with crayons, colored pencils, or watercolors. All of these "fun games" were remedial, and the changes in this girl were exciting to her parents.

Sensory integration is the term used when we are able to process things that we experience through our five senses. We can then integrate them into our mind. If a child has a Sensory Integration Disorder (SID), she may be unable to process or identify what she sees, hears, smells, touches, or tastes. She may be impervious to pain or extremely sensitive to it. She may have a very minor problem with these issues or a major one. SID is usually associated with autism. For example, a child with autism usually doesn't like to be touched, but she may enjoy touching objects or people because she is obtaining a sensory pleasure. There are many exercises to enhance the sense of touch, identification, and memory. Two of the activities for Monica consisted of identifying objects by touch that were hidden under a towel (this is described on page 296 of Part Two) and identifying objects drawn on her back.

After less than two months of sensory integration, creative therapies, and Touch and Tone, plus a great deal of dialogue, her teachers noticed that she was beginning to play nicely with her peers. After three months, the changes in her behavior and grades were dramatic.

nature and create conditions that bring us more deeply into materiality. These three powerful emotions affect our breathing, which becomes rapid and shallow, and most people—especially children on the Autism Spectrum—experience at least one of them on a daily basis. Nightmares often result from this imbalance, disturbing a child's sleep and wakening concerned parents. Soon, this unbalanced breathing becomes the norm and causes nervousness and illness in some form.

Poetry and Oral Sculpting

Speech and breath affect every aspect of our three-fold nature of thinking, feeling, and willing. Every time we speak, we alternate cadence, vowels, and consonants to form a balance. Poetry, like music and art, affects us in different ways. It may stimulate our desire to think or imagine, or it may bore us. Some verses are soothing and peaceful; others are fiery and excite our will. Some of the great poets, such as Goethe and Browning, wrote with an awareness of the effect of their words.

> When we articulate with speech, we become a sculptor as we create form, tone, and meaning, which are expelled or projected in our exhalation.

Just as therapists selectively provide remedial art and music to children, so should poetry be selected to strengthen the developing child. It does not matter that the child appears deaf to your words. At some level she hears, understands, appreciates, and is strengthened by your efforts.

As we begin to read and listen to poetry with consciousness and recognize a child's physiological responses, we can provide the proper poetic "remedy" to children according to the needs of their temperaments. (See Chapter 8.) The rhythm and cadence of our speech affects a child in the same way that music does: It balances the body's natural rhythm.

When we articulate with speech, we become a sculptor as we create form, tone, and meaning, which are expelled or projected in our exhalation. Imagery such as this is very helpful in understanding the power of the word. If we can imagine our impressive ability to create with words, we can more readily understand why speech is important.

WHAT CAN I DO?

As a teacher, you might be the first person to identify a speech, hearing, or sensory disorder in a child. Parents may suspect a problem but believe it is a condition that will correct itself and fail to seek help. In the classroom, you have the opportunity to notice a potential concern and bring it to their attention. Your observation and conversation may be exactly what parents need to acknowledge a problem and be spurred to contact a medical professional.

If you are a therapist, the unconventional methods described in this book will offer some food for thought when working with children on the

Autism Spectrum. Everything can be seamlessly integrated into your existing programs. The seemingly minor improvements observed by therapists will be seen by parents at home. This often has the effect of changing their attitudes towards what they may perceive as a program that isn't working if progress is slower than expected.

Activities to Enhance Communication

Children's progress is much more rapid when their parents are actively involved. There are many opportunities for family members to touch, stroke, and massage the child, which is a wonderful way to communicate their love.

Simple home exercises, such as those involved in the processes of breathing and speaking, can help increase gross motor capacity. Singing is a fun activity that can help a child become more comfortable with expressing herself and moving beyond her inner world. Singing together as a family is beneficial for everyone, but especially for a child who has breathing difficulties. Singing helps to open up the lungs and strengthen the entire respiratory system.

Playing classical music and doing a group relaxation is a great family activity. Do simple breathing exercises and say "Inhale" as you breathe in through your nose and "Exhale" as you breathe out through your mouth, each for about three seconds. Children will imitate the rhythm of your breathing; shallow breathing becomes deeper and it soon regulates itself to a normal and healthy rhythm. You can then either remain quiet for a few minutes or do a simple visualization, depending on the attention span of your children.

Children's progress is much more rapid when their parents are actively involved. There are many opportunities for family members to touch, stroke, and massage the child, which is a wonderful way to communicate their love. A tactilely defensive child will want to be touched very gently at first but may soon welcome a warm embrace. She may not return it, which is typical of an autistic child, but she will enjoy it—especially when it is done with love. If it is thought of as a duty, she will know and she will reject it.

Turn to page 287 of Part Two for an exercise that will enhance a child's verbal dexterity and communication.

It is up to us, as parents, to do everything we possibly can to help our children. We know now how we create with our words, but do we really understand how damaging thoughtless and sarcastic comments can be? Those words can hurt for decades, until we learn to let go of the situation that created them.

WORDS CAN HURT

Most parents want the best for their children but are unaware of the effects of their words upon a sensitive young person. People think they are being amusing when they make sarcastic comments. Often these are said with a chuckle, to soften the cutting edge of the knife. Some examples are:

The Power of Patience and a Soft, Kind Voice

Elliot, an intelligent nine-year-old Aspie, loved the books I brought each week for him to look at. He was fascinated with trains, planes, trucks, fire engines, and anything that had complex parts and purposes. Although he read very well, he mispronounced words and was annoyed if I corrected him, even softly. He would say, "I know! I know!" and quickly turn the page. The first few times he was irritated that I had the audacity to correct him, since it was a new experience for him. He soon realized that I was not ridiculing or scolding him. He would ask, "Can I read this sentence over again?" and he would, correctly. I found it interesting that he wanted to read the entire sentence instead of just the word.

The next step was to ask if he understood what the word meant, and this was always followed by an interesting exchange of questions and answers that stimulated his inquiring mind. Although he stumbled over some relatively easy words, he clearly knew the names of every dinosaur in his dinosaur book.

Elliot's appreciation of reading and articulation was enhanced by his freedom to ask questions without feeling he was being judged, and also by his strong desire to learn. It is important for us to remember that a child will respond to a soft, kind voice but shut down if he feels he is being scolded, misunderstood, or patronized. Even at a young age, children are that perceptive.

Mother to child with dripping ice cream cone: "What a little slob. I can't take you anywhere." (chuckle)

Grandma to thirteen-year-old girl: "Well, you're no beauty, but you get good grades and some boys like that." (smile)

Father to son who trips over a rug in a dark hallway: "What a klutz!" (ha ha)

Sibling to curly-headed sister: "Hey, Brillo-head!" (entire family laughs)

Have you ever said something similar to a child? If so, she'll remember it. The following is an exercise for parents (or anyone) that can help them identify some of the ways they may have been injured by thoughtless comments and how they may be doing the same thing to children.

Take a minute to think about something that was said that hurt your feelings. If you're still holding on to it (and you probably are, since you remember it), it's time to let go. Hanging on to anger and resentment does not hurt the offending person; it hurts only you. It will literally destroy you. As you think about the most hurtful comments made to you, keep in mind that they were probably said in a moment of thoughtlessness. Look at the comments and let them go or the pattern will, in all probability, be passed on to your children. Children learn by your example, and you are their role model.

We can hope that people will soon realize that verbal abuse and emotional abuse are every bit as destructive as physical abuse and break the pattern. As adults, we can release our anger and hurt, but autistic children do not know how to do that. It is far better to consider our words before we say them, because once said they cannot be taken back.

Changing Your Words

Now that you have examined some of the painful comments that have been stored away for years, it is time to look at the things you may say and do to your children. It is important that you do not feel overly guilty about this. There are very few parents who never feel twinges of guilt about some of the things said and done in moments of anger that caused tears to well up in their child's eyes. And yet, most parents do the very best they know how, making mistakes and perhaps learning from them.

A simple rule of thumb is to remember that most statements made in anger that start with "You" are attacking, and those that begin with "I" are non-threatening. For example:

"You make me so angry, I could scream!"

"I really feel angry right now."

"You're so loud! Can't you pipe down?!"

"I'd really appreciate it if you would lower your voice a little."

This may not be as easy as it sounds. Breaking patterns is often difficult, but it can be done. You first have to become sensitive to your child's reaction to you. When you say something, does she look hurt, about to cry, scared? If so, you need to ask yourself, "What did I say to make her afraid of me?" If you cannot come up with the answer, maybe you should ask your child, remembering the rule of thumb of "you" and "I." How about, "I noticed that you were hurt by what I said, and I'm sorry. Can we talk about it?" instead of "You're such a baby! What's the matter now?" It really works, and everyone's feelings of value remain intact.

SUMMARY

Speech is a powerful tool. Used by someone with the right motive, it can move mountains. Used by someone who seeks to seduce and manipulate, it can destroy lives. An understanding of the whole speech process encourages us to seek a rhythmical balance of speaking, hearing, and breathing.

By substituting "babble" for "speech," the average healthy baby, unfettered by experiences in the outside world or by physical limitations, achieves this balance quite naturally. We should not be surprised that babbling is the same in all cultures. It is, after all, part of the growth process and a precursor to speech, regardless of our locale. These undecipherable sounds strengthen muscles that will be needed for speech development. When we think of babbling as early speech and bodily movement, we become fascinated—even awed—by the entire process of orderly childhood development.

We must remember that deaf children can "hear" by placing their hand on a piano being played or through touching a speaker. They can also feel the beat through their feet on the floor. Like a sponge, the skin soaks up everything that we put on our body, just as the entire body consumes what we take in through our mouth.

Children with ADD and Asperger's clearly understand rules and limitations when they are rationally explained. Yelling does no good; it is a disrespectful use of the power of the word and eventually is ignored. This sets up a cycle that may be very difficult—or impossible—to break. It creates an imbalance of rhythm in a child's breath. Choose your words carefully. Negative, mean-spirited words can literally hurt the person on the receiving end.

In the next chapter, you will learn how puppetry is helpful to children with neurological disorders and how you can easily implement this art in your home along with speech and massage.

CHAPTER 13

*T*he Power of Puppetry

Puppetry is a fun and effective way of helping children articulate their true feelings. All concerns of young people—from silly to serious—are more easily approached through a non-threatening and non-judgmental "person" in whom a child can confide. Puppetry is often helpful to parents who may be uncomfortable discussing certain topics, such as sexual abuse, or who may have suppressed emotions of their own, in which case a dialogue between parent and child, each with a puppet, may be cathartic for both.

Autistic children who seem uninterested in the world around them are actually observing everything in their environment. It is sometimes difficult to get a child's attention by speaking to him, but when a lifelike puppet is introduced, he is—even momentarily—curious about this new person he hasn't seen before. Even that brief encounter can be a gateway to a sustained focus during which the puppet begins to open a channel of communication, one-sided though it might be.

The child within us has never lost its affection for puppet shows—one of the oldest forms of entertainment—which have evolved from the ever-popular traveling shows to the sophisticated Muppets. As an educational vehicles, dialogue in puppet shows conveys morals and legends just as fairy tales do. They therapeutically encourage communication and provide solutions to problems that many children experience but are unable to solve or even discuss.

Although all of the arts offer the opportunity for the spirit to emerge and make its presence known, severely affected autistic children do not respond to puppet shows as do other children on the Spectrum. Since they have difficulty relating to other people and themselves, they cannot identify with characters in a play and are therefore distanced from the messages contained in the stories. However, autistic children who are high-functioning will usually respond to questions asked by the puppets, and repeated play may help them to speak more freely.

ROLE PLAY

Working with puppets is a spirit-to-spirit communication through a third party, the puppet. This is often the only way of truly reaching a child, and easily the most effective, since it is a game and the puppets are toys to the child.

Role play is a safe, non-threatening way of telling a story that comes alive and reveals deep-seated emotions. Puppetry provides a release of pent-up emotions, and the spirit can more readily exert itself in the presence of a well-trained therapist or an educated parent or teacher. Puppets are successfully used in therapy when children will not—or cannot—speak. Puppets of people often take on a life of their own with non-verbal boys and girls, who begin to impart messages in their own way. Speech often becomes more fluid and meaningful when a child is using a puppet, since the object is removed from his own physical body, which provides a sense of detachment and safety.

Puppets become non-judgmental and non-threatening confidants of children who are eager to express their feelings but who hesitate because of troublesome experiences with adults who may have been offended, shocked, hurt, or uninterested. Puppets display none of these reactions, and children often speak freely to them. Adults are also less inhibited when speaking through a puppet, and certain topics, such as sexual abuse, are more easily addressed through "play." When two people talk to each other through puppets, feelings that often surprise both people are aroused and brought into the open.

Puppets and role play are natural companions. There is no better way to reach children than through these enjoyable "games." Because puppets are toys, their clinical and educational purpose is more effective. Children more readily respond because they are not being directly interrogated or lectured. Puppetry is a highly effective method of working with children who have been abused sexually, physically, mentally, emotionally, or spiritually. Puppets, these little people, are used successfully with autistic children who may be non-verbal but whose spirits are sensitive, functioning, and responsive. Some children with autism are able to sustain a dialogue with a puppet, and their comments may surprise therapists or parents who are working with them.

Puppet therapy is an enjoyable and effective "game" that allows a child to speak from the feelings in his heart. Whether he plays alone or two play together with puppets, the child's imagination is limitless, and the puppets provide an outlet for internal thoughts and feelings.

Working with puppets is a spirit-to-spirit communication through a third party, the puppet. This is often the only way of truly reaching a child, and easily the most effective, since it is a game and the puppets are toys to the child. However, when you realize the efficacy of the interaction, you will find that this form of therapy is useful in obtaining information that enhances the therapeutic process. At the same time, it triggers something in the spirit that brings peace and awareness to the child.

Puppets are an ideal way of introducing children to hospital procedures so they know what to expect when they need to go to the hospital. In developing countries, where vaccinations are often largely unfamiliar, fears can be put to rest by telling the importance of being vaccinated through the power of puppets. These versatile little people can be used in almost any situation where a lesson must be conveyed in a way that is acceptable to both children and adults.

Puppets can be used to educate young children, since almost every child will respond to a question or instruction from a puppet. They forget everything when watching a puppet show and focus entirely on the puppets, especially on the main character, who, to them, is a living person.

Children with Asperger's Syndrome and ADD/ADHD understand the stories and can identify with many characters or situations. They are often eager to communicate with the therapist through an inanimate object, the puppet, which is given life for a few short minutes. They feel a sense of freedom, as if their boundaries have been stripped away so that they can be absolutely honest and open.

It is interesting and revealing when a child holds a conversation between two puppets. It may be the only time he can speak his mind to an abusive father, a neglectful mother, or a resentful sibling—as is shown in the inset "Adam and His Father" on page 246.

THE PSYCHOLOGY OF PUPPETS

Children often feel like puppets insofar as they have little control over their own lives. They feel as if others are pulling the strings and talking for them. They feel they are at the mercy of their condition. Puppetry is a very effective method of offering a fun opportunity to speak without fear of recrimination. Puppets talk to each other, yell, cry, and love each other according to the whims of the child who is "pulling the strings."

We must always remember that children on the Autism Spectrum are very intelligent and understand every word that is said to them, even though this may not appear to be so. The assumption that they don't hear or comprehend intensifies the feeling that they have little control over, or voice in, their lives. When angry words are spoken in their environment, they feel them deeply. When people talk about them, they hear the hurtful comments and may appear to be unaware of them, but they shape their opinions about themselves and their capabilities. When a puppet speaks from the stage, children believe what is being said, and for that reason puppeteers need to be particularly cognizant of their words. This is especially true if the speaker is an authority figure such as a mother, father, teacher, doctor, or minister or other religious leader.

Adam and His Father

A bright and personable eleven-year-old child with autism, Adam found that he was constantly compared to his younger, neuro-typical, athletic brother—a situation that is not uncommon.

Ungainly and little interested in sports, Adam could not measure up to his father's ideal of a son. He was very sensitive and aware of this disparity of love and affection, and one day this came to the surface during a session with puppets. I brought out a boy puppet and a father puppet that resembled Adam and his father.

As we sat side by side on a futon, I held both puppets and began a dialogue between them. It was innocuous, not designed to focus on any situation in real life. After several minutes, I gave the boy puppet to Adam, and the father began asking him questions that could be easily answered. When Adam was comfortable with this "game," I gave him both puppets. This changed the dynamics completely, since Adam was now both father and son, speaker and listener, threat and threatened. **A** represents the Adam puppet and **F** represents the Father puppet. Holding both puppets in front of him, facing each other, he immediately began:

A: Dad?

F: (Silence)

A: Dad?

F: (Silence)

A: Dad!

(Father puppet turns his back on the boy.)

A: Dad! Talk to me!

F: (Silence)

A: Why won't you talk to me? (He begins to cry.) You never talk to me. Why don't you talk to me? Please talk to me.

I gently removed the puppets from his grip and held him, trying to comfort him. Like all of the sessions, this one was taped, and I debated whether to share this tape with his mother, who was in denial about her husband's favoritism. I decided to make a copy for his mother, who listened to it in stunned silence. She confronted her husband, who said he was unaware of the intensity of his son's feelings, and after a lively conversation he agreed that he had indeed been treating Adam unfairly. Unfortunately, he never accepted Adam as he did his athletic son.

An interesting shift takes place in the child's response depending on who is holding the puppets. When a child is using two puppets and creating a dialogue between them, the inner nature of the child is often revealed, allowing us—and him—to learn what is hidden. Suppressed emotions and thoughts and feelings can emerge from deep within his subconscious, which is suddenly being given freedom to speak. The child also becomes a more active participant in identifying his situation and expressing his emotions verbally through the puppets. Children face many challenges, but working with puppets is fun both for them and for adults, and creating your own puppets can be an enjoyable project.

Creating the Puppets

As a puppeteer, you become a writer, actor, director, educator, and friend to the audience. The more childlike you are, the more readily you can relate to—and communicate with—the children. You need to be as spontaneous as the children are in their play if you hope to communicate with them.

Puppets can be as inexpensive as drawing faces on your finger or spending fifty dollars in a toy store. You don't need to spend a lot of money to make puppets. They are only a tool for the message. Keep them simple, especially if you enlist a child's help, because children are apt to become frustrated when confronted with a project they feel is beyond their ability. Also, you don't want children to be so mesmerized by the puppets' appearance that they neglect or fail to hear the lessons of the scripts.

Paper lunch bags are easily transformed into puppets by drawing a mouth with red marker on the fold, which then opens and closes, and adding eyes, yarn hair, and a nose. Styrofoam eggs are great for eyes, nose, and mouth. You can color popcorn kernels with tempera paint, and press the pointed side into the egg for features. Paper plates, a crayon, and a craft stick are all you will need to create a child's first puppet. Cut smaller circles out of paper plates for faces, and attach to the craft sticks. Add the features and hair using whatever creative medium you choose. A two-sided puppet helps non-verbal children to communicate. (See page 290 for more on this.)

You can build a puppet stage out of foam core, which is found at craft stores, or out of a refrigerator carton (or similar large box), which you can find at appliance stores. Let your child help "decorate" it any way he wants. You can make drapes out of velveteen or similar fabric and attach it to the top of the stage. A scrim helps to hide the puppeteer, although you will find that this is not necessary for children to enjoy a puppet show.

Four puppets are all you need to start performing puppet shows. A mother, father, boy, and girl puppet are usually sufficient to use initially in storytelling and role play. In fact, you will probably rarely use more than two at a time. These "people" help children talk about serious issues that may be affecting their lives.

When using puppets, make or buy puppets that look like people. As one boy said, "I don't use animals. Animals don't talk." Have on hand an assortment of styles, ages, and occupations, both male and female. Men can have beards and moustaches and wear cowboy hats. Both men and boys can wear baseball caps. All puppets can have long hair or short hair in an assortment of black, brown, gray, white, red, and yellow yarn or similar hair-like material available in craft stores. Ladies can wear jewelry or glasses and a variety of hats or headscarves. Be sure to have puppets that look like nurses, police officers, firefighters, doctors, and religious figures.

> As a puppeteer, you become a writer, actor, director, educator, and friend to the audience. The more childlike you are, the more readily you can relate to—and communicate with—the children.

With this variety, you will be able to address just about any situation that may arise, since role play with puppets is an immediate way of treating a problem with a non-threatening approach. Keep the puppets where they can be easily reached for an impromptu show or role play when you feel a child may want to talk about a difficult topic.

Difficult Topics

A variety of topics that may be too confusing, painful, or embarrassing for both adults and children to discuss can be approached through puppetry. The following is a list of important subjects, some or all of which may need to be addressed with your child:

- Adoption
- Alcoholism
- Alzheimer's disease
- Anger
- Cheating in school
- Child abuse
- Dealing with bullies
- Death
- Disabilities
- Divorce
- Earthquakes or tornadoes
- Fear of the dark
- Jealousy
- Lying
- Making decisions
- New siblings
- Racial prejudice
- Self-esteem
- Serious illness
- Sibling rivalry
- Substance abuse
- Talking about problems
- Trip to the hospital

Most children experience one or more of these situations in their daily lives. This can be traumatic. Use your imagination and creativity to develop a script that is personal to a particular child, and use puppets that resemble him and his family members.

Bringing the Lifeless to Life

Puppetry, like other art forms, brings the lifeless to life. It is the enthusiasm of the puppeteer that animates the puppets and activates qualities of curiosity, respect, and appreciation in the child. If you can speak in an accent, an added quality is introduced into the play. Puppet shows are magical to the young mind. The dolls come alive because they look like real people. They move and talk with each other as well as to each child.

A skilled puppeteer can do all of this without a stage, in full view of his audience, because children focus on the puppets, not the puppeteer.

Just as the storyteller must be spirited and able to hold the attention of his audience, so must be the puppeteer. There will be times, often in a large group of preschool children, when the entire group's attention will wander if they lose interest. When this happens, chaos can ensue. If the puppets themselves cannot restore order, a very effective technique is to have the puppets drape forward over the edge of the stage. It may take a minute or two, but one by one, the children will see that something different has occurred.

"What's wrong with the puppets?" is whispered throughout the audience. Curiosity and concern bring quiet to the room as the puppets slowly straighten and explain that they cannot continue to talk when everyone else is talking. When asked, "Do you want to go on with the puppet show?" the answer is a resounding, "Yes!" and order is restored.

Fairy tales can be presented to children by way of puppet shows because puppetry easily combines the fascination of puppets with the spiritual tales of self-realization and values. Stories acted out by puppets may be more meaningful than narrated stories since children fixedly listen to puppets. In the timeless story of the boy who cried wolf, people and animals combine to create action, drama, anxiety, relief, and ultimately the lesson about the importance of truthfulness and the consequences of lying.

If the stage is large enough, two or three people can operate up to six puppets, although two or three at a time would be less distracting or overwhelming to young or autistic children. The content of puppet shows is rarely for mere amusement; stories present morals and messages in an amusing way.

> Stories acted out by puppets may be more meaningful than narrated stories since children fixedly listen to puppets.

Some puppets are designed solely for children with disabilities. There are puppets specifically designed for discussion of physical disabilities, such as dolls in wheelchairs or wearing braces, casts, or bandages. Large puppets may be in wheelchairs or on crutches or have casts on their limbs. All of these lend themselves to a discussion of disabilities. Every child has seen other boys or girls with a limitation that may be only temporary—for example, a broken arm or leg. His curious nature wants to know what caused this condition, but a reluctance to ask questions may mean he never gets satisfactory answers. Puppet shows can explain certain medical problems and let children know it is acceptable to ask questions in a respectful way.

Helping the Blind "See"

One of my most rewarding experiences was when I was asked to do a puppet show for a group of five- and six-year-old children. As I set up the stage, the children entered the room with their teacher and sat in a semicircle in front of the stage. When I was told they were blind, I was concerned because so much of a puppet show is visual, and I had also planned a puppet-making party.

However, I knew they were very tactile and invited them to come up to the stage to feel its size and shape, the drapes, and the scrim. When they sat down again, I passed the large, soft-sculpted puppets around so they could feel their features. All of the puppets had hair, and some had hats, moustaches, jewelry, or glasses. The children were captivated by the actual show and could not have been a more attentive audience.

Feeling more confident after the show, I described the puppets we were going to make and gave each child a styrofoam head and a craft stick. They felt the eyes, nose, and mouth that would make a face and the yellow, red, black, and brown yarn hair. They knew there were fabric squares for clothing that would be attached to the craft sticks with a rubber band.

Their skill at assembling the puppets was amazing. They were firm about what color hair they wanted for their puppet. Every child created a puppet he or she was proud of, and when one girl said, "Let's do a puppet show," they all thought it was a great idea. The teacher and aide put together two tables for the stage. They draped a tablecloth between them as a scrim to "hide" the children. Then all the boys and girls took turns thinking up and performing puppet shows that were moving experiences for all of us. This was one more example of the creativity of children who have been labeled "handicapped" or "disabled."

Becoming Verbal

It is not unusual for autistic children to begin speaking articulately after working with puppets. They may have previously spoken a few disconnected words that communicated their needs, but the start of full, articulate speech can be a welcome surprise.

It is not unusual for autistic children to begin speaking articulately after working with puppets. They may have previously spoken a few disconnected words that communicated their needs, but the start of full, articulate speech can be a welcome surprise. Erika's story is an example of an autistic child's successful communication through puppetry (see page 251).

Parents and teachers may talk to, preach to, and punish boys and girls who simply don't want to hear any more lectures on manners or morals. However, one puppet show or one session of role playing may accomplish more than any other effort to convey messages of truthfulness, peer-pressure resistance, decisionmaking, or other areas of concern for children, parents, educators, and therapists.

This "game" allows a child to speak from his heart. Whether a child plays alone or two children play together with puppets, the imagination knows no bounds. Adults, hearing the conversation, may think it is "cute," but observation will detect words and scenarios that may be profound and spiritual in nature. Children may talk about what it was like before they were born or be very articulate about their surroundings and their families. To understand the way a child thinks, we need to put ourselves in his shoes and feel like a child. There is a difference between being childish and being childlike.

BE THE CHILD

You need to be as spontaneous as children are in their play if you hope to communicate with them. You need to be childlike and excited about everything in order to explore everything and give your imagination free reign; otherwise, you are an authority in a "me/you" relationship.

The most effective teachers and therapists are inspired, just as great musicians or artists are. This inspiration derives from their spiritual nature; it is not something that can be learned from reading a textbook. When instructors and therapists are inspired, so is everyone they come in contact with, although it may not be immediately apparent or dramatic. In fact, the changes brought about as a result of these relationships are often subtle.

To be effective in any work with children, you must not only think like a child but also feel like a child. That is, try to understand their feelings about what is happening to them and to everything around them. Try to feel their childlike innocence, their complete abandon as they play, and their enjoyment in a simple toy.

It isn't easy to think like a child. Our adult intellect constantly gets in the way and creates problems when we try to establish a relationship with

Communication Through Puppets

Autistic, eight-year-old Erika was virtually unable to hold an intelligent conversation for more than a few seconds. However, she was immediately attracted to puppets and would hold brief conversations with them. Because she was so verbal with these figures, I made a pair of puppets that looked like Erika and her mother, who was very enthusiastic about her daughter's ability to "converse" with these little people.

One evening as they played with the puppets before bedtime, her mother asked her a question that had been asked and unanswered numerous times: "What do you want to do when you grow up?" This time Erika answered the puppet seriously, "I want to grow up and sell Girl Scout Cookies!" This unusual response began the first of a series of intelligible conversations between the puppets although direct one-on-one dialogue did not occur for several months.

young people. However, it can be done, and those who are able to do it find a joy that they haven't felt in many years—the joy of childhood. This joy springs from our spiritual nature, as does our feeling of awe when seeing a sunset or listening to a well-orchestrated piece of music.

PLAYFUL PUPPETS

Puppets seem to come alive and breathe, dance, stomp, and glide. They hug and kiss, much to children's delight and giggles. Children like to see puppets performing everyday acts because they appear more like real people. Use the puppets to pantomime a variety of actions, such as waving, clapping, talking, hugging, arguing, telling a secret, pushing, dancing, jumping, sneezing, or lifting a heavy object.

As part of a preschool presentation, two puppets were attempting to lift an invisible box. When the preschool children were asked what they thought was in the box, a boy shouted, "A puppy!" and a girl, clearly upset, cried, "No, it wasn't! It was a kitten!" This is the magic of puppetry. This was interesting and amusing because of their unawareness that there was no box at all.

Children may want to name the puppets, especially if they resemble someone they know. Young people often have extraordinary memories and can accurately remember the names of each puppet weeks after their last session. Children speak freely about angels and some claim to have seen one. An angel puppet is a trusted figure to a child, who will be attracted to it as to a very special person.

We know that changing from one activity to another during a therapy session strengthens the child's three-fold nature. As Marjorie Spock wrote in *Teaching As A Lively Art:* "In accordance with human nature which lives quite differently in thinking, feeling and willing, or motor experiences, activities of the (classroom) period strike a rhythmic balance between mental effort, artistic creation and motor activity."

During all remedial and artistic sessions, children alternate between active and passive activities by standing, sitting, lying down, and using fine and gross motor skills. A session with puppets uses similar transitions. For example, sitting passively watching a puppet show is very different from painting a stage, helping to write a story, or holding and speaking through a puppet. Each calls upon different forces and sensory experiences that bring out inner dialogues that may have been hidden behind a façade or mask.

PUPPETS AND MASKS

Like people, puppets have characteristics that can be altered by either adding or taking away something that reveals their occupation, hobby, status, gender, or age. For thousands of years, masks have been used in religious and cultural celebrations or ceremonies for the same purpose. They can be held in front of the face, be fitted to the face, partially cover the face, or cover the entire head as seen in traditional African and Asian cultures.

In the same way, puppets are able to perform while the puppeteer is hidden behind a scrim or black porous fabric. People are able to hide behind puppets and masks, as their true self is provided the anonymity to speak of subjects that may be considered tactless or unmentionable, such as abuse and fear. Because our faces reveal who we really are, and often our true feelings, we are able to assume a persona that is given permission to speak freely even though we may feel inhibited about certain subjects. We mask ourselves, if only for a few minutes. When we are behind a mask or using a puppet, we can be silly, serious, or menacing, which may be the opposite of our usual demeanor, just as Halloween masks transform people for a short time.

We do not know exactly when puppets were first used, but masks have a 20,000-year history that is documented by drawings and carvings on the walls of tombs and caves. Egyptians adorned themselves with half- or full-head masks of animals and birds in the belief that wearing them invoked the gods they symbolized. Death masks have been found in tombs, and today masks are still worn in religious ceremonies in tribal societies. The familiar twin masks of comedy and tragedy probably started in early Greek theater.

People wear different "masks" that they put on as they begin their day and have to interact with others. We may be irritated by something said to us by a superior but have to maintain our composure by keeping on the mask. At home, most people remove the mask and "be themselves." Some are well thought of during the day as kind people but abuse their children and spouse in the evening. With a mask, we can appear to be whatever we want to project as our true self.

ADULTS AND PUPPETS

Puppet therapy is beneficial for both adults and children. It helps with anger management, problem solving, and the building of social skills. Children enter into role play more easily than adults do, though, because adults have had many years' experience of establishing denial, secrecy, and defense mechanisms. However, as those in both age groups learn to trust the therapist, their defenses are eventually lowered.

Parents of children with autism or Asperger's are often in need of counseling, too. They have been dealt a serious blow with the diagnosis of these disorders, and it may take some time to accept the fact that their

People are able to hide behind puppets and masks, as their true self is provided the anonymity to speak of subjects that may be considered tactless or unmentionable, such as abuse and fear. Because our faces reveal who we really are, and often our true feelings, we are able to assume a persona that is given permission to speak freely even though we may feel inhibited about certain subjects.

child is not perfect. Unfortunately, some never do face the fact that their child is not like his siblings, cousins, or other kids on the block, and that he never will be. Using puppets in counseling helps them to distance themselves and speak through the puppets. This often helps them deal with the situation and is revealing both to the counselor and to themselves.

This type of therapy works well with adults who feel frustrated, angry, and directionless in their lives. By placing their personalities aside, they are able to have a two-way conversation with their true selves, a situation that would be unthinkable without the aid of puppets. Some adults who have had such a spiritual experience state that it has been a catalyst for a major transformation in their lives.

Puppets provide an opportunity to contact one's higher self, or spirit. They open up children and adults alike to their inner child—their childlike, trusting, intuitive nature that slowly diminishes as one matures. Because for children up to the age of twelve this is still a powerfully operative force, they are much more willing to enter wholeheartedly into this therapeutic exercise.

Adults have built many layers of protection around themselves over the years simply by living in the world. This is especially true in our high-tech society, where television and computers occupy so much of our time that they smother the creative, imaginative, intuitive aspect of the three-fold human being. There is no need for conversation or communication, and the result is a lack of satisfaction for everyone. Known as "Divine Discontent," this is what happens when we continually suppress our intuitive urgings that would propel us towards personal growth.

> Puppets provide an opportunity to contact one's higher self, or spirit. They open up children and adults alike to their inner child—their childlike, trusting, intuitive nature that slowly diminishes as one matures.

Parents often see a side of their personality that is hidden from their spouse, children, and themselves. When used in therapy, puppets are a key ingredient in the realization and acceptance of one's faults. Adults are no different from children in this regard. They feel they do not have to take responsibility for what the puppet is saying, and they feel free to speak. Naturally, this is noted by the therapist, who can address the issues either through direct conversation or, again, through puppetry.

As adults, we communicate mostly through words, while children communicate through play that might include painting, dancing to music, sand play, or puppetry. Most therapists don't use sand play, but it is a very effective, fun, and messy way of allowing children to create something physical and to engage in storytelling. For this, you will need an oblong plastic storage box, sand (available in toy stores), and miniature figures. These could include houses, animals, boys, girls, men, women, food, etc. The process is simple: The child is encouraged to do whatever he wants using either wet or dry sand. That is usually the only direction necessary for play and fantasy to engage him for a long time. Often, suppressed emotions surface, such as those associated with a father hitting or pushing a child, which may indicate a need for additional therapy. In each of these activities, children are calling upon different forces that invigorate muscles, senses, memories, and realization.

WHAT CAN I DO?

Be a child with your child, and have fun while you are playing with him. It will be relaxing for you and make it much easier to use the puppets. Be honest and sincere even when speaking through the puppets. If you feel it is a chore or a duty, your child will know it and refuse to cooperate. He may show his displeasure by pulling the puppets apart or throwing them around the room. You may feel he's "acting out" when, in reality, he knows what is going on but can't tell you that he is bored and wants to do something else.

Do shows that might include one of his siblings as a character. Parents' feeling of inadequacy often limit them in working with their child. Instead of thinking of the desired result, for example in role play, just be spontaneous and see what happens.

Like any other tool for capturing your child's attention, a puppet should be used occasionally and for incrementally longer periods of time—from perhaps one minute to five or ten, depending on the child's attentiveness. The purpose is to intrigue him and leave him wanting more. This process is based on your observation and perception and knowing when it is time to move on to another activity.

Exercises for Communication Through Puppetry

There are a variety of specific activities you can do with your child using puppets. These exercises will help your child express feelings that may otherwise remain hidden inside him. Don't be reluctant to get started. The results are often amazingly insightful.

Turn to page 289 of Part Two for specific exercises using puppetry.

SUMMARY

Puppets are therapeutic, entertaining, educational, and fun for children of all ages. Children will relate to characters that look like real people. They listen to—and believe—what puppets say, and for that reason puppeteers must be aware of the power they wield through inanimate dolls.

When children use two puppets, role play takes a new direction because they are no longer responding to questions from a parent, therapist, or another child. They are having an internal dialogue that is verbalized and brought to the surface through the puppets. These little people can be very elaborate and costly or very simple and inexpensive. Children care more that puppets seem real, not about their cost or quality.

Puppets are often used by professionals in cases of child abuse, but puppets are very effective when talking about other subjects that boys and girls face during their young years. Children confide in puppets, knowing that their secrets are safe. Yet at the right time and in the right place these "secrets" can be revealed to a parent or therapist who is able to help the child work through concerns, fears, anger, or jealousy.

There is obviously more than play involved in puppetry and other creative therapies, as the spirit desires to bring the child to his ultimate potential despite any limitations imposed on the body by heredity, birth, or environment.

You have learned that puppets, music, color, and art are among the effective, well-known creative therapies. Less well-known therapies, such as knitting, sculpture, and horseback riding, are described in the next chapter.

CHAPTER 14

*S*upplemental Therapies

This section includes therapies that don't "fit the mold" of traditional therapies found in schools and clinics. They're all fun and effective for children on the Autism Spectrum. These non-traditional therapies include knitting, sculpture, and horse therapy, among others.

There is no reason you shouldn't use as many methods as you feel will help your child. They all have something to offer, and a combination of therapies, along with necessary medical care, will form a comprehensive and integrated treatment plan for your son or daughter.

You may be given suggestions about therapies that you have never heard of, but the decision is ultimately yours and will be based, in large part, on your inner sense of whether it is appropriate for your child. There are many words for this small voice within, which is your intuition being called into play. Some may call it a hunch or gut feeling. Whatever the name, rely on it. Some therapies are wonderful and perfectly safe; others are dubious or dangerous. Granted, the latter are not accepted therapies, but desperate parents often want to try anything and everything for their child without thoroughly checking them out. Please do your homework; the Internet is invaluable for this.

Every therapy in this book has been proven effective for over twenty-five years, including the following supplemental therapies. The therapies listed in this chapter are implemented occasionally, unlike the ones in previous chapters, which are a regular part of weekly sessions. For example, knitting is often frustrating for children, and insisting that they stay with a task they dislike is tantamount to closing the door to any further communication and improvement. With any therapy, rely on your perception, observation, and intuition to know when to stop what you're doing and move to something else, preferably in a different location.

HANDWORK

Handwork includes such creative activities as knitting and crocheting. These activities can be challenging but fun and provide a sense of accomplishment. Knitting and crocheting are closely associated with speech and thinking. As a child learns a new skill that requires concentration, her mind is working in a different mode; that is, she is learning something new. The brain is energized, new brain cells are produced, and many areas of behavior improve, including speech. The more nimble the fingers, the more articulate the speech. Due to the nature of such craft, handwork develops perception, fine motor skills, focus, patience, observation, imagination, and self-worth.

All therapies depend on your observation and perception of the child, her demeanor, her physical condition, and her emotional state of mind.

Not all children on the Autism Spectrum will be able to learn how to knit or crochet, but for those who would like to try, handwork opens up new, creative possibilities. Therapists and parents don't have to be very good at knitting or crocheting. If you know the basics, that's enough to get children started creating a long, narrow strip that can become anything they want it to be. In fact, a seven-year-old boy made a scarf for his puppet, while a six-year-old girl, who had greater ambitions, said she was knitting a sweater for her father. It came as no surprise when that failed to happen, but she enjoyed the effort. Her father was surprised, delighted, and proud of what his daughter had accomplished.

First show your child precisely how knitting or other handwork is done, and then ask whether it's okay that you hold her hands to guide her. Always ask permission; people generally don't like to have their hands grabbed by someone without being prepared. Hold both of her hands, and begin to knit. With your hands covering hers, she will gain an idea of the movement necessary to manipulate the needles and the yarn in order to knit properly.

Always be sure the child can see exactly what you're doing. After a few stitches, she'll probably shake off your hands and say, "I can do it myself." If she drops a stitch, calmly point it out and ask if she would like to fix it. If she says "Yes," you can hold her hands and show her how it's done. If she says "No," then let her do it herself, regardless of the mistakes. In any case, she'll probably soon ask for help, and if she doesn't, that's fine, too—the important thing is that the child is engaged in a new and challenging activity.

Her handwork should be brought out once in a while and only for a short time during sessions because the child is bound to make mistakes that might frustrate her. She may lose interest and never want to try again. This is particularly true of a child with ADD/ADHD, who quickly loses focus. She will often want to quit any project or activity if it's not going smoothly or if she's distracted. Whether to introduce handwork into the session depends on your sense of the child at that particular time. You should ask yourself: Should she knit? Should she sculpt? Should she dance? What does she need today? All therapies depend on your observation and perception of the child, her demeanor, her physical condition, and her emotional state of mind.

SCULPTURE

Even at a very young age, the need to sculpt shows in a child's love of building. Children love to play in the dirt with trucks, cars, and shovels, and to make sand castles at the beach. Older children enjoy working with clay to sculpt cars, trucks, people, and buildings. They become sophisticated architects working on more complex concepts and stimulating a more active inner life.

Sculpture brings clay to life for a child just as it brings marble to life for a sculptor. In both cases, a tangible object is transformed from its original state into something entirely different. We rarely think of playing with clay as sculpture because in our programmed minds sculpture means a marble or bronze statue. It's a rare artist, though, who begins to chip away at a block of marble without first having made a clay model.

Sculpting with clay has many benefits. It improves perception, spatial recognition, imagination, creativity, and fine motor skills. Working with clay is fun for children with neurological disorders who are able to overcome their aversion to tactile substances. Clay feels unpleasant at first; it's cold and sticks to the hands. Overcoming the reluctance to touch clay is a huge step for autistic children, who may have previously refused to touch this unfamiliar material as well as many other substances.

Beeswax is often used instead of clay for sculpting and is preferred by many remedial therapists because of its texture. It's not as messy as clay and may appeal to children for that reason alone. Like clay, beeswax is always warmed with the hands before it is worked with.

Tactilely defensive children who overcome their aversion to clay or beeswax may appear to be simply playing as they roll the material into balls; but in reality they're having an inner struggle between their repulsion to the texture and the artistic impulse of their spiritual nature. Working with clay helps to ground a child. It gives her a feeling of being connected to something firm and secure.

When a child works with clay and seems to be finished with her project, she may take another look, scrutinize her creation, and then change part of it or roll it all into a ball. She has a feeling of control when she can make changes based on what she wants and not on what someone else tells her to do. She soon realizes she can do the same within herself and, in effect, is the architect of her life.

When working with clay, children with ADD/ADHD and Asperger's Syndrome are doing more than playing: They're learning, imagining, and growing. They're able to create by adding and removing at will and bringing the subjective into the objective by the use of their mind and hands.

Every child is a potential artist. Children may enjoy such creative activities as painting, drawing, and movement, but sculpture is totally different. Sculpture is the only way of creating three-dimensional forms from a solid material. Even tactilely defensive children who don't like to get their hands dirty are fascinated with the idea of making something out of "nothing."

It's best not to have an agenda when introducing clay, especially to children who are tactilely defensive. If you have decided that this is the day Frankie will make something with clay, Frankie may have a different agenda that doesn't include touching something that feels repulsive to him. Instead, be a role model. Get down on the floor with paper or plastic and put the variously colored clay between you. Take a small piece of red clay and, talking constantly about what you're doing, roll it into a ball and describe what you have made: a red ball. Roll it into a rope and talk about how it is a rope; then make it thinner and bend it into various shapes, telling him that you have now made a red snake.

It may seem that Frankie is ignoring you and refusing to touch the clay, but he is watching and listening to everything you do and say. Eventually—and it may take weeks—he will tentatively touch the clay, and then, imitating you, create a rope and a snake. This is a huge accomplishment for a child who is tactilely defensive, and he should be sincerely praised for it.

HORSE THERAPY

Horse therapy is a non-traditional form of therapy, and not everyone may have access to this joy. Most children—and many adults—are intimidated by the sheer size of a horse, but once they overcome their fears, they often find riding horses their most fun-filled therapy.

During Equine Therapy, children are always accompanied by a trained therapist and are mounted on a horse, which has likely also been trained to work with people of all ages with disabilities. The therapist may encourage boys and girls to help groom the horse after a ride. Most children enjoy this part of their session as much as the ride itself. All of the sensations felt by children during horse therapy, from movement to grooming, help them to develop qualities that enhance sensory perception, fine motor skills, observation skills, affection for an animal, and responsibility.

Children with autism have shown improvement in coordination and balance after a few sessions with an Equestrian Therapist. The gentle rocking of the animal's body stimulates the muscles of the child's upper body, which becomes stronger and more flexible.

While there are many ways to paint or draw—such as with watercolors, acrylics, crayons, or pencils—there's only one way to participate in horse therapy: to get on a horse. There's no substitute for the calm nature of a well-trained horse and the rolling movements of its body, which are reflected in the motions of the child. Children form an emotional attachment to "their" horse, and some who had been non-verbal begin to speak after only a few riding sessions.

We don't know why this occurs, other than because the child is being balanced by the side-to-side movement of the horse. Here's an example: Three-year-old Allison was autistic and non-verbal. Her mother decided to try horse therapy in the hopes that her daughter would benefit from it. This very petite little girl was frightened at first, probably by the sheer size of the horse she had been placed upon. After several sessions, she no longer resisted, nor did she show any indication that she enjoyed this new therapy.

On the next day of her regular session, her mom had an errand that took her past the ranch. Allison suddenly became agitated, pointed out the window, and said excitedly, "Horse! Horse!" Her mother couldn't believe what she was hearing from her child—who had never spoken before. This was true testament to Allison's intelligence—as well as to the effectiveness of Equine Therapy.

MOVEMENT

Until we became mainly a society of mechanized urban dwellers, most people lived on farms and worked from dawn till dusk doing hard physical labor. Activities of the entire family, regardless of age, required constant movement of the body. In general, children today have very little physical exercise, which causes a loss of muscle strength and a tendency towards obesity.

When guided by an experienced movement therapist, dancing or moving to music is very effective in helping children on the Spectrum become aware of their body and the space around them. As the limbs are energized, the child's arms, legs, and torso become more flexible and in tune with one another.

Music is an important part of movement because of its rhythm. Limbs are strengthened by hearing music with a pronounced beat during listen-

When guided by an experienced movement therapist, dancing or moving to music is very effective in helping children on the Spectrum become aware of their body and the space around them.

ing or reading time because the feet and legs unconsciously keep time to the music. Back and neck muscles are also engaged.

Movement activities have many benefits for all children. In general, all exercises and artistic therapies help the brain to grow in size. The heartbeat increases and gives needed blood and oxygen to the brain. New neuropathways are created. Specific movements from one side of the body to the other—known as cross lateralization—balance the hemispheres of the brain. Gross motor muscles are strengthened throughout the body.

Cross lateralization can be done either by physical touch or by specific exercises, such as those described in this book. It simply means shifting the focus from one side of the body to the other, from the right to the left and back again, each time crossing the mid-pole of the brain. Cross lateralization stimulates the creative aspects of Aspies, who are very literal and whose drawings tend to be rigid. This fact is seen in their pictures, which change from black robots and monsters to flowers and colorful animals. This change also becomes obvious in their schoolwork, social skills, and ability to articulate their feelings.

When we exercise, our breathing changes and comes into a natural, balanced rhythm. Movement doesn't have to be just dancing. It can be stomping, jumping, skipping, hopping, clapping, or stretching. It can be all of these and more for a good group activity. Obviously, when movement is done in a group setting, social skills improve, too.

Turn to page 293 in Part Two for an exercise involving the use of sounds, movement, and music.

RHYTHMIC MASSAGE (RM)

Rhythmic massage therapists are trained and licensed in this specialized form of therapy. However, you can learn the basics of massage and use them to help your child. Rhythmic massage is different from traditional massage as we know it. The purpose of RM is to balance the body and brain by crossing the mid-pole through stimulation of the sensory system. RM is done systematically from the top of the body to the bottom and then from bottom to top. It's done from the left to the right side of the torso and then from right to left. Rhythmic massage stimulates the senses and circulation of the body with its upward and downward, side-to-side movement. This excites the brain by providing needed nourishment. The brain is constantly at work, even as a child is totally relaxed. Rhythmic massage reduces hyperactivity, improves sleep patterns, increases appetite, releases stress, relaxes muscles, and increases circulation.

Children who overcome their aversion to being touched like massage; they relax and let down their defenses. Although it's pleasurable, rhythmic massage is more than a few minutes of rest and a nice feeling. It brings together those of the child's forces that have been dormant since birth—namely, the abilities to feel, sense, and balance herself.

Children with autism who are tactilely defensive instinctively reject the idea of being touched. It may take weeks—possibly months—to gain the trust of a child who experiences touch as painful. It's a slow process of desensitization that starts with the first meeting of therapist and child, when she decides whether to trust this stranger.

When there's a feeling of trust and respect, it's easier for a child to allow someone to touch her. This doesn't automatically mean she'll let you massage her, but it's a beginning. Start by "accidentally" touching her hand as you're both painting. She'll pull away a few times but soon won't mind it as much. Move to touching her arm, then stroking it, and then touching her shoulder and back. By this time, she will trust you and may actually turn her back to you as a way of saying, "Please rub my back." It's difficult to actually massage most children with autism. Kids with Asperger's and ADD/ADHD love it and look forward to it, but again, trust and mutual respect have to be present.

Children feel (and are) very vulnerable when they're lying face down and can't see what's about to happen. If you're a therapist, be sure to ask the parents for permission to massage their child; some therapists have them sign an agreement. Explain the benefits and methods and invite them to observe so they can massage their child at home.

Before you begin a session, ask the child if it's okay to touch her. Explain clearly what massage is and how it's done. Ask if she has any questions. Select a soothing piece of classical music for this session. Kids with Asperger's Syndrome and ADD/ADHD can articulate how they feel after a massage, but some children with autism are unable to put their feelings into words. Instead, they may show their pleasure by their reluctance to get up from a relaxed state, in which case they often fall asleep. They may turn from their stomach to their back and lift their shirt as a sign that they want you to continue.

The back is a large and major part of the body that sends signals to the organs and to related brain sites. Stimulation of the nerves of the back helps to balance the three-fold nature of a child. This, in turn, activates her will, which moves her to action either consciously or unconsciously. By crossing from one side of the back to the other (also known as patterning), you stimulate nerves in the area. This stimulation is transferred to the brain, or the will aspect, which, in turn, is energized. This encourages motion and, in turn, movement, whether intentional or not.

In other words, movement can be an intended and considered action or one that is instinctive, done without thinking. Frequent stimulation and cross lateralization strengthen the will feature of the body, mind, and

Frequent stimulation and cross lateralization strengthen the will feature of the body, mind, and spirit, or three-fold nature, of a child, who will be more decisive in her movements.

spirit, or three-fold nature, of a child, who will be more decisive in her movements.

Touch and Tone can be used following rhythmic massage, since the child's senses are heightened. Turn back to page 231 for information on Touch and Tone. Whether combined with other therapies or used alone, rhythmic massage is a beneficial, relaxing, and pleasurable experience for most children.

SUMMARY

By adding knitting and sculpture to your treatment plan, you will be learning along with your child. More than that, you will be having fun with her. Equine Therapy is best left to the experts, who have had intense training in how to work with children who have neurological disorders. This isn't something that can be taken lightly; putting your child on an untrained horse with untrained personnel is courting disaster. This is the only supplemental therapy that you will not be able to do yourself.

Rhythmic massage is more effective when performed by a therapist who has had training in the technique, but don't let that deter you from working with your child. Children love to be stroked and touched. If you do nothing more than a basic massage, both of you will gain from the pleasure you are giving your child and the time of closeness.

All of the therapies in this chapter can be included in the program you have planned for your child. By including the activities and exercises that are detailed in Part Two, you will have a well-rounded program that is easy and fun for everyone.

PART TWO

Activities to Enrich Body, Mind, and Spirit

In Part One, we explored facts, theories, research, characteristics, criteria, and therapies pertaining to ADD/ADHD, autism, and Asperger's Syndrome. Part Two will show you how to put these creative therapies, designed to nurture and enrich a child's physical, mental, and spiritual nature, into practice.

As you begin to read Part Two, suspend analytical thought and allow your feeling nature free reign. You may be wondering, "Why?" The answer is that once our concrete mind tries to grasp and analyze something as nebulous as the effect of music and art on a sensitive child's body, mind, and spirit, we no longer sense; we think. We do not feel; we dissect, and then we cannot enter into a child's rich world of fantasy and color.

Some of the creative therapy exercises in this section may seem very basic to you. But you must remember that the goal is to reach children on the Autism Spectrum, for whom social interaction, expression, and communication beyond their inner lives is difficult. Of course, there are varying degrees of disorders on the Autism Spectrum. Your child may have a mild case of ADD or a severe form of autism. There are only a few exercises that may be too challenging for severely affected autistics. Otherwise, these are excellent methods for all children. Use your observation skills and intuition (as always) to gauge your child's reaction to a certain exercise. However, don't give up; remember, progress is often gradual.

These are unfamiliar ideas because they are not conventional methods learned in the classroom. Instead, they were developed—and continue to be developed—through an understanding of the spiritual nature of children, who respond to truth, beauty, and goodness.

These innate qualities cannot be investigated scientifically, as can Autism Spectrum Disorders; rather, they appeal to our sense of beauty. For example, music cannot be seen or touched; it must be experienced. Our feelings (which are spiritual qualities) are aroused by listening to the great classics, just as our emotions (which are physical and mental responses) are by popular music.

Although the techniques described in Part Two may seem unfamiliar, they aren't new, having been used, written, and talked about for years. In today's world, they have been implemented by teachers, therapists, doctors, and parents who clearly understand the hidden impact of the arts on a child's sensitive, spiritual nature. This section provides concrete examples of uses of these timeless art forms, which have such a positive therapeutic effect on children on the Autism Spectrum.

The activities and exercises that follow will be enjoyable for you and for your child. Your child will think you are only playing a game; however, you will be helping him learn, grow, and strengthen his body, mind, feeling nature, and, most important, his spirit.

Each activity lists a stated goal or objective for the child (beyond the obvious task at hand), any materials needed for the exercise, and instructions or examples to guide you. Parents can easily do all of these enjoyable activities with their child at home. Teachers and therapists will also find this to be a useful guide of practical examples for use in their classrooms or sessions. By implementing these exercises as part of an integrative therapeutic program, you will help balance your child's three-fold nature of body, mind, and spirit.

You'll find the following exercises and activities grouped according to the chapter with which they correspond. At the end of Part Two, there are some exercises that are not necessarily associated with one particular chapter in the first part of this book and are labeled as such.

The exercises and activities in Part Two gain new meaning when we keep the spiritual nature of children in mind. We develop within us a feeling entirely different from the one we would if we were to watch children simply draw a picture of their family, or if we were to test their memory. There's a stream of creativity and intuition that springs from children's innate sensitivity, and we need to recognize and work with that while we play these games so that we can ultimately help our children nurture and balance their three-fold nature of body, mind, and spirit.

Drawing Exercises

Introduced in Chapter 7, the following exercises incorporate drawing activities that help children understand spatial relationships as well as the concepts of duplication, reversal, and the identification and completion of what is incomplete.

SPATIAL RELATIONSHIP EXERCISES

Gain Familiarity With Shapes, Symmetry, and Balance

MATERIALS NEEDED
- Marker board, paper, or blackboard
- Non-toxic markers or colored chalk

1. Start by asking the child to draw a vertical line down the center of a square marker board, blackboard, or paper. Doing this, he has created two rectangles; when he bisects that line with a horizontal line, he has created four squares. When he draws lines diagonally to connect the corners, he has suddenly formed eight triangles. After he has drawn these lines, the child may fill in each triangle with a different color. The color doesn't matter, and there is no right or wrong choice. The object is to encourage decisionmaking and a sense of color.

A hyperactive child is often calmed by drawing a horizontal or vertical line on a blackboard or marker board because doing so draws upon the forces of his will to do this exercise, the performance of which crosses the mid-pole of the brain. It takes concentration and purposeful effort for a hyperactive child to draw a straight line from a point on one side of a marker board to a point on the opposite side. His determined struggle is obvious in his facial expressions, as is his delight when he successfully achieves his task. It is quite an effort for a child with autism to draw a vertical or horizontal line freehand on the marker board or on paper. When we employ such exercises in symmetry, we are calling up the forces of balance—the same that helped the child lift himself erect and that were used in learning to walk.

GOAL *Recognize Right and Left*

MATERIALS NEEDED
- Marker board, paper, or blackboard
- Non-toxic markers or chalk
- Eraser

2. Draw a line down the center of the paper or board. Point to each side and say, "This is the left and this is the right." However, a more impressive teaching method is to begin by saying, "I'm going to draw on the right side of the paper, and you can draw on the left side, okay?" The child then has to think much more actively about this idea: "What does that mean? What does she mean? What is right? What is left?" After you draw a simple picture on the right side of the board or paper, say, "Now, it's your turn." He will clearly see that his left side is blank, waiting for whatever he wants to draw or scribble.

When that exercise is completed, erase it from the board or use a clean sheet of paper. Ask the child to draw a line down the middle of the page and ask, "Which side would you like this time, right or left?" This provides the opportunity and necessity to make a decision, which is very difficult for some children since they must first determine which side they want and then suggest you use the other. A great deal of processing takes place in decisionmaking, and although most people are able to choose rapidly, many children on the Autism Spectrum feel totally unable to make a decision of any kind.

GOAL *Recognize Above and Below*

MATERIALS NEEDED
- Marker board, paper, or blackboard
- Non-toxic markers or chalk
- Eraser

3. Draw a line down the middle of the board or paper. To refresh the child's memory of the previous exercise, point to each side and indicate the left side and the right side. Then ask, "Which is the left side?" and "Which is the right side?" Tell him, "They're side by side," and "They're next to each other," pointing to each.

Erase the board or take another sheet of paper and draw a horizontal line across it. Explain, "There are two sides to the board, but instead of being side by side or next to each other, now one is above and the other is below." Or you could say, "One is on top and the other is on the bottom." Alternatively, you could say, "One side is over the other," or, "One side is beneath the other." Then point to the appropriate area. These simple, precise explanations are extremely helpful.

You can then draw a moon with a house below it and say, "The moon is over the house," or, "The moon is above the house." Then point to the house and say, "The house is under the moon," "The house is beneath the moon," or, "The house is below the moon." Give several other examples to illustrate this principle, and then ask the child to offer his own example of the polarity of above and below. He probably won't grasp the concept immediately, but he probably will after several tries, after which it becomes an enjoyable game.

DUPLICATION EXERCISES

Follow Directions and Gain Perception of Form GOAL

MATERIALS NEEDED

- Marker board, paper, or blackboard
- Non-toxic markers or chalk
- Eraser

4. Draw a straight line on a paper, blackboard, or marker board. Tell your child to try to draw the same type of straight line you have just created. Next, draw a curved line on a clean paper or board, and then direct him again to attempt to duplicate what you have just drawn. This type of line will probably be more difficult for the child to copy, at least at the beginning of the process. Repeat this exercise as often as necessary in accordance with the needs and ability of the child, alternating the use of straight and curvy lines and telling the child to duplicate your drawings each time.

He may clearly understand the exercises suggested and believe that he has produced exact duplications of the lines you have drawn; however, when asked to look first at the examples and then at his drawings, the child may find that he is surprised to see that they are not precisely identical. Repeating this exercise during weekly sessions will produce a dramatic improvement in his ability to copy your drawings. The child will be glad to see his improvement as time goes by.

GOAL *Improve Observation, Action, and Independence*

MATERIALS NEEDED
- Marker board, paper, or blackboard
- Non-toxic markers or chalk
- Eraser

5. As your child becomes more familiar with the duplication exercise above, you can say, "Let's play a game. Would you like to play a game on the board?" He will invariably be pleased and say, "Yes!"

Tell your child, "First, I will draw a straight line from here to here." (Point to the left and right sides of the board.) "Ready?" (Draw the line, near the top of the board.) "Now you draw the same thing I just did."

This will be done by your child either slowly or rapidly, depending on his progress, but rarely will it be the same length as the example. This is repeated with vertical lines as you say and then demonstrate that your line will be from top to bottom. It is not unusual for a child to start his line where the parent ended hers. It is unnecessary to point this out on his first attempt, since the objective is to introduce the concept. If he continues to do this, it's perfectly okay to place his hand with the marker near the top (or left side) of your line and repeat the directions. Remember—always courteously ask permission to hold his hand, even if he is your own child. Say to your child, "That's great! Now I'm going to erase it; is that okay?" (A child invariably will agree, and the board is cleared.) "Great! Now, it is your turn to draw something that I have to copy."

A child's first attempt is often tentative, but when he draws a line or circle or a series of both, he is jubilant, especially if the parent appears to have difficulty duplicating it. (At first, it might be helpful to hold his hand and guide the chalk or marker. Again, never grab a child's hand without permission; you want to help him, not impose your will on him. Always respect and regard him as an individual with a disability, not as a disabled child.)

Some children will say, "I can't," at which point you may say, "Yes, you can. I know you can." Some will try, and others will say, "I need help. I need you to help me." You can reply, "I will help you if you really need it at first. Would you like me to help you get started?" And then ask if you may hold his hand.

Many children with autism are not given the chance to act independently, and believe they are incapable of doing anything without the help of their mother or therapist. This exercise will help strengthen their sense of independence and give them greater confidence in their capabilities. They are more capable than they are given credit for.

CIRCLE EXERCISES

Increase Awareness of Form in Preparation for Writing   **GOAL**

MATERIALS NEEDED
- Marker board, paper, or blackboard
- Non-toxic markers or chalk

6. Perhaps because the majority of people are righthanded, most people draw circles in a counterclockwise direction. To break imbedded patterns, ask a child to draw a circle on the paper or board in a clockwise direction—that is, beginning at the top and moving to the right and down, then to the left and up, connecting the two ends. This is more difficult than it sounds and is similar to drawing lines from left to right and right to left, an activity that crosses the mid-pole and helps to balance the hemispheres of the brain.

The exercise of creating a circle is an excellent precursor to writing because a child will be more conscious of the need for form; he won't be just "scribbling." He becomes aware of the rhythm of a curve, an oval, or a wavy line. This rhythm cannot be taught; it must be sensed. When a child draws a circle, his whole body feels the circular motion and his eyes follow the line from beginning to end.

Children should learn to make flowing lines well before they are taught to write. We know that handwriting gradually becomes illegible in a person experiencing a mental decline. When we deliberately try to improve our writing, it has a positive effect on our personality, which undergoes changes as a result. We should prepare children to write by having them draw lovely, flowing lines. By doing this, children intuitively feel and see the beauty of this form as opposed to that of jagged, straight lines with points, which hint at a more rigid or negative energy. They won't be perfect, of course, but they will be good representations.

Move Beyond Boundaries   **GOAL**

MATERIALS NEEDED
- Marker board, paper, or blackboard
- Non-toxic markers or chalk

7. After a child achieves the goal of creating circles, he can gradually learn how circles become a spiral. Show him how your hand stays in contact with the paper or board as you flow smoothly from one circle into another, making a spiral. Tell him how the circles don't have to—and shouldn't—be the same size. Emphasize the flow and interconnectedness of the circles.

Autistic children aren't always relaxed when creating spirals. It may be because they are in a rather heightened state when doing something, which indicates their readiness to move beyond the boundaries of a circle. The concept and creation of a spiral is usually difficult for a child with autism. For a long time he may try to duplicate your spiral but be unable to do more than circles upon themselves. Keep working with him, and point out the differences between your spiral and his.

When he is able to draw a spiral with a broad base and narrow top, he is usually ready to "move up and out" into the world, to communicate with and trust others. This simple exercise is more difficult than it sounds, because a child who has low self-esteem or fear of an adult world may be reluctant to break through his barrier of isolation, which provides a certain measure of security.

When he is able to duplicate geometric figures, wavy lines, and spirals, he may feel encouraged to do something he's never done before, such as dancing, singing, or taking part in a play. Participation is a major accomplishment for a withdrawn child and indicates a willingness or eagerness to be part of the world around him that is being enjoyed by other children.

COMPLETION EXERCISES

GOAL *Identify What's Missing and Actively Work to Complete*

MATERIALS NEEDED
- Marker board, paper, or blackboard
- Non-toxic markers or chalk
- Eraser

8. Draw a circle with a gap at the top. Ask your child if the circle is complete or finished. If your child does not see that the circle is incomplete, show him the space and draw the missing part. Repeat with a gap at the bottom, sides, and in between. Do the same with a triangle, drawing only two sides, and draw a square and rectangle with three sides. After drawing each, ask him if the object in the drawing is complete or incomplete.

The following week, start with each symbol and say you are going to do something different. Draw a circle and as you add eyes, eyebrows, ears, nose, "smiley" mouth, and hair, say the name of each feature.

A good exercise for helping Spectrum kids identify whatever is "missing" is to complete a drawing that is missing a part of the face. Tell your child you are now going to erase one part of the picture of the face, and he has to guess what was removed. Proceed to erase, for example, an eye, and tell him that something is missing. Ask if he knows what it is. If not, point to the missing eye and draw it in. Do this with several parts of the face, erasing and drawing one feature at a time.

Then, erase the entire face and draw another, but with one piece missing. Ask him if he knows what part of the face is not there. This is a little more difficult, but after a few attempts, he will recognize the feature that was left out.

After that, ask him to draw in the missing part. It is not unusual for a child to draw an eye or an ear in various places on the face until he becomes familiar with the "game," spatial reality, and the human face. When he becomes proficient in this fill-in-the-blank exercise, it is time to ask him to draw a face and leave off something.

Obviously, this is even more difficult. As your child strives to perfect his circle and to fill in the missing parts of a face, he is developing his moral forces—an understanding of right and wrong—as well as forces of cognition or perception, which will carry over to his other tasks and exercises. These social and moral forces should be allowed to develop naturally and without explanation or apparent expectations your child should simply be observing and emulating you.

Discover the Concepts of Mirror Images and Balance   GOAL

MATERIALS NEEDED
- Marker board, paper, or blackboard
- Non-toxic markers or chalk
- Eraser

9. This is more difficult than completing the faces, as in the exercise above, and is more applicable to kids with ADD/ADHD and Asperger's than it is to those with autism.

Draw half of an object and ask your child to draw its missing mirror image immediately to the right. (A line can be drawn down the center of the page to separate the two images.) Show him how to do this the first few times, and he will grasp the concept of reversal and mirror images. This is rather easy for kids with ADHD or Asperger's to comprehend. It's not as hard as it sounds, once a child understands what you're looking for.

For example, start with half of an oval, and then half of a square. Eventually move to more difficult images, such as brackets: < | > or (|). Other suggestions for reversal are letters and numbers, such as E and 3. As you move from one object to the next, either erase the board or use a clean sheet of paper. There are no firm rules with this exercise, so you can use your imagination.

It is important to remember that it is your enthusiasm about continual discovery that is transferred to your child. At the same time, we need to be realistic and accept that although one's spirit is balanced and wants the physical body and brain to be balanced as well, sometimes this goal may never be attained. This does not mean you should stop trying, because at some level and to some degree even the most unresponsive child will understand.

*F*airy-Tale Exercises

The following six activities are meant to be done right after listening to a fairy tale (see Chapter 9), and they share the same objective. These exercises help children to develop memory, creativity, imagination, and the ability to verbalize their thoughts and recollections. They also help reinforce the moral of the fairy tale that the child has just heard. In addition, social and fine motor skills are enhanced when the children interact through role play and puppetry.

Increase Creativity and Memory and Understand Morals of Fairy Tales GOAL

MATERIALS NEEDED
- Hat, scarf, or mask (optional)

1. **Role Play:** Role play can be done with two children who have just heard the story. They can take turns being the "hero" and "villain" as they recreate the plot. Young boys and girls love playacting and fantasizing. A fairy tale is a great vehicle for their urge to act. If you have costumes, it will be even more fun. They don't have to be fancy; a hat and scarf or a mask the child has made may add to the drama.

Tell them to use different voices for each character and demonstrate what you mean. They will likely forget the voice they should be using and/or fall down on the floor and laugh.

Of course, role play doesn't have to require two children; a child can role play with anyone—parent, therapist, grandparent—or even alone.

MATERIALS NEEDED

• Two puppets

• Puppet stage (optional)

2. **Puppet Show:** A puppet show can be done with one child using two puppets, or with two children using one each. They create a puppet show based on the story they have just heard. However, they may want to do an entirely different fairy tale, which is fine. In fact, this shows a spark of imagination and individuality. They may argue over which fairy tale to "produce" but come to an agreement when told they can do both.

A simple puppet stage adds a nice touch but is not necessary. It can be a large box that the children have decorated with paints and markers, or it can simply be a piece of fabric taped to both sides of a doorway.

MATERIALS NEEDED

• No materials necessary

3. **Retelling the Story:** Ask your child to tell you the story he has just heard, and then ask, "Did you learn anything from this fairy tale?" He will probably say, "Yes!" Then you might ask, "What do you think was the lesson of the story?" This encourages his ability to recall facts and to articulate the meaning of the story.

MATERIALS NEEDED

• No materials necessary

4. **Memory Game:** This is a good activity for strengthening your child's memory and determining his level of focus. Ask him questions based on the details of the fairy tale he has just heard. For example, if you have just read the story "The Wolf and the Seven Goats" (see page 178), ask:

How many baby goats were in the story?

What are baby goats called?

Where did the mother goat go?

What did she tell her children to do?

One goat was saved because he hid someplace. Where did he hide?

Obviously, base the questions that you ask on the particular story you've just told him. You'll be able to see both how well he understands what he hears and the attention he has been paying to the story.

MATERIALS NEEDED

- Paints
- Paintbrush
- Paper

5. **Art:** This exercise in creating artwork can be quite revealing, as it will show you which elements of the fairy tale have made an impact on your child. As soon as you finish telling the story, bring out paints and paper and ask your child to paint a picture about the story. Tell him that it can be of anything he wants from the story and that he can have as many pieces of paper as he needs for his painting—he doesn't have to squeeze the figures together. When doing this kind of art with him, you may even want to use a long sheet of paper, such as that from a fax roll. He can then draw many different scenes.

MATERIALS NEEDED

- Pencil
- Paper

6. **Writing:** If your child is old enough and able to write, remind him what the fairy tale he just heard was about and the lesson he learned. Ask him to write about a time when he encountered a dilemma (telling a lie, being unkind, etc.) similar to that of the character. What he writes should be based on the moral or message of the particular tale. Again, using the story "The Wolf and the Seven Goats" (see page 178) as an example, ask him to write about a situation where he disobeyed his mother and got in trouble. Remind him that this particular story was about seven children who did not do what their mother told them to do. After he writes and you have read his story, ask: "What did you learn from your experience?"

Exercises With Music

The following exercises encourage the recognition and expression of children's feelings and reactions to music (see Chapter 10). The activities also contribute to a child's sense of awareness and strengthen memory skills.

Recognize and Creatively Express Feelings and React to Music   GOAL

MATERIALS NEEDED
- Short selections of several different kinds of music
- Crayons or colored pencils
- Paper

1. Here is a group exercise that is fun for all children, both with and without developmental disorders. However, if it's just you and your child, feel free to participate in this activity. Grownups enjoy it because they can visibly see the effect of music on their emotions.

Play two or three minutes each of different kinds of music: rock, classical, country western, blues, and jazz. Give each child crayons or colored pencils and a supply of plain white paper that will be labeled according to the style of music played. Suggest that the children draw anything they want to as they listen to each selection. Tell them not to think too deeply about what they create, but just to put their reactions and feelings onto the paper without analyzing them. The goal is to create with feeling and spontaneity. At the end, ask which music they liked the best. Contrary to popular thought, kids don't always like rock the best and classical the least.

Have them hold up the pictures they drew in response to each kind of music. They will probably find that, to their surprise, many creations will be very similar to one another. An interesting part of this activity is their realization of how they are affected by the different music and how this, in turn, affects their artwork. Jazz and rock generally produce jagged lines, many angles, and dark colors, while the classics and blues produce softer, curved lines with lighter colors.

GOAL *Express Mental and Emotional Reactions to Music in Writing*

MATERIALS NEEDED
- Classical music selection, relaxing but not melancholy
- Pencils
- Paper

2. This exercise is most appropriate for children who are able to focus and understand instructions, such as those with ADHD and Asperger's. It can be done with a group of children or just one child. Play a short classical piece that is relaxing but not melancholy. Have children sit with their eyes closed while listening. When it ends, ask if they liked it and if it reminded them of anything. One child may say he thought about a circus while another might comment that it reminded her of a vacation last year when everybody was singing in the car and having fun.

Then ask them to write about what they felt. This can be in a few words or in a few lines; length doesn't matter. Speaking and writing are two different forms of communication, and each provides its own method of describing our thoughts, feelings, and impressions.

GOAL *Associate Movement and Hearing With Music*

MATERIALS NEEDED
- Classical music selection
- Cymbals
- Gong
- Recorder

3. An interesting game for kids with ADD and Asperger's is an exercise called "Dancing with Music," in which classical music is played and the addition of live instruments suggests different ways of moving the body. Reverberating gongs may bring to mind slow, long, gliding steps; the clash of cymbals may encourage children to march. The sounds of the recorder may make them want to swirl in soft, gentle movements.

This is a fun activity for kids to do with their friends and siblings, but you can also do it alone with your child. It is a good idea for the mom and dad to be actively involved in all of their children's exercises. Groups of children may be self-conscious about dancing to different sounds or tend to act silly at first. As they begin to join in, they will enjoy it but may still giggle at the movements of the other children.

You will need musical instruments of good quality so that the tones are pleasing to the ear. For example, as mentioned, small cymbals, a gong, and a recorder can be used in this exercise. Explain that everyone will dance to the music that will be playing until they hear the sound of the gong or the cymbals or three notes on the recorder.

Demonstrate the different sounds each of these instruments makes and the movements that go with it. The gong will be the signal for dramatic sweeping movements about the room, while the cymbal is a call to march in place. The recorder has a lighter sound that encourages slower and gentler movements. Each of these movements should last for no more than a minute or two at a time.

Play a piece of classical music, and encourage everyone to move or dance to it. At some point, strike the gong. The children should begin their swooping and gliding movements. You might next strike the cymbals, to which everyone marches as if in a parade. They should stop when you strike them a second time. Repeat with three notes on the recorder, and the children should now swirl and float about the room rather than glide to the gong or march to the cymbals.

Children with a short attention span may enjoy dancing for a very short time and quickly tire of it. Others may like to continue the dance, but if you extend it much longer than a few minutes the newness of the game quickly wears off and they may not want to do it again.

Develop Memory and Sense of Awareness GOAL

MATERIALS NEEDED
• Musical instrument (optional)

4. Point out two or three locations in a room that your child can easily remember, such as couch, door, and windows. Tell him to close his eyes and stand still, and then tell him you are going to move around the room and stand in front of one of those spots and snap your fingers.

First, be sure to show your child how snapping your fingers is done so he knows the sound. You cannot just say you are going to "snap" your fingers. He will probably not know what you mean. (Snap—Break in half? Snaps on his jacket?)

Tell him to point to the area of the room where he thinks you are standing. (Remind him—no fair peeking!) This strengthens his sense of hearing, memory, and general awareness of his surroundings.

This exercise can also be done using the sound of an instrument instead of snapping your fingers. Try different instruments for variety.

GOAL   *Increase Awareness and Strengthen Memory*

MATERIALS NEEDED
- Small plastic containers with lids
- Rice, uncooked
- Beans, uncooked
- Sand
- Another small, light object

5. For this activity, you will need several small plastic containers with lids. These will be filled with uncooked rice, beans, sand, or any other small, light object you may have on hand, each in a separate container and shown to your child so he knows what they are. Shake them to let him hear the different sound each makes. Some will have a higher "tone" than others do. Tell him to close his eyes and then ask him to identify the contents of one of the containers you are shaking near him.

These filled containers can also be used as inexpensive, homemade rhythm instruments.

*E*xercises With Color

The following exercises, for use with Chapter 11, utilize color in various fun ways to help children enhance memory, observation, imagination, and creativity.

Expand Visualization, Imagination, and Memory **GOAL**

MATERIALS NEEDED
- Paints
- Paintbrush
- Paper

1. This is a favorite of both children on the Spectrum and their neurotypical siblings and friends. There are no set rules to follow—just a suggestion for getting started. It is a good exercise for expanding your child's imagination. Ask him to close his eyes and listen as you tell a story. After saying each sentence, pause for two or three seconds and continue. Speaking softly and slowly, begin a fairly short story that may sound like this:

"Pretend that you are in a forest with many green trees. They are very big trees, and in one of them you see a beautiful red cardinal. If you listen, you can hear it singing. As you look further up the tree, you can see a blue sky with white clouds. You look down at your feet and see that you are standing on a yellow road with a purple stripe down the middle. You start walking down the road and see a little white house with a purple door. It is a very pretty house and you wonder who lives there. As you walk up to the porch, you see that the door is open. When you look inside, *[pause]* what do you see?"

Tell him to open his eyes. Ask him to tell you what he saw in this forest. If he misses something, ask if he saw the "_____." He will probably then say "Yes." If he hasn't already described it (for example, the bird), ask what color it was. This is a powerful exercise for stretching his imagination and memory.

Finally, ask what he saw when he looked in the open door. The answer may surprise you. (I have done a similar exercise with groups where many of the children "see" the same thing.)

Vivid imaginations are a part of childhood, and even preschoolers enjoy visualizations. The storyteller's mention of green grass and a tree with a red bird singing in it may be embellished with other colorful details, such as yellow and blue flowers, as the child experiences and remembers more vivid imagery.

After this exercise, ask your child to paint what he felt was the most important, or the prettiest, thing he saw. Note the colors and details he gives to his chosen object. An interesting and fairly common response is the addition of an object or person that wasn't mentioned.

Make up your own stories to provide variety, but always be sure to keep them short and very colorful.

GOAL *Develop Creativity and Imagination*

MATERIALS NEEDED

• No materials necessary

2. Children love silly questions and will often give silly answers. Ask your child a few "silly" questions, and tell him that there are neither right nor wrong answers to these. This exercise can be done anywhere and everywhere.

Start with the following questions as a base:

What color is happiness?	What does a ray of sun smell like?
What color is Monday?	What color is a thunderstorm?
What does a peach sound like?	What does rain feel like?
What does yellow feel like?	What color is a siren?

You may then think of similar ones you'd like to ask, based on his responsiveness and ability to understand the activity.

When various games and exercises are alternated with other activities, they can often be combined in a casual way. For example, if your child is coloring a balloon blue, you can take that opportunity to ask:

What do you think blue smells like?

What color is a smile?

What does a rainbow sound like?

And so on. The number of possible questions is limitless.

Improve Observation Skills **GOAL**

MATERIALS NEEDED
• No materials necessary

3. This game is an excellent color and memory activity that can be done with one child or with a group of children. Ask them to close their eyes and not to peek. Ask them specific questions, such as the ones listed below, and after each question, ask them to say their answers aloud and then open their eyes to see if they are correct. If they are, they will be delighted. If they are incorrect, they will be encouraged to be more observant of their surroundings in the future.

What color are your shoes?

What color is the carpet?

What color is my shirt?

What color are the chairs?

What color are the drapes?

Who is sitting to your left?

What color shirt is the child who is sitting to your right wearing?

Where is the clock?

How many doors are in the room?

What is on the wall behind me?

Again, for variety, you can always substitute similar questions that also have to do with memory and basic awareness. Introducing new questions helps remind children of the broad possible scope of observation they can apply to their world.

GOAL

Improve Verbal Expression

MATERIALS NEEDED
• No materials necessary

4. Ask your child if he dreams in color. Most children will say they do and will describe their dreams in graphic, colorful detail. If your child doesn't immediately share his dreams with you, ask him, especially in the morning, what he dreamt about last night. Asking a specific question is better than asking a general one, and asking it in the morning makes it less likely that he will have forgotten his dream. Listen to what he tells you. Pay attention to the specifics.

A dream is an example of the unconscious mind making itself known to conscious awareness, and a child's recollection of his dreams is a key to understanding his unconscious mind. When a child can articulate and discuss his dreams, a perceptive parent or therapist will discover layers of the child he didn't know existed.

GOAL *Improve Spontaneity and Imagination*

MATERIALS NEEDED
- Slides or sheets of paper of different,
  pure solid colors

5. Left-brained children usually prefer to trace pictures, do follow-the-dot or paint-by-number pictures, and/or copy what someone else has drawn. They often lack or suppress spontaneity and creativity.

A good group activity that encourages spontaneity in, and stimulates the imagination of, all children involves showing them a slide of a pure solid color and asking: "How does this make you feel?" or "What does this remind you of?" Show them several different slides of nothing but a solid color, and ask them these questions for each. The responses will indicate the effect of the various colors upon the child as an individual and as part of the group.

GOAL *Improve Expression Through Music and Color*

MATERIALS NEEDED
- Music, any type
- Assortment of various solid-colored,
  three-foot fabric squares or scarves

6. Children love to dance to music, even if it is only by slightly moving their feet or twirling colored scarves around their head or body or simply waving them in the air.

For a fun group activity in color therapy, each child should be allowed to choose a scarf from a large assortment of various solid-colored, three-foot squares. It is interesting to see if there is a correlation between the color a child chooses and his degree of activity.

Play music in the background and let the children "dance," using the scarves however they'd like. Some may swirl the scarf around themselves as they jump around. Some may choose to lie down and drape the scarf over their head or body. They may even want to wrap themselves in it as they rest. Allow this to happen. Children know at what point they need rest, and the use of music and color creates a peaceful, non-threatening environment. They know when they have had enough "color therapy," at which point they may simply stop.

Verbalization
Activity

The following exercise encourages verbal expression in your child (see Chapter 12).

Improve Vocabulary, Verbal Skills, and Imagination **GOAL**

MATERIALS NEEDED
- No materials necessary

1. Young verbal children love words. They like the sound of their own words but do not always want a dialogue with you. Sometimes they just like to hear themselves talk.

They like to make up stories, and one of the most effective activities for combining words, color, shapes, and imagination is to tell a story and have them fill in the blanks.

For example, begin with: "A lady was walking down the street and she saw a _____." As your child fills in the blank, you continue with more sentences and word pictures as you ask him to describe:

the color of a flower	the shape of a building
the design of a restaurant sign	the number on a house
the color of a dog	the shape of a cloud

The possibilities for this exercise are endless. You can encourage children's imaginations with stories that begin with a child walking through a zoo, a family gathering for a particular holiday, and so on. As children form clear images of each object, they are enriching their imagination, vocabulary, and verbal dexterity.

*E*xercises in Puppetry

These activities employ puppets so that children will be able to communicate in ways that were impossible without them (see Chapter 13). The exercises encourage personal expression and make difficult topics easier to discuss as children experience a sense of comfort and safety.

Improve Interaction and Communication Through Puppetry **GOAL**

MATERIALS NEEDED
- Two puppets
- Music, any type

1. If your child seems uninterested in puppets, don't give up. He may not look directly at them, but that doesn't mean he is unaware of them or your voice. To help your child become more comfortable using puppetry as a way to interact and grow, start off simple.

Hold two puppets, and make them perform common, everyday activities, such as waving, clapping, and sneezing, and tell your child what they are doing. Alternate the puppets' actions and ask him what he thinks the puppets are doing. Play music as the puppets glide, stomp, and dance around. Then ask your child again what the puppets are doing. Encourage your child to mimic what each puppet does.

Progress From Observer to Participant **GOAL**

MATERIALS NEEDED
- Two puppets

2. Many parents and therapists are not familiar with working with puppets and may need some ideas to start the process—especially to learn how to get a child to use the puppets actively.

It usually works best to start off with the adult using two puppets and supplying the voices and dialogue for each. Then, parent/therapist and child each can hold a puppet and engage in a dialogue—often, at first, a repetition of the previous puppet show. Examine how your child responds in order to determine how quickly you can progress through each step.

Finally, the child can be given both puppets to hold. At this point, he is no longer simply replying to questions but actually creating a dialogue within himself. Through this exercise, suppressed emotions are brought to light. Consider the following example, and use it as a guideline when introducing puppetry to your child.

Rebecca's mom is using two puppets and putting on a little show to help her daughter learn about how "Angry Andrew" was able to control his anger. During this show, Rebecca is a passive observer.

Then, Rebecca's mom gives her one puppet—the "Angry Andrew" puppet—and they repeat the show. Rebecca can readily relate to Andrew and enjoys her part in the story. Rebecca is now both an active and a passive participant in the action.

Finally, Rebecca's mom gives her daughter both puppets. Now Rebecca has no one else to ask the questions or set the stage. She is entirely on her own and needs to create dialogue between the two puppets. At this point, true emotions usually surface, and, in this case, the cause of her anger becomes clear. Rebecca is now an active participant both in identifying her anger and in the puppet show. And she is often able to deal with her feelings by verbalizing them through the puppets.

GOAL *Express Feelings*

MATERIALS NEEDED
- Two plain paper plates
- Scissors
- Non-toxic markers, pens, or crayons
- Yarn in color of child's hair
- Glue
- Tongue depressor or similar flat, wooden stick

3. If your child is non-verbal or has difficulty expressing his feelings, he will probably appreciate this simple puppet that offers an easy and fun way for him to communicate with you. In this exercise, remember that children on the Spectrum are very curious and will watch everything you do and listen to everything you say.

As you begin this exercise, tell him exactly both what you are about to do and what you are doing as you construct the puppet. Describe how he will be able to use the puppet to answer whether he is happy or sad.

Cut the center of two paper plates into four-inch rounds. On one circle draw a happy face with a big smile, and on the other draw a face with a sad, down-turned mouth. Glue lengths of yarn for hair on each side. Paste these two faces together with two inches of a tongue depressor between them for a handle.

Demonstrate both the happy face and the sad face with your expressions. Explain that if he wants to tell you how he is feeling, all he has to do is show that side of the puppet. He will probably understand this simple concept very quickly and realize that by holding the tongue depressor and turning the puppet to the appropriate side he will have a means of communicating with you.

You will find that if he is happy and having fun, he will show you the smiley face. If he feels ill, angry, hurt, hungry, or anything other than happy, he will show that face to you. When your child shows you the puppet with the sad face, ask if he feels, for example, sick or angry or hungry or hurt. By a process of elimination, you will usually be able to determine what is causing his distress or discomfort—something he cannot otherwise express. This exercise is also helpful with children who do not speak English but do know the expressions of happy and sad.

Prepare for Hospital Visit and Become Less Anxious GOAL

MATERIALS NEEDED

- Two puppets—one a child and one a nurse

4. If your child has to be hospitalized, you can help prepare him by using puppets to describe the process—from going to the hospital to being discharged. Hospitals often encourage children to take a tour of their unit and ask whatever questions they may have in mind.

You can supplement these measures by using a nurse puppet and a child puppet. The nurse puppet can talk about the benefits of surgery and how much better your child will feel when it is done. If he doesn't have any questions, it may mean he is afraid to voice his fears. In this case, the "nurse" should ask simple questions and make simple statements like these:

I wonder who will be in the room with you. Don't you think it will be fun to make new friends?

Just think! You won't have any more sore throats like you've had. Won't that be nice?

You probably won't feel like eating much when you wake up, but I heard the food is really good in the hospital and you can order whatever you want.

It will be for only one night and then we can go have fun.

Naturally, you should adjust the statements based on your child's condition and length of stay. In all events, keep the puppets' conversation upbeat and positive.

GOAL *Become Less Tactilely Defensive and More Affectionate*

MATERIALS NEEDED

• Various puppets, of both children and adults

5. Many children with autism resist both hugging or touching others and being hugged or touched, even by a loving parent. They simply don't know how to show affection or hug another person—but they can learn. Puppetry can help.

Use the puppets you have in your collection. Have them act out everyday situations—saying hello or goodnight, sharing, comforting another's skinned knee, etc.—in which it would be appropriate for a child and parent, siblings, or friends to hug each other. You can even make up silly stories and have the puppets hug each other. Puppets can demonstrate the process with their arms, and you can intrigue your child by using various voices, accents, and tones. Encourage your child to feel free to copy what the puppets are doing.

Activity Using Movement and Sound

Your children will enjoy this seemingly "silly" game that incorporates physical movement, music, and verbalization of sounds (see Chapter 14).

Increase Motor Skills and Expand Verbal Skills **GOAL**

MATERIALS NEEDED
- Picture of elephant
- Classical music, slow and somber
- Music, any type

1. Children with autism usually like music, especially music with a beat. They may dance vigorously around the room or simply stand in place and move their bodies gently in a swaying motion.

We know from experience that all children like silly sounds such as a cow's "moo," a horse's "neigh," or a lamb's "baa." They often try to imitate the sounds, which is great for their vocal cords.

In order to encourage expression and physical activity, sing songs to children that incorporate both sounds and movement. Encourage them to imitate silly actions at first.

For example, start by showing children a picture of an elephant and explaining what its trunk is. Then, bend over slightly and, using your outstretched arms, move about the room as if you're an elephant as you slowly swing your arms from side to side. While doing this, tell them that you are pretending to be an elephant and pretending that your arms are its trunk. Then, ask the children to mimic the movements of an elephant swinging her trunk. It helps to play music that is slow and dirge-like for this short exercise in imitating such a ponderous, huge animal.

Children may also like to pretend they are a giant taking huge steps that cause the forest to tremble—or that they are birds flying and flapping their wings.

Ask them what noises a cow, horse, elephant, or chicken makes, and incorporate them into the song as everyone dances around. Act like a train making a "choo-choo" sound as you "chug" around the room with your arms pumping like the wheels of an engine.

You'll be able to think of even more sounds for this exercise, which is especially good for children who have limited verbal skills. They'll try to make these sounds, and they often surprise themselves when they manage to do so.

*G*eneral Exercises

The following exercises do not correlate to any specific chapter in Part One. In many ways, these activities overlap in their goals, helping children in a variety of ways—strengthening motor skills and observation skills and encouraging general mental gymnastics.

Develop Association Skills; **GOAL**
Strengthen Perception and Mental Acuity

MATERIALS NEEDED
• No materials necessary

1. This exercise is a lot of fun and strengthens a child's sense of association and perception. Say the first part of a pair—for example, "salt"—and ask your child what goes with it. (Giving a child a couple of examples first makes this easier for him.) Pairs can include common words that often go together (like "shoes and socks") or opposites (such as "long and short"). The following is a list of words that can be paired up:

Salt	Pepper	Rich	Poor
Up	Down	Thick	Thin
Hammer	Nail	High	Low
Wash	Dry	Push	Pull
See	Hear	Hat	Coat
Arms	Legs	Day	Night
Give	Take	In	Out
Stop	Go	Read	Write
Win	Lose	Sun/Son	Moon/Daughter
Yes	No	Soap	Water

Work	Play		Bat	Ball
Fast	Slow		Knife	Fork
Bread	Butter		Pail	Shovel
Lock	Key		Sad	Happy

There are countless other words that can be paired together. You can play this game with your child anywhere, even while stuck in your car in traffic.

GOAL *Become Less Tactilely Defensive and Better Able to Identify Through Touch and Recalled Image*

MATERIALS NEEDED
- Paper bag
- Five or six small, familiar objects

2. Gather five or six small, familiar objects, such as a key, paper clip, watch, coin, etc. Place the objects in a paper bag and ask your child to reach in without looking, select one, and identify it by touch alone. He should then remove it to see if he is correct. Put the object aside and repeat the process until all objects are removed from the bag.

If your child had trouble identifying one or more objects, put all of them back in the bag and have him try again. He'll make many mistakes at first but will soon be able to identify the object by touch because he will remember what it looks like. You can introduce and eliminate a variety of objects over time.

GOAL *Develop Observation Skills*

MATERIALS NEEDED
- Tray or tabletop
- Six or eight small, familiar objects
- Towel

3. Gather six or eight small, familiar objects, such as a key, pen, coin, playing card, etc. Place the objects about two inches apart on a tray or tabletop in front of your child and identify each one. Cover with a towel. Remove one object without the child seeing which one, and uncover the rest. Ask your child if he knows which item has been removed.

A variation is to place three objects on the tray or tabletop in front of your child and cover with the towel. While the objects are covered, add another item the child has not seen previously. Remove the towel and ask him to identify the new object.

Both of these are usually fun for children. However, if your child has trouble with these activities and becomes frustrated, move on to something else after a few attempts. Repeat the game every few sessions. He'll gradually improve his ability to observe and identify things both in front of him and elsewhere in his environment.

Develop Observation Skills and Ability to See Beyond the Obvious GOAL

MATERIALS NEEDED

- Children's books that have colorful, complex pictures within pictures

4. Gather any children's book that has colorful, complex pictures, such as one with an animal or person hidden within the scene. (An alligator hidden in the leaves of a tree would be one example.)

Tell your child which object in the picture you're looking for, and point it out to him when you find it. Ask the child if he can find a picture in which there is something "hiding" or not immediately obvious. This is also a good exercise in learning to take turns. ("I found the turtle in the rock; now it's your turn.")

Develop Fine Motor Skills and Prepare to Spell and Write GOAL

MATERIALS NEEDED

- Follow-the-dots coloring book
- Paper
- Crayons

5. Many children who for various reasons are unable to write or print can learn to print their names by following the dots. Begin by introducing the child to follow-the-dots coloring books. Through such activities, he will learn to be observant. As he colors in the picture he outlined through following the dots, he will further learn that boundaries are there for a reason. He will also sharpen his fine motor skills.

As a child becomes more proficient at connecting the dots, you can outline a few letters of the alphabet with dots on a sheet of paper. Have him follow the dots as he forms the letters. Then outline the letters of your child's first name. By connecting the dots, the child is on the way to spelling his entire name. After he understands the process, ask him to print his name without dots.

He'll probably object and say that he can't do it. Encourage him by saying that you know he can. Tell him, "It's the same thing as doing your name with the dots, but this time you're not using the dots. You're printing like a grownup." Children usually like that idea.

(Note: A ten-year-old girl with autism learned how to spell by using this method and, several years later, began using a computer to write a monthly column for the local autism society's newsletter.)

GOAL *Develop Fine Motor Skills,*
Patience, Ability to Take Turns

MATERIALS NEEDED
* Small alphabet blocks

6. Begin by putting one block on top of another to show your child how it's done.

Put a block on the table and then say, "Your turn." After asking permission, gently hold your child's hand and grasp a block, placing it on top of your block. As you place your child's hand back on the table, pick up a block and say, "It's my turn." This is repeated, each time talking with your child, telling him, "It's your turn," and, "It's my turn now." Children learn this concept fairly quickly.

When the blocks reach a certain height, they will fall over. The inattentive child will be startled, which brings him back to the present, and you should say something like: "Uh-oh! It fell down, didn't it? Let's build another one, okay?" He will probably say "Okay," nod his head, or in some way let you know he is all for it. This is particularly important for a child who doesn't like change and has a need for perfection. He probably wants the tower of blocks to remain standing, regardless of how many are placed on top of each other.

He will soon learn how many blocks he can add before it topples, and he may even push the tower so that it falls. This gives him a sense of control, of building and rebuilding. He also learns the process of taking turns, and he will wait for you to put your block on the pile before adding his own. It's not uncommon for a non-verbal child to say, "Uh-oh!" as he topples his tower. He is obviously not parroting this exclamation. It is being used intelligently at the appropriate time.

A particularly observant child may soon notice the letters on each side of the block as he stacks them or lines them up in a row. He may spell words with the blocks—usually, his name. This is the beginning of a new game and a new accomplishment.

Improve Gross Motor Skills, Perception, Turn-Taking, Agility **GOAL**

MATERIALS NEEDED

- Soft, medium-sized rubber ball (not a hard soccer ball)

7. Ask your child if he would like to play with the ball. Most children with autism don't know how to catch or throw a ball but soon learn to do so and enjoy it.

Depending on the child's degree of understanding, you may introduce this concept of catching or throwing a ball by sitting opposite the child on the floor. Roll the ball slowly towards him, saying, "Catch the ball." When he touches or grabs the ball, say, "Good for you! Now, roll it back to me." Use hand and arm motions to mimic rolling it. Be patient; it may take several weeks for a child with autism to understand this concept and begin the effort to return the ball.

For a more advanced exercise, stand about eight feet apart from your child and gently toss the ball so it bounces just once about three feet in front of him. At first the child will make no effort to catch it, but eventually he'll get the idea, catch it, and make an attempt to throw the ball back. It's exciting for both the therapist or parent and the child when he's successful.

Depending on the weather and your location, you may eventually decide to go outside and play kickball. A few minutes of this activity, when done regularly, will help strengthen arm, leg, back, and eye muscles. This is more fun if the ball can be kicked against a wall, because this way it rebounds and can then be caught.

Improve Awareness of Color, Shape, Order; Develop Fine Motor Skills and Memory **GOAL**

MATERIALS NEEDED

- Jigsaw puzzle with number and size of pieces appropriate to age and ability

8. The process will vary depending on the age and ability of the child. Older children or those with ADD/ADHD or Asperger's Syndrome should begin by finding all the pieces with a straight edge, which will form the border, and then sort the remainder of the pieces according to color.

For younger children or those with autism, select a puzzle with fewer pieces. Pick up one piece and put it on the picture of the puzzle on the box top. Do this several times, and your child will understand what you're trying to show him. He will attempt to imitate you.

Wooden puzzles are great for young children because the pieces are large and easy to pick up. Children often have an idea where a piece goes and push it around on the board until it happens to fall into place.

A child can work on a jigsaw puzzle by himself or with another child. It's not necessary to take turns with this game because sometimes finding a piece is a matter of luck. Besides, it's more fun for two people to work a puzzle together.

Memory skills come into play when looking for a specific piece. For example, if he's missing the tail of a cat and the child remembers seeing it "someplace," a strong memory will help him to recall where it is in the remaining pieces.

*C*onclusion

The book you have just read is the culmination of a lifetime of work dedicated to children with autism, Asperger's, and ADD/ADHD. The programs I developed in 1981 were considered so revolutionary in Phoenix, and most other cities in Arizona, that they were ridiculed and dismissed—until the improvement in children could no longer be denied. As you have discovered, there is nothing odd about either the rationale or the exercises. If I could do it, you can too.

The only thing that may have set me apart at the time is that I knew, without a doubt, that the autistic children I worked with were highly intelligent and very aware of their surroundings. I continually told them that I knew they understood every word I said to them and that I respected them. I told them I loved them and was proud of them. I reassured them that I knew they could do the exercises and that if they needed help I was right there to help them.

Because I was communicating with their sensitive nature, these wonderful boys and girls responded rapidly and, at times, dramatically. They trusted me and knew I was trying to help them live as normal a life as possible.

It is common sense that if we respect someone we will receive respect in return. If we love someone, she will return that love. If we communicate with a child, even non-verbally, she will respond. A child knows if people around her are sincere or simply talking for the sake of talking. You cannot fool a child. She has a sixth sense, or intuition, that is attracted to the spiritual nature of art—and people.

Mutual trust and respect will work wonders for both you and your child. It will open up a whole new world—as long as you are sincere and remember the three major attributes of an integrated, respectful person: truth, beauty, and goodness. What you think is more important than what you say or do, because what you say and do is the result of what you think. Energy follows thought. If you don't practice truth, beauty, and goodness in your life, they will not become part of your spiritual nature, which is what communicates with your child's sensitive inner spirit.

When you live your life according to those three spiritual qualities, you will be correspondingly able to help your child balance the hemispheres of her brain and create new brain cells through therapeutic, remedial, and creative activities.

Although the diagnosis of autism is devastating, it is not a life-threatening disease. It is, however, a life-changing disorder that uproots the family structure and the ideal of "perfect" children.

When you first hear that your child has autism, you will want to know what caused it and how she can be healed. Yes, changes will have to be made in your home, but the first changes will have to be in yourself. Before you can learn how to address a child's body, mind, and spirit, you have to rid yourself of crystallized thoughts. If you remain set in your old ideas, teachings, and beliefs that you're never allowed to change and grow, you will always be unable or unwilling to experience anything new. Abandoning crystallized thoughts and patterns brings us all a little further down the road of our own spiritual growth so that we can help children through natural, creative means that were once widely used and respected.

It had previously been thought that only trained art, music, or play therapists were capable of using the basic techniques taught in college courses; however, in these times, we need to call on all of our resources to help children who cannot help themselves. Due to the global phenomenon of children on the Autism Spectrum, parents without specialized training—but with compassion, sensitivity, awareness, and knowledge of the basics—are able to use remedial therapies in their practices and homes successfully. We all want the best for our children, and oftentimes the best is in our own home.

> When parents discover they can be an integral part of their child's development, they truly begin to know their child and discover the innate intelligence that had not previously been seen.

When parents discover they can be an integral part of their child's development, they truly begin to know their child and discover the innate intelligence that had not previously been seen. Engagement in a daily routine of activities, such as those provided in this book, strengthens the relationship between these children and their parents, siblings, and other relatives, all of whom will want to take part in these "new games."

WHERE TO BEGIN?

Autism knows no boundaries. It affects children worldwide, and the symptoms are generally identical. It cannot be blamed on one thing that they eat, drink, or have injected into them. There is no apparent common denominator that links children in every country. Their environments are different, so there must be another cause.

We don't know what the cause is, but we do know that kids on the Autism Spectrum are sensitive, intelligent, and aware young people who are different in many ways from their peers. "Different" doesn't necessarily mean "peculiar" in a bad way; it means they have something extra—something unusual and puzzling to add to our society.

An integrative, comprehensive approach is recommended for treating a child on the Autism Spectrum. The exercises and activities in this book are fun—in fact, they may seem too easy and too much fun to be effective. By combining medical treatment with the creative, remedial remedies you have learned in this book, you will be able to work with your child at a very early age.

Since children on the Autism Spectrum, particularly those who are autistic, have little or no connection with the outside world, early intervention is an absolute must in order for them to learn how to live in their environment. As soon as you see any indications of abnormal behavior, have your child seen by your doctor, who should refer you to a Developmental Pediatrician for testing and recommendations. For maximum effectiveness, it is ideal to begin therapeutic methods before the age of twelve, since patterns in the brain are formed by that age.

All children on the Autism Spectrum present challenges to parents, therapists, and teachers alike. Such children also tend to want things their own way, which can be frustrating for everyone. After reading the previous chapters, therapists should see how these methods can be integrated into their current therapeutic regime, while teachers should be able to identify children on the Spectrum by their characteristics. Knowledge of the temperaments is helpful to everyone who works with, cares for, or teaches children with or without neurological disorders.

Each category of Spectrum Disorder is composed of unique individuals, so there is no panacea. Every child on the Spectrum has her own personality and temperament. Understanding her inherent disposition and acquired personality is a key to communication. Her moods will vary from hour to hour; therefore, she will need variety throughout the day.

GETTING TO WORK

All children on the Autism Spectrum respond to the creative arts. They should be provided with the proper tools to explore creative activities. It is never too early to play classical music in your home. Music and art are two of the most effective forms of therapy for every child. Photographs taken of their artwork are testament to what autistic children are capable of if given the right tools and encouragement. Autistic children can even overcome an aversion to clay.

It took months, but a very tactilely defensive boy apparently was determined to work and play with this odd substance. He rolled long ropes of different colors into an arc on his mother's dining room table. Underneath, in letters he had made, was the word "rainbow." This was a boy whose mother was convinced he was severely retarded and non-verbal; fortunately, she was impressed enough with his accomplishment to take a picture of his art. There are many forms of communication, and his rainbow was a wonderful statement.

Children with autism want to communicate but often are unable to verbalize their feelings. Although they may not be articulate in expressing their wants, needs, fears, or sensations, they are sentient human beings who can speak through painting, music, sculpture, and movement. They need to be supplied with the tools that will help them experience the spiritual nature of art.

If you are told by a doctor that your child will outgrow her behavior, but your "gut feeling" tells you otherwise, go to another doctor. Persist in an accurate diagnosis and then persist in finding therapies that are right for your child.

Remember, your first impression is usually the right one. You need to follow your intuition. Otherwise, intellect gets in the way and supplies all kinds of reasons why you should or should not do something. Your intuition is your higher self or spiritual nature. Do not dismiss your feelings about the care of your child. Above all, follow your intuition when working with your child in your home. Know when something isn't working and smoothly but quickly transition to another activity.

Be observant and perceptive and you will know what your child needs from you. You will have the opportunity to take a pro-active stance in your child's improvement through an understanding of her three-fold nature of body, mind, and spirit. Remedial, creative therapies are the key to balancing a child and ultimately bringing order out of disorder and functionality out of dysfunction.

Both articulate and non-verbal children on the Autism Spectrum are curious, observant, perceptive, and independent. Because they are so gifted in various ways, they respond the beauty of the arts and are eager to experience it all. So provide them with the opportunity to experience, and express themselves through, creative therapies and activities.

The methods detailed in this book were carefully developed over a period of more than twenty-five years. Parents who believe in their children and see the spark of intelligence that perhaps others miss are encouraged to use all of the exercises and activities listed in this book. Major breakthroughs are possible at all levels of your child's body, mind, and spirit. Without synchronicity, wholeness will always remain just an ideal.

Additional Resources

In 1981, when I began my work with children in Arizona, factual sources of information about autism were almost nonexistent. Most people had never heard of Asperger's Syndrome. Fortunately, that has changed, no doubt because of the explosion of Spectrum Disorders, which, in turn, has demanded answers, leading parents and professionals to explore all possibilities.

In today's computer-savvy culture, we can search the Internet for information about anything and everything. Because of the millions of documents that are easily found by a search, I have listed only a few online websites and sources to get you started.

The books listed below have been in my library for many years, many of them from the date of publication. They are groundbreaking works by experts in their fields, and I owe them all a debt of gratitude for their insights and compassion for children who face the daily challenges of neurodevelopmental disorders. Because of their efforts, my work has been able to help young boys and girls achieve their fullest potential through the arts. Best of all, you, the reader, having finished this book, will have the benefit of their wisdom as well.

BOOKS

Bauer, Alfred, PhD. *Healing Sounds: The Fundamentals of Chirophonetics*. Rudolf Steiner College Press, 1993.

Bennett, William. *The Book of Virtues*. Simon and Schuster, 1997.

Cousens, Gabriel. *Conscious Eating*. North Atlantic Books, 2000.

Grimm Brothers. *The Complete Grimm's Fairy Tales*. Pantheon Books, 1944.

Heline, Corinne. *Color and Music in the New Age*. New Age Press, 1980.

Holtzapfel, Walter. *Children's Destinies*. Mercury Press, 1977.

Husemann, Friedrich and Otto Wolff. *The Anthroposophical Approach to Medicine, Vol. 2*. Anthroposophic Press, 1987.

Konig, Karl. *The First Three Years of Life*. Anthroposophic Press, 1969.

Lorenz-Poschmann, Agatha. *Breath, Speech and Therapy*. Mercury Press, 1982.

Meyer, Rudolf. *The Wisdom of Fairy Tales*. Floris Books, 1981.

Neiderhauser, Hans and Margaret Frohlick. *Form Drawing*. The Rudolf Steiner School, 1974.

Ott, John N. *Health and Light: The Effects of Natural and Artificial Light on Man and Other Living Things*. Ariel Press, 2000.

Scott, Cyril. *Music: Its Secret Influence Throughout the Ages*. Samuel Weiser, Inc., 1958.

Spock, Marjorie. *Teaching as a Lively Art*. Anthroposophic Press, 1978.

Steiner, Rudolf.

The Arts and Their Mission. Anthroposophic Press, 1964.

Curative Education. Rudolf Steiner Press, 1981.

Education As An Art. Steiner Books, 1970.

The Essentials of Education. Rudolf Steiner Press, 1926.

The Four Temperaments. Anthroposophic Press, 1980.

The Inner Nature of Music and the Experience of Tone. Anthroposophic Press, 1983.

A Modern Art of Education. Rudolf Steiner Press, 1981.

Woodward, Bob and Mara Hagenboom. *Autism: A Holistic Approach*. Floris Books, 2000.

WEBSITES

The following are excellent general Internet resources.

The Naked Scientists Online: www.thenakedscientists.com

NeuroScience for Kids: faculty.washington.edu/chudler/neurok.html

Hundreds of great sources of information are available on the Internet by doing a search for autism, ADHD, and Asperger's. Here are a few of them.

ADD/ADHD

About ADD: add.about.com

ADD/ADHD Online Support Group: www.adders.org

Attention Deficit Disorder Association: www.add.org

LD Online: www.ldonline.org/indepth/adhd

ASPERGER'S

Mayo Clinic: www.mayoclinic.com/health/aspergers-syndrome/DS00551

National Institute of Neurological Disorders and Stroke: www.ninds.nih.gov/disorders/asperger/asperger.htm

O.A.S.I.S. Online Asperger Syndrome Information and Support: www.udel.edu/bkirby/asperger/moreno_tips_for_teaching.html

Web MD—Asperger's Information: www.webmd.com (*Search for Asperger's.*)

AUTISM

Autism Network International (ANI): ani.autistics.org

Autism Research Institute: www.autismresearchinstitute.com

Autism Society of America: www.autism-society.org

National Institutes of Health (NIH): health.nih.gov/result.asp/62

Web MD—Autism Information: www.webmd.com (*Search for autism.*)

E-NEWSLETTERS

These two are excellent sources of information. You will find additional free newsletters on many websites.

About.com. Choose a topic of interest from the website: talk.about.com

The Shafer Autism Report. Submit request to: editor@sarnet.org

OTHER PRINT RESOURCES

Centers for Disease Control and Prevention, 1993 UN Report.

Dairy Forage Research Center, University of Wisconsin.

Food Research Institute, Dept. of Food Microbiology/Toxicology, University of Wisconsin.

Mayo Clinic, Archives of Pediatrics and Adolescent Medicine, March 2000.

Nutrition and Stimulants, Biodynamic Farming and Gardening Assoc./PA, 1991.

Pediatrics, April 2004.

References

Chapter 1

Courchesne, E.; Carper, R.; Akshoomoff, N. "Evidence of Brain Overgrowth in the First Year of Life in Autism." *Journal of the American Medical Association (JAMA)*. 26 Jul 2003.

Chapter 2

Ashford, Nicholas A. Multiple Chemical Sensitivity Symposium. Canada. 16–17 May 2001.

"Autism and ADHD Linked to Addictive Food Additive." La Leava di Archimede—Association for freedom of choice and correct information. 15 Mar 2004. 9 Oct 2007. www.laleva.org/eng/2004/03/autism_and_adhd_linked_to_addictive_food_additive.html

Bernard Weiss, B. and Landrigan, P.J. "The Developing Brain and the Environment: An Introduction." *Environmental Health Perspectives*. Jun 2000; 107(3).

Direct Laboratory Services, Inc. Newsletter. 27 Feb 2004. 7 Feb 2007. www.directlabs.com

Folstein, S. and M. Rutter. "Genetic Influences and Infantile Autism." *Nature*. Feb 1977.

Hadjivassiliou, M.; Grünewald, R.A.; Davies-Jones, G.A.B. "Gluten Sensitivity as a Neurological Illness." *Journal of Neurology, Neurosurgery, and Psychiatry*. 30 Apr 2002.

Lazaroff, Meredith. "Heavy Metal Toxicity and Autism." Developmental Disabilities Center. Aug 2005. 11 Oct 2007. www.ddrcco.com/neurology_Aug.htm

McFadzean, Nicola. Personal communication. 12 Oct 2007.

McNeil, Donald G. "When Parents Say No To Child Vaccinations." *New York Times*. 30 Nov 2002.

Mehl-Madrona, Lewis. "Prenatal Aspartamate Exposure." 2 Feb 2007. www.healing-arts.org/children

Mezey, E., et al. "Transplanted Bone Marrow Generates New Neurons In Human Brains." National Academy of Sciences. 4 Feb 2003.

Neubrander, James. "Methyl B-12: Making It Work For You!" Autism One Conference. Chicago, Illinois. 29 May 2005.

Norwegian Directorate of Health and Social Welfare. "A National Clinical Guideline for the Use of Dental Filling Materials." 7 Feb 2005. www.shdir.no

"The Safety and Efficacy of Chelation Therapy in Autism." *Autism Research Institute Newsletter*. Mar 2006.

Wakefield, A., et al. "Enterocolitis in Children with Developmental Disorders." *Am J Gastroenterol*. Sep 2000; 95(9).

Chapter 3

American Journal of Psychiatry. Jun 2000.

Dawson, Geraldine. "Early recognition of 1-year-old infants with autism spectrum disorder versus mental retardation." *Journal of Autism and Developmental Disorders*. 2000; 30(2).

Palmer, R.F., et al. "School District Resources and Identification of Children with Autistic Disorder." *American Journal of Public Health*. Jan 2005; 95(1).

Pevin, Joseph. Personal email correspondence with author. 28 Feb 2007.

Samuels, Jack. "Significant Linkage to Compulsive Hoarding on Chromosome 14 in Families with Obsessive-Compulsive Disorder: Results from the OCD Collaborative Genetics Study." *American Journal of Psychiatry*. Mar 2007.

Shugart, Yin Yao. "First Whole-Genome Scan for Links to OCD Reveals Evidence for Genetic Susceptibility." The Mental Health Research Association. 6 Oct 2007. www.narsad.org

Volkmar, F., et al. "Defining and Quantifying the Social Phenotype in Autism."

Wrong Diagnosis. 28 Feb 2007. www.wrongdiagnosis.com/a/autism/stats-country.htm

Chapter 4

American Psychiatric Association. *Diagnostic and Statistical Manual of Mental Disorders (DSM-IV)*. American Psychiatric Association, 1994.

Christakis, Dimitri A. "Early Television Exposure and Subsequent Attentional Problems in Children." *Pediatrics*. Apr 2004.

Feingold, Ben F. *Why Your Child Is Hyperactive*. Random House, 1973.

Genetic Science Learning Center. University of Utah. 7 Mar 2007. learn.genetics.utah.edu/units/addiction/issues/ritalin.cfm

The Greater Dallas Council on Alcohol & Drug Abuse. Personal email correspondence with author. 6 Mar 2007.

Oski, Frank A. *Don't Drink Your Milk!: The Frightening New Medical Facts About the World's Most Overrated Nutrient*. Simon and Schuster, 1977.

Ritalin Source. 7 Mar 2007. mayoclinic.com

Chapter 5

Silverman, Steve. "The Geek Syndrome." *Wired*, Dec 2001.

Chapter 6

Hagler, Louise. *Tofu Cookery*. The Book Publishing Company, 1982.

Roberts, H.J. Report to Hearing on "NutraSweet: Health and Safety Concerns." Committee on Labor and Human Resources, United States Senate; Washington, DC. 3 Nov 1987.

World Environmental Conference Report. World Environmental Conference on Aspartame. Elizabeth City State University, North Carolina. 2 Dec 1995.

Chapter 8

Spock, Marjorie. *Teaching As A Lively Art*. Anthroposophic Press, 1978.

Steiner, Rudolf.

The Essentials of Education. Rudolf Steiner Press, 1926.

The Four Temperaments. Anthroposophic Press, 1941.

A Modern Art of Education. Rudolf Steiner Press, 1981.

Chapter 9

Almon, Joan. Personal email correspondence with author. 1 Feb 2007.

Chapter 10

Gimzewski, Jim. *Smithsonian Magazine*. Mar 2004

Peterson, E.A., et al. "Noise raises blood pressure without impairing auditory sensitivity." *Science News*. 27 Mar 1981

Chapter 11

Gill, Donald W. 5 Oct 2007. www.alba-julserras.com/site/437024/page/113343

Koewler, Kathy. Personal email correspondence with author. 1 Jul 2007.

Chapter 12

König, Karl. *The First Three Years of Life*. Anthroposophic Press, 1969.

Chapter 13

Spock, Marjorie. *Teaching As A Lively Art*. Anthroposophic Press, 1978.

Chapter 14

The Yarn Company. 4 Aug 2007. www.theyarnco.com

About the Author

At an early age, Janet Tubbs showed an interest in what would become her life's work. She was influenced in many ways by her father, whose hobby was performing magic tricks and puppet shows with large Punch and Judy puppets. By the age of eight, she was performing her own shows for friends in the basement of her home. At age nine, she was sharing the stage with her father and knew the secret of "mind-reading" and pulling rabbits out of a hat. By ten, she was proficient in dance, piano, singing, and the flute.

Janet's father was a hospital administrator at a children's hospital, where her interest in medicine and ill children was sparked as a teenager.

She had four children who all played instruments; when they were in school, Janet taught herself to play the violin, trombone, trumpet, and clarinet. In addition, she bought and played a guitar, hammered dulcimer, and piano.

As her children grew older, Janet volunteered for the American Red Cross in its program for children with disabilities. It wasn't long before she was inspired to combine her love of children and the arts in order to develop a program for young boys and girls with emotional and behavioral problems. While working with children in the child development center at a Phoenix hospital, she began to enlarge and modify her program to specialize in services for children with autism.

At that time, using music and art therapeutically in the Phoenix area was considered strange, unworkable, and "New Agey." Despite this skepticism, Janet persisted and formed Children's Resource Center, a nonprofit organization for helping children with disabilities attain their fullest potential through various forms of art.

With unmistakable and rapid signs of improvement in children, she soon was presenting her work at state, national, and international conferences. In addition, she was invited to speak to doctors and nurses at all the major hospitals in the area; twice to the Naturopathic College of Medicine in Tempe, Arizona; and twice to the medical school at the University of Arizona, Tucson.

Janet has designed a line of lifelike, soft-sculpted puppets that have proven successful in reaching and teaching children with Autism Spectrum Disorders.

She is the author of several books, including *Don't Worry, They'll Grow Up—A Parent's Survival Guide; Middle-Aged Children—Getting Through the Tough Preteens; The Mind Garden—A Supplemental Curriculum; The ABC's of Animals—A Dictionary From A to Z;* and *If You Can't Pronounce It, Don't Eat It—A Vegetarian Cookbook.*

Janet has eight grandchildren and one great-grandchild. She now lives in suburban Cincinnati, where she is working on her next book of tips for successful parenting.

*I*ndex

DOES YOUR BABY HAVE AUTISM?
Detecting the Earliest Signs of Autism
Osnat Teitelbaum and Philip Teitelbaum, PhD

For many years, the diagnosis of autism has centered on a child's social interaction—from poor eye contact to lack of language skills. Although the autism community agrees that early intervention is key to effective treatment, the telltale signs of this disorder usually don't reveal themselves until the age of two or three. But what if it were possible to detect the potential for autism within the first year of life? That is the basis of Osnat and Philip Teitelbaum's book, *Does Your Baby Have Autism?*

This dedicated wife-and-husband team has worked for nearly two decades to develop ways of detecting signs of potential autism or Asperger's syndrome by examining a child's early motor development. By studying the patterns of righting, sitting, crawling, and walking in typical infants, and comparing them with those of children who were later diagnosed with autism, the authors have been able to pinpoint movement patterns that appear to be the precursors of autism and Asperger's.

Does Your Baby Have Autism? first provides general information about the history of autism, followed by a discussion of The Ladder of Motor Development. Each of four chapters then examines one motor milestone—righting, sitting, crawling, or walking—contrasting typical development with atypical development. Finally, parents are guided in finding professional help for a child whose motor skills may indicate a problem.

$17.95 • 160 pages • 7.5 x 9-inch quality paperback • ISBN 978-0-7570-0240-3

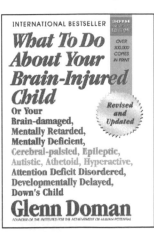

WHAT TO DO ABOUT YOUR BRAIN-INJURED CHILD
Glenn Doman

In this updated classic, Glenn Doman—founder of The Institutes for the Achievement of Human Potential and pioneer in the treatment of the brain-injured children—brings real hope to thousands of children who have been sentenced to a life of institutional confinement.

In *What To Do About Your Brain-Injured Child,* Doman recounts the story of The Institutes' tireless effort to refine treatment of the brain injured. He shares the staff's lifesaving techniques and the tools used to measure—and ultimately improve—visual, auditory, tactile, mobile, and manual development. Doman explains the unique methods of treatment that are constantly being improved and expanded, and then describes the program with which parents can treat their own children at home in a familiar and loving environment. Included throughout are case histories, drawings, and helpful charts and diagrams.

Twenty thousand families from over one hundred nations have brought their children to The Institutes. The great majority of these children have done better than their parents had hoped, and for each of these families, this book was the starting point.

$18.95 • 336 pages • 6 x 9-inch quality paperback • ISBN 978-0-7570-0186-4

HOW TO TEACH YOUR BABY TO READ
Glenn Doman and Janet Doman

As the founder of The Institutes for the Achievement of Human Potential, Glenn Doman has demonstrated time and again that young children are far more capable of learning than we ever imagined. In *How To Teach Your Baby To Read,* he and daughter Janet show just how easy it is to teach a young child to read. They explain how to begin and expand the reading program, how to make and organize necessary materials, and how to more fully develop your child's reading potential.

By following the simple daily program presented in *How To Teach Your Baby To Read,* you will give your baby a powerful advantage that will last a lifetime.

$13.95 • 288 pages • 6 x 9-inch quality paperback • ISBN 978-0-7570-0185-7

HOW TO TEACH YOUR BABY MATH
Glenn Doman and Janet Doman

Glenn and Janet Doman have not only shown that children from birth to age six learn better and faster than older children do, but have given it practical application. *How To Teach Your Baby Math* demonstrates just how easy it is to teach a young child mathematics through the development of thinking and reasoning skills. It explains how to begin and expand the math program, how to make and organize necessary materials, and how to more fully develop your child's math potential.

By following the simple daily program in a relaxed and loving way, you will enable your child to experience the joy of learning—as have millions of children the world over.

$13.95 • 240 pages • 6 x 9-inch quality paperback • ISBN 978-0-7570-0184-0

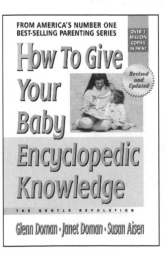

HOW TO GIVE YOUR BABY ENCYCLOPEDIC KNOWLEDGE
Glenn Doman, Janet Doman, and Susan Aisen

How To Give Your Baby Encyclopedic Knowledge shows you how simple it is to teach a young child about the arts, science, and nature. Your child will recognize the insects in the garden, learn about the countries of the world, discover the beauty of a painting by Van Gogh, and more. This book explains how to begin and develop this remarkable program, how to create and organize necessary materials, and how to more fully cultivate your child's learning ability.

Very young children not only can learn, but can learn far better and faster than older children. Let *How To Give Your Baby Encyclopedic Knowledge* be the first step in a lifetime of achievement.

$13.95 • 318 pages • 6 x 9-inch quality paperback • ISBN 978-0-7570-0182-6

HOW TO MULTIPLY YOUR BABY'S INTELLIGENCE

Glenn Doman and Janet Doman

Too often, we waste our children's most important years by refusing to allow them to learn everything they can at a time when it is easiest for them to absorb new information. *How To Multiply Your Baby's Intelligence* provides a comprehensive program that shows you just how easy and pleasurable it is to teach your young child how to read, to understand mathematics, and to literally multiply his or her overall learning potential. It explains how to begin and expand a remarkable proven program, how to make and organize the necessary materials, and how to more fully develop your child's learning ability, preparing him or her for a lifetime of success.

$15.95 • 400 pages • 6 x 9-inch quality paperback • ISBN 978-0-7570-0183-3

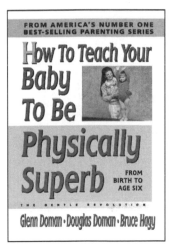

HOW TO TEACH YOUR BABY TO BE PHYSICALLY SUPERB

Glenn Doman, Janet Doman, and Bruce Hagy

The early development of mobility in newborns is a vital part of their future ability to learn and grow to full potential. In *How to Teach Your Baby To Be Physically Superb*, Glenn Doman—founder of The Institutes for the Achievement of Human Potential—along with Douglas Doman and Bruce Hagy guide you in maximizing your child's physical capabilities. The authors first discuss each stage of mobility, and then explain how you can create an environment that will help your baby more easily reach that stage. Full-color charts, photographs, illustrations, and detailed yet easy-to-follow instructions are included to help you establish and use an effective home program.

$29.95 • 296 pages • 7.5 x 10.5-inch hardback • ISBN 978-0-7570-0192-5

HOW TO TEACH YOUR BABY TO SWIM

Glenn Doman, Janet Doman, and Susan Aisen

Teaching an infant or toddler to swim is not only a matter of safety, but also a great way to stimulate the child's physical coordination, concentration, and intelligence. That's right. By teaching your baby the proper swimming techniques, you can actually enhance his or her learning ability. You will also make your child happier, healthier, and more self-confident. Based on the revolutionary learning principles developed at The Institutes for the Achievement of Human Potential, *How To Teach Your Baby To Swim* is a clear and easy-to-follow guide to teaching your child swimming basics.

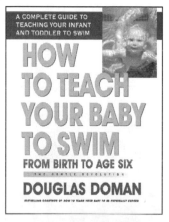

$14.95 • 128 pages • 7.5 x 9-inch quality paperback • ISBN 978-0-7570-0198-7

MASSAGING YOUR BABY
The Joy of Touch Time
Dr. Elaine Fogel Schneider

The power of touch is real and has been scientifically shown to have remarkable effects. For infants, it encourages relaxation; improves sleep patterns; reduces discomfort from teething, colic, and gas; strengthens digestive and circulatory systems; and does so much more. For parents, it nurtures bonding, increases communication, promotes parenting skills, and actually reduces stress levels. Now, massage expert Dr. Elaine Fogel Schneider has written the ultimate guide to using infant massage at home. *Massaging Your Baby* begins by explaining how and why massage is so beneficial. It then provides an easy-to-follow step-by-step guide to effective massage techniques.

$15.95 • 224 pages • 7.5 x 9-inch quality paperback • ISBN 978-0-7570-0263-2

POTTY TRAINING YOUR BABY
A Practical Guide for Easier Toilet Training

Katie Warren

Contrary to traditional belief, the transition from diaper to potty can be started even before your child's first birthday—and completed by the second! Katie Warren advises taking advantage of the early months, when babies do most of their communicating on an emotional level, as children understand things intuitively much sooner than they understand words. *Potty Training Your Baby* provides information on everything from where to buy a potty to dealing with those inevitable little "accidents." Perhaps most important, the author shows you how to turn this often dreaded and frustrating task into a time of growth and learning for both you and your child.

$9.95 • 104 pages • 6 x 9-inch quality paperback • ISBN 978-0-7570-0180-2

HOW TO MAXIMIZE YOUR CHILD'S LEARNING ABILITY
A Complete Guide to Choosing and Using the Best Computer Games, Activities, Learning Aids, Toys, and Tactics for Your Child
Lauren Bradway, PhD, and Barbara Albers Hill

Over twenty years ago, Dr. Lauren Bradway discovered that all children have specific learning styles. Some learn best through visual stimulation; others, through sound and language; and still others, through touch. In this book Dr. Bradway first shows you how to determine your child's inherent style. She then aids you in carefully selecting the toys, activities, and educational strategies that will help reinforce the talents and traits your child was born with, and encourage those skills that come less easily.

$14.95 • 288 pages • 6 x 9-inch quality paperback • ISBN 978-0-7570-0096-6